An Englishman in Patagonia

An Englishman in Patagonia

John Pilkington

Best wishes,
John Pilkington

CENTURY
London Sydney Auckland Johannesburg

First published in 1991 by Century
Random House, 20 Vauxhall Bridge Road, London SW1V 2SA

Random House Australia (Pty) Ltd
20 Alfred Street, Milsons Point, Sydney, NSW 2061, Australia

Random House New Zealand Ltd
18 Poland Road, Glenfield, Auckland 10, New Zealand

Random House South Africa (Pty) Ltd
Endulini, 5 A Jubilee Road, Parktown 2193, South Africa

Reprinted 1999

Random House UK Limited Reg. No. 954009

A CIP catalogue record for this book is available from the British Library

ISBN 0–7126–3582–3

Set in Linotronic Palatino by CentraCet, Cambridge
Printed and bound by Professional Book Supplies Ltd, Oxon

For Liz

Contents

Maps

John Pilkington's route through Patagonia

Acknowledgements

Any traveller who ventures, even briefly, among such generous people as the Patagonians will carry home a hoard of fond memories. Singling out individuals seems absurd; but chance did bring me together with one or two special people, who responded exceptionally to my needs.

Among those in Chile I'd like to thank Marcela and Gianni Biggi and Francisco Valiente of Santiago; Renato Cárdenas and Cathy Hall of Castro on the island of Chiloé; Juan Cárcamo and Johnnie MacLean of Coyhaique; Verena and Gunter Schäfer of Estancia Buena Vista near Cochrane; and Gabriela Neira, Gustavo López and Danka Ivanoff of Chile Chico. In Punta Arenas I'm especially grateful to the directors of Adventure Network International, especially Martyn Williams and Hugh MacLeay; Adventure Network's office manager Tony Piggot; Peggy and Helen Fell; Margaret Harper; Peter Dooley and his staff at the British School; and Bill Matheson, the Honorary British Consul.

On the Argentine side, I'd like to express my appreciation to Naomi and Pat O'Byrne of Estancia Cullen on Tierra del Fuego; Héctor Peña and Derick and Malena Pickering of Río Gallegos; Alcira Rogers and the staff of Río Gallegos's British College, in particular Marjorie de Oliva; Jean and Jack Halliday of Santa Cruz; Lidia Mann Pickering of San Julián; Suzana and José de Santos and Mair Davies of Trelew; Cristina and Jorge Fernández of Esquel; Jane Williams and Jim and Anne Wood of Estancia Huechahue in the province of Neuquén, and especially Jorge Fernández, Paula Gutnisky, Jorge Insua, Mercedes Pereyra and Alfredo Boillat, all of Buenos Aires.

Several British companies generously provided equipment for the trip. Phoenix Mountaineering's foul-weather clothing easily met the challenge of the Patagonian and Antarctic climates, and the carrying cases donated by Camera Care Systems took care of my photographic and sound equipment. As on previous occasions, Vango (Scotland) Ltd came up with something for me to test, this time a pair of tough Excell boots; and Arran Poyser sponsored further items of clothing. Kodak and the Royal Bank of Scotland also helped handsomely in appropriate ways.

I'd like to record my special thanks to Nicholas Whines of the BBC, who made possible the radio programme which has accompanied this book; to Anthony Lambert, my ever-diligent editor; and to Liz Berryman, without whose support this (and other adventures) would never have happened.

I left Patagonia in humble admiration for a people who are holding their own in a tough neck of the woods. A single book can barely do justice to their mettle. But if I've stimulated some interest in them, my intention will have been achieved; because in a humdrum world the Patagonians are an example to us all. My final acknowledgement goes – with gratitude and respect – to them.

'A Land of Monsters'

One Saturday morning in 1989, on BBC Radio 4's *Breakaway* programme, Bernard Falk was trying to describe something boring. Eventually he gave up. 'It sounds as much fun as a package holiday in Patagonia,' he concluded.

I pricked up my ears. Radio presenters weren't often so disdainful. Anywhere with an image that bad must, I thought, be rather special.

I knew that in the eyes of the British writer Bruce Chatwin, Patagonia had been a country of black fogs and whirlwinds at the end of the inhabited world. Chatwin's American contemporary Paul Theroux summed it up as a 'fanciful blur of legend, the giants on the shore, the ostrich on the plain, and a sense of displaced people, like my own ancestors who had fled from Europe'. To the nineteenth-century naturalist W.H. Hudson it had a look of antiquity, of eternal peace, 'of a desert that has been a desert from of old and will continue a desert for ever'. 'Patagonia?' screamed Lady Florence Dixie's friends when she announced her expedition with Lord Queensberry in 1879. 'Who would ever think of going to such a place? Why, you will be eaten up by cannibals! What on earth makes you choose such an outlandish part of the world to go to? What can be the attraction?'

Such dismissive remarks haven't diminished with the passing years. The historian Michael Mainwaring observed as recently as 1983 that the name still mystifies outsiders. 'It is thought by some people to be a fictitious country like Ruritania, or somewhere near the Amazon, or next to Mesopotamia, or somewhere off the Hebrides, or a disease. . . . It is the back of beyond, a nowhere place.' Such a nonentity, in fact, that when awarded the 1979 Booker Prize and asked what importance she attached to such

1

literary awards, Iris Murdoch replied that they mattered as much as if it was raining in Patagonia.

But if Iris Murdoch hadn't found inspiration there, other novelists had. Patagonia's typecasting as a place unspeakably remote and teeming with danger prompted Jules Verne to locate *The Children of Captain Grant* and *The Lighthouse at the End of the World* there. James Joyce made a cursory reference to 'the terrible Patagonians' in *Dubliners*. And Sir Arthur Conan Doyle used turn-of-the-century reports from Patagonia as his basis for *The Lost World*.

But for me, on that spring morning in 1989, the name Patagonia meant simply a land that must hold some surprises. From the 40th Parallel to Cape Horn it beckoned: almost half a million square miles. Like Tartary or Siberia, this southernmost tip of South America tantalizingly resisted definition. It was neither a country nor a province, but included bits of both Chile and Argentina; and though a glance at my atlas disclosed the label 'Patagonia' stretched generously across that turnip-shaped appendage to the continent, it looked almost like an afterthought. I rummaged in vain for evidence that the name had ever enjoyed any solid political status.

Most historians agree that Patagonia was so christened in 1520 when Ferdinand Magellan took shelter from South Atlantic storms during his round-the-world voyage for the Spanish Crown. He noticed to his surprise a gigantic figure on the shore. The man, we're told, wore only a guanaco hide and rough moccasins, and was dancing, leaping and singing in a most extraordinary way. When at last this Tehuelche Indian was persuaded to come aboard Magellan's flagship the *Trinidad*, the expedition's chronicler Antonio Pigafetta was greatly impressed. 'So tall was this man that we came up to the level of his waist-belt. He was well enough made, and had a broad face, painted red, with yellow circles round his eyes, and two heart-shaped spots on his cheeks.' Pigafetta added later that even the shortest of the Tehuelche stood taller than the tallest man of Castile. But what most staggered Magellan about this Indian was the immensity of his feet. '*Ha, Patagón!*' he cried – which, allowing for his archaic Spanish and some corruption in telling the tale, may be translated as 'Wow, Bigfeet!' With the arrival of Europeans the days of the Tehuelche were numbered, but their homeland achieved immortality as Patagonia – 'Land of the Bigfeet'.

A package holiday appealed to me no more than to Bernard Falk; but the idea was born. Later that year I'd planned to do some walking in Peru – but within a week of arriving I found myself in Chile, heading with a growing curiosity towards Santiago and the south. It was November; the southern summer stretched before me. I took my map of Patagonia, marshalled what crumbs of information I'd managed to collect, and sketched out a rough route.

Of all things guiding my pencilled line, perhaps the most important was the realization that I was looking at not one Patagonia but two. On the Chilean side, densely forested peninsulas and islands squatted in the teeth of the Roaring Forties, separated by winding fjords whose vertiginous shores sheltered seal colonies, foresters' cabins and the occasional rain-sodden fishing hamlet. Broad rivers tumbled down from the Andes to disgorge themselves into these inlets, their names unexpectedly familiar to a British ear. Simpson, Baker, Cochrane. . . . My pencil strode confidently across them (on no evidence whatsoever that I'd be able to do the same) and came to rest on the great triangular island of Tierra del Fuego – 'Fireland'.

East of the Andes, by contrast, Patagonia was by all accounts made up of rolling, virtually treeless grasslands, the home of guanaco, ostriches and twenty million sheep. The pencil crept up its eastern seaboard, making surges inland where, for instance, a Welsh name like Trevelin stood out among the Río Negros and the Santa Cruzes.

How long would such a journey take? Six months? Six years? Having given up my job in England, for the first time in my life I had no deadline. The Patagonian winter would doubtless propel me towards more temperate latitudes after six months or so. But for all practical purposes I could take as long as I needed.

I ruminated on the enormity of this new-found freedom, as my pencil hovered back to its starting point, where the Chilean railway system and the Pan-American Highway came to an abrupt end in the old provincial capital of Puerto Montt.

Geographically and politically, Chile is the enigma of Latin America. Stetching from the tropics to Antarctica, from sea level to over 22,000 feet, it encompasses almost every climatic variation on earth. Its people are equally varied: immigrants from the Spanish colonial period mix with twentieth-century settlers from a score of European countries; and a tiny Indian population remains around the city of Temuco.

Some observers, studying this fragile ribbon between the Andes and the Pacific, have wondered how it can survive at all. 'You have to be thin to be Chilean,' I was once told. 'Otherwise you fall off.' But despite the lunacy of its boundaries, from 1818 till 1973 Chile enjoyed continuous and mostly peaceful civilian rule – the longest such period of any country on the continent.

I'd visited Santiago briefly ten years previously, so on reaching the city centre I made for Calle Londres, a street I remembered with affection. In 1979 this winding lane had been the centre of a run-down quarter: a district of dark shadows, rotting rubbish and crumpled bodies in corners. Turning the corner, I was amused to see that it had now been declared a conservation area. The tramps had been replaced by fake Victorian lamp-posts, the potholes by reconstituted cobbles. Tourists were poking around where prostitutes had once flaunted their charms; and nearby I found a craft market and a bistro.

Many of the older hotels had become pay-by-the-hour establishments, accommodating the displaced ladies and their clients. Only one, the Londres, remained an authentic *residencial*. By chance this was where I'd stayed on my previous visit. It seemed unchanged – indeed, undusted – and the ring echoed up its marble stairway as I leaned on the bell.

The Residencial Londres occupied a corner building of honey-coloured stone, dating from the final years of the last century. It had once been a private house, and indeed still boasted some finely proportioned rooms. To my disappointment I was shown to a cubbyhole down a dark corridor; but at breakfast next morning I found myself looking out over a fine stone-flagged courtyard, one of the city's surviving examples. Sunshine streamed through the dining room, dancing on the sideboard and highlighting the cobwebs on the marmalade pots.

At my table sat two elderly ladies, white-haired and so thickly made-up that their faces looked as if they would crumble if touched. '*Buenos días, caballero*,' said the taller, sterner of the two. 'This is Hilda and my name is Greta.'

The pair spoke in a distinctive, heavily accented Spanish, and I was sure I recognized them from my previous visit. 'You're from Germany, aren't you?' I ventured.

'*Ja, ja!*' replied the one introduced as Hilda.

'How long have you lived here?' I asked, meaning in Santiago.

'Twenty-three years in this house!' replied Greta proudly. 'And before that, across the street. We were exiles, you see – refugees from the Third Reich. We had no family, so for company we stayed together.'

'Didn't you ever think of going back?'

'Oh, many times – but we were afraid of what we might find. You must understand that Germany wasn't a good place to be just after the war. Then, as the years went by, it seemed to us that Chile might prove a better home than the Fatherland.' Greta's lips showed a trace of a pout. 'There are many Germans here, you know.'

I knew something of Chile's German community, most of whom lived in the far south. 'But they're hundreds of miles away,' I protested.

'*Richtig!*' She thumped the table triumphantly. 'Which is exactly why we remain in the capital. Far enough from the disgusting beer and sauerkraut – but close enough to hear all the gossip!'

Unusually for Latin America, Santiago enjoys a mild climate, and now, in late spring, the weather was at its best. I strolled in shirtsleeves, enjoying the relaxed atmosphere, the ready smiles, and the tomfoolery as youngsters sprayed passers-by from newly restored fountains.

Chile was reportedly at last emerging from its recent traumatic years, and I was exhilarated to see this evidence of it in the capital; but at the same time I felt restless to carry on south. With an increasing sense of urgency I rummaged for facts about Patagonia. I'd always thought the place to be somehow more imaginary than real: a kind of never-never land, quite disconnected from the rest of the world, and desolate in a schoolboy-fiction kind of way – like the moon. So I was surprised to find ordinary Chileans quite well informed on the subject. 'Patagonia,' announced the Residencial Londres receptionist, 'has the worst weather in the whole of South America. It appears on the television forecast every day. Wind and rain. Wind and rain.

Even when the rest of us are sweltering, the forecast for Patagonia is always wind and rain.

Some equally startling information was thrown up at the Chilean Society for History and Geography. In a splendid Edwardian chamber, distinguished past members squinted down at me from gilt-framed portraits as I waited for an interview with one of its vice-presidents. After a few minutes the oak door creaked open to reveal a rotund figure. Like his predecessors on the wall, he was amply waistcoated, and out of a well-worn wing collar rose an equally ample face, wrinkled and bewhiskered like the Walrus in *Alice Through the Looking Glass*. 'You were asking about Patagonia?' he wheezed.

The vice-president listened to my questions with the patience of a man for whom time was no longer measured in minutes or even hours. 'Patagonia,' he remarked finally, 'is unique in all the world. Do you realize it has no capital, no government, no boundaries and no flag? It takes up more than a quarter of my country's territory, and the same of Argentina's; but after a lifetime of studying history and geography I've yet to put my finger on what exactly Patagonia is.'

'Hasn't anybody ever fixed its boundaries?' I asked.

'Many have tried. On the Chilean side, some say it starts at the River Bío-Bío south of Concepción; others at the 40th Parallel; yet others at the boundary between our so-called tenth and eleventh regions beyond Puerto Montt. Yet ask in Chaitén – a Patagonian town by two of these definitions – and they'll say they want none of it! On the Argentine side the choice is between the Río Colorado, the Río Negro and the 40th Parallel again. But I've spoken to Argentines from the province of La Pampa, north of all these boundaries, who consider themselves Patagonians through and through.'

'It sounds as if being a Patagonian is more a matter of how you feel than where you live?'

'You could say that. It's certainly something to do with the way Patagonia has been settled. Its original immigrants had to overcome untold obstacles, and the survivors developed a common bond, an understanding which united them over great distances. If you want my opinion – and remember I'm not a Patagonian – anybody whose parents, grandparents, or great-grandparents suffered as those pioneers did will carry Patagonia

6

in their blood, wherever they may live and whatever comforts they may enjoy today. Conversely, Patagonia's newcomers will never be true Patagonians – however much they may try to convince you otherwise. Patagonia itself may be undefinable, but you can tell a Patagonian by the sweat and the tears.'

We sat in high-backed, exquisitely carved chairs, facing each other across an antique mahogany table in one of the most sophisticated cities in Latin America; yet my mind was already hundreds of miles south. Patagonia was beginning to look like more than Chatwin's black fogs and whirlwinds; more than Theroux's giants on the shore; more even than Hudson's 'desert from of old'. Not only did it defy physical description, extending as it did from the wet, fjorded, forested Pacific seaboard, across several thousand square miles of ice-cap, to a virtual desert where it reached the Atlantic. But for the first time I also glimpsed a more metaphysical attraction. A thousand human tragedies must have been played out on this desolate stage.

So much for Patagonia's past. What, I asked, about its future? The vice-president smiled. 'Look closely at the trees along the shore,' he suggested. 'The far south is being engulfed by the sea. I know this is something you're also concerned about in Europe, but here it's happening rather faster. If you know where to look, you'll see that much of the coastal vegetation is drowning before your eyes.'

It was true that some European governments – the Dutch in particular – had been expressing anxiety about the shrinking polar ice-caps. The resulting rise in sea level would presumably hit Patagonia as elsewhere. But what about the Patagonian Ice-Cap, the greatest body of ice outside the polar regions? Like those at the poles, it had supposedly been showing signs of melting. Wouldn't a reduction in the ice-load counterbalance the rising of the sea?

The old man weighed his reply. 'As a scientist, I'd like to be able to answer that,' he said at length. 'But as a realist, I have to say that it's in the lap of the gods.'

We climbed a staircase to a musty gallery, home of the society's geographical archives. Chart after chart bore the annotations of eighteenth-century navigators: 'This Channel May Have Outlet', 'Peaks Not Surveyed' and the ominous 'This Coast Unexplored'. They were smeared with the stains of salt water and had the yellowed edges of documents left too long on wheelhouse tables. These were no mere reprints. We pored over them like school-boys, the vice-president straining to read the spidery flourishes almost as excitedly as me.

Eventually we turned to the topographical sheets of Chile's official mapmakers, the Instituto Geográfico Militar. Some of the Patagonian ones hadn't been revised for 50 years. 'Look here,' urged the vice-president suddenly, pointing to the vast Lake Viedma, over the border in Argentina, which was shown as draining to the Atlantic. 'Do you see how this lake is dammed up against the ice-cap? Its outlet is to the east, but can you imagine what would happen if the ice-cap were to shrink?' He paused a moment and looked me in the eye. 'Why, the waters would drop straight down to the Pacific!'

With the maps in front of us I could see the logic of his argument. What was more, there were other lakes along the frontier in the same condition. If even one of the great ice dams were to rupture, drainage would be altered over thousands of square miles. Forests, wildlife and any pockets of human settle-ment would be decimated. For the first time I began to grasp the immensity of things in this region on which I had set my sights. I also realized how very few of its shores had felt the wash of the surveyor's skiff, the tread of the explorer's boot. The thought was chilling; those yellowing charts might just as well have borne the words 'Here Be Dragons'.

In the Natural History Museum, a classical pile crumbling to dust, I came face to face with some of the extraordinary monsters which have inhabited Patagonia through the ages. Their size seemed in scale with the land. After inspecting the leg bones of a *ligua*, a kind of dinosaur, I entered a room to find a reconstruction of a *chacabuco*, fully eight feet tall, gazing questioningly down at visitors like a camel that had lost its humps. In a gallery the size of a small aircraft hangar there followed the complete skeleton of a blue whale – 90 feet long, and in its living state weighing 120 tons.

But I had to hunt for the animal I most wanted to see. After an hour's pursuit I found Patagonia's oddest creature of all in a corner, hidden amongst the stuffed steamer ducks. To be exact, it was hardly more than the ghost of an animal: a piece of pelvis, a bit of jawbone, a vertebra, a photographic montage and a thick, brittle, curling fragment of hairy reddish skin. These relics represented almost all that is now left, anywhere in the world, of the Giant Ground Sloth or *milodón*. They were discovered in 1895 in a cave near an inlet called Last Hope Sound, together with several thousand years' worth of sloth droppings. The montage showed a figure looking rather like King Kong, perhaps ten feet tall, advancing on hind legs with an evil look in its eye. Three-clawed feet left huge pancakey impressions in the ground. The sloth's curled upper lip was extended like a salamander's tongue, catching the insects and grubs on which it subsisted. A scaly skin completed the hideous picture.

It was this gross animal which had first aroused Bruce Chatwin's interest in Patagonia. A fragment of skin had been brought home by his mother's seafaring cousin, Charley Milward. In 1974 Chatwin conceived the idea of going to look for further evidence, and at the same time seeing if Milward's outrageous tales had any truth in them. Like others before him, Milward had painted a picture of empty plains stretching to a craggy horizon of windswept, untrodden peaks – the ultimate wilderness. For Chatwin it was a heady mix. What lured him even more was the fact that Patagonia seemed to have provided a last refuge, not only for the *milodón*, but also for a number of outcasts and oddballs of the human kind. In the twelve years since it had been published, his book *In Patagonia* had done much to nurture this impression of a land peopled by eccentrics. I relished the thought that I would soon be among Patagonians and could draw some conclusions for myself.

The southbound traveller from Santiago is treated to a succession of visual delights. For the first 300 miles the view is of wheatfields and vineyards – a Loire Valley complete with arrow-straight avenues of Lombardy poplars – and in the towns a visitor with time and curiosity will find the *bodegas* of Chile's most famous winemakers. But the distant Andes are a constant reminder of a harsher land, and crossing the Bío-Bío one gradually becomes more aware of its volcanoes and dogtooth peaks. The gap between mountains and sea narrows, and bit by bit the forests and lakes close in on the Pan-American Highway, overwhelming its tacky roadside trappings.

For me southern Chile evoked sensations already forgotten.

After the long desert journey from Peru I relished the whiff of rain in the air; the feeling of renewed energy now that my body was no longer clammy and hot; and, most of all, the sight of a landscape no longer biscuit-coloured but green. My eyes feasted on green pasture, green verges, green beech, oak and elm: a dozen glorious shades at every turn.

My bus rolled southward. Coffee was brought, and I sipped it slowly, staring at a notice above the driver's head. 'God is my Co-driver', it read. A watery sun showed briefly amid gathering rainclouds; then the first fat drops hit the windscreen. For ten deafening minutes the vehicle echoed to staccato drumming as the driver peered frowning through the spray. It all seemed decidely European, until I remembered that unlike in Europe these raindrops were pure. The trade winds which cross the Pacific encounter no cities and carry hardly any pollution. The only way the industrial world could ruin this land would be by melting the ice-caps and drowning it.

Nearing Puerto Montt, I had the unsettling impression that I'd stepped into Germany before the First World War. Men with Teutonic faces, bristling moustaches and flat caps walked arm-in-arm with women in headscarves. Tired-looking horses drew carts down gravel lanes through countryside which, to my European eye, looked vaguely neglected. The fields here had been hacked out of the forest by hand; so they were small, and full of abandoned patches where the drainage was poor. Vast areas were given over to rough grazing. Southern Chile's farmers, not having the capital or chemicals available to their Western European counterparts, were working their land more gently.

I always find it difficult to pinpoint the subtleties of the southern seasons. My diary told me that it was 1st December – equivalent to 1st June north of the Equator – but at this latitude spring had only just given way to summer. On all sides, nature seemed to be hurrying to make the most of it. Hedgerows were full of energy, young green tendrils reaching out luxuriantly to wave in the slipstreams of passing vehicles. Roadside verges were thick with buttercups and ox-eye daisies; copses were almost choking with dog-rose. And just to remind me that this was Chile, at the corner of a field stood a monkey-puzzle tree.

Puerto Montt, where road and railway ended their 660-mile journey from Santiago, was on the receiving end of a cloudburst when I arrived. I hurried through deepening puddles to Raúl Arroyo's tumbledown guesthouse, a shack at the foot of a bluff. In the dining room a dozen drenched travellers were sitting on rucksacks, tucking into mountains of fish and chips. 'Come in, come in,' urged Raúl – then, seeing that the room could hold no more, he shrugged his shoulders with a grin. 'You think this is a squeeze? One day last year I had 40.'

But though he made the most of his modest guesthouse, Raúl was no Rachman. His charge was minimal, his hospitality generous. 'I just can't turn people away,' he told me. I chose a secluded eight-by-four-foot cupboard, dumped my luggage on the bed, and left the others to their fish and chips. The rain had eased; so I ran the two blocks to the promenade, sea shells crunching under my feet. Clambering onto a parapet, I let my gaze revolve slowly across the 180-degree horizon. To the west, the wet, green island of Chiloé lay diffidently in the shadow of the receding storm. East, the 9,000-foot volcano Osorno shimmered in bright sunlight like a heap of gems. And straight ahead – due south – my eyes drifted beyond the leaden and forbidding waves towards a place whose secrets might, I hoped, soon be revealed.

Puerto Montt was a monument to the versatility of timber and corrugated iron. Founded in 1852 by German colonists, it had made certain concessions to the twentieth century, but they were widely spaced and grudging. Timber, especially, was everywhere: in the painted shingles of the houses tumbling down to the shore; in the horse-drawn carts which rumbled along the Costanera; in the old railway carriages, pensioned off on a siding beside the railway station; and piled high on the lorries chugging in from the forests to fuel the ovens and stoves of the town's 120,000 inhabitants. All this wood gave Puerto Montt a grainy look, enhanced by the corrugated roofs whose red, green and orange surfaces were thrown into dramatic relief when the sun shone low in the west. Their roughness mimicked the ever-turbulent waters to the south.

Back at the guesthouse, I found the next cubicle occupied by a young German, dishevelled and staring dreamily through the polythene-covered hole which passed for his bedroom window. Fritz was waiting to buy a boat. He'd left home four years previously with his life's savings in the heel of his shoe. For a while he'd wandered aimlessly around Peru and Bolivia; then, on a friend's recommendation, drifted into Chile and hitchhiked south. Reaching the forests east of Puerto Montt, he found at last what he was looking for. 'It's like Tyrol without the people,' he grinned, still gazing through the window.

Fritz had spent his first summer hiking from lake to lake, asking directions from farmers with names like Zimmerman or Reichert, who had pointed towards hidden passes and pressed jars of honey and home-made cottage loaves into his hand. Here was somewhere, he thought, where a man could live unmolested and perhaps find peace of mind. He began to hatch a plan.

He was no farmer, but he knew he had a practical streak and was good with his hands. 'Here in Puerto Montt I took the plunge,' he continued, turning to face me at last. 'An estate agent was offering 100 hectares of rough country by a lake, two days' walk from the nearest road – so I invested what was left in my shoe.' Within two summers he'd built a house, planted cereals and fruit trees, and filled his farmyard with hens, geese, pigs and a horse.

At first he'd been absorbed by the tasks, content with his own company and confident of success. But then his luck ran out. The second spring brought almost continuous rain – not unusual in that part of Chile, but sufficient to wash away his seedlings and cut him off completely from the outside world. 'No one came to ask how I was. My friends in Germany stopped writing; then, would you believe, the farm became infested with rats!' He winced at the memory. 'Do you know, I spent the whole summer hunting and trapping those bastards, sometimes 100 of them each day. For me it was a very bad year.'

But Fritz remained a dogged optimist. After finally exterminating the rats, he borrowed some money to finance the new boat. The holding would produce a surplus in the coming year – he was sure of it – so he'd need the boat to ferry the produce across the lake. 'Next year will be the turning point,' he insisted. 'And just to make sure, I've ordered a kilo of rat poison.'

By any definition of Patagonia, I was now on its brink. But before continuing south I wanted to visit an island whose history has been linked with Patagonia for more than 100 years. Chiloé, half the size of Wales, separates Reloncaví Sound from the Pacific. Lying in the teeth of the Roaring Forties, it's a stormy place – the name means 'Land of Seagulls' in the language of the Mapuche Indians, suggesting that seabirds are often driven far inland. Over the centuries its several thousand 'Chilote' farmer/fishermen have developed an abiding *esprit de corps* and a judicious distrust of mainlanders. In 1826 they were the last in the whole of Latin America to join the liberators and boot out the Spanish.

In 1834 Charles Darwin, arriving on HMS *Beagle*, found the Chilotes well fed but miserably lacking in creature comforts to improve their damp lives. They would eagerly barter a duck or goose for a little tobacco. Castro, the island's capital, he found 'a most forlorn and deserted place . . . the streets and plaza coated with fine green turf, on which sheep were browsing.' There was not a watch or clock in the whole town, he observed caustically. 'An old man struck the church bell by guess.'

News of Patagonia reached the Chilotes in the 1870s, when the first of the great 'estancias' or sheepfarms were being established in the far south. The pioneer ranchers were desperate for farmhands. Although it would be many years before the Chile/Argentina frontier was properly defined, most of the estancia lands had been granted by the Argentine government, so their new owners looked first to Buenos Aires for their labour.

Display advertisements were placed in Argentine newspapers, offering handsome wages for anyone prepared to make the move to Patagonia. People consulted ships' captains and ticket agents. Where were Río Gallegos, Punta Arenas, Ushuaia? What, indeed, was Patagonia? Some thought it was an Argentine province, others a foreign country. Within a few months Patagonia became the talk of the Buenos Aires cafés and bars. But the call to the south happened to coincide with a period of relative prosperity in the capital, and few workers actually made the trip. The rigours of Patagonia, it seemed, held little appeal for townsfolk.

The Chilotes on the other hand were used to hardship. Their island's fertility had proved to be a mixed blessing; farmers battled constantly with dense forests which, brought on by copious rains, forever threatened to engulf their fields. Being natural seafarers, Chilote men were also used to being away from home. They soon began to spend their summers in Patagonia, joining the teams of sheepshearers who moved from farm to farm. Later, many settled there permanently. Some encouraged their families to join them; others preferred the single life, sending monthly allowances back to their loved ones rather than lead them to what for many years was thought of as 'a man's place'.

I was taken to the island by Pedro Bórquez, a chocolate salesman. He was in a great hurry, but not too great to swing his car to a spectacular halt at the sight of a hitchhiker on the outskirts of Puerto Montt. We caught the Chiloé ferry with moments to spare, and crossed in a heavy swell with dolphins pitching round the bows. Chilote folklore maintains that these waters are haunted by *El Caleuche*, a ghost clipper whose great translucent sails lure fishermen to put to sea on stormy nights. Invariably the victims are never seen again. Some Chilote sailors are still said to make a point of locking themselves inside their cottages on blustery evenings, just in case.

After the Pan-American Highway, Chiloé's roads seemed uncannily quiet. They reminded me of the lanes of Pembrokeshire, and in fact the landscape was like west Wales too: a hotchpotch of small fields, whose freshly-turned soil would soon be covered by the deep, luxuriant green of potato crops brought on by spring rains. Many of the clapboard houses were gaily painted and could be approached through twin rows of whitewashed stones. Others stood empty and derelict. If their owners hadn't left for Patagonia, they must certainly have decamped to Puerto Montt, and their once productive plots were reverting to wet grassland and sphagnum bog.

We arrived at the port of Ancud, and Pedro rushed off to sell chocolate. After our high-speed journey I was happy to pass an hour by the quayside, watching the fishermen unload their catches from brightly painted *chalupas* and listening to the seagulls screaming as they fought for scraps.

There wasn't much to explore. Although more than 200 years old, Ancud was largely destroyed by an earthquake in 1960. A few buildings survived the tremors, only to collapse under the tidal wave which followed them. Chile's earthquakes are legendary, but this one seems to have taken everyone by surprise. The main road to Castro remained impassable for months, and the island's only railway never operated again. Ancud's stately nineteenth-century cathedral, one of its few stone buildings, was reduced to rubble, to be replaced years later by an inconsequential wooden one – the only single-storey cathedral I've ever seen.

Wandering later in the surrounding countryside, I chatted to a farmer putting out silver milk churns to be collected later by the dairy dray. The roadsides were home to a giant species of rhubarb, which he told me Chilotes eat raw with salt. I replied that in my country we prefer to boil it and add sugar, a comment which so amused him that he nearly split his sides. Like many Chilotes, he kept a dozen or so pigs in his yard, and as we talked they scampered at our feet, piglets squealing after their mothers as they rooted among the wild fuchsias.

The Chilotes excelled themselves when it came to giving lifts. I walked out of Ancud on the Castro road, and no sooner had I left the town than a lorry pulling a heavy trailer ground down through innumerable gears and hissed to a halt. A door swung open. Familar music wafted from the cab. Two young faces grinned down. 'Castro?' they called. I nodded, and strong arms leaned down to take my rucksack. Carlos and Mario were carrying fish, but they were too full of questions for me to discover much about them. When Mario found that I could translate the English lyrics of one of his cassettes, I was immediately set to work. He explained that he'd fallen in love with the singer, Tracy Chapman, and his inability to understand her words had been causing him great distress.

Carlos and Mario's lorry was a modern one, equipped with the latest gadgets, and after I'd completed my translation the CB radio was brought to life. '*Naranja Mecánica. Atentivo Spártacus. ¿Copias?*' Crackle. '*Spártacus. ¡Atentivo! ¿Copias?*' More crackle. To distract them from the tiresome thing, I mentioned that *Una Naranja Mecánica*, or *A Clockwork Orange*, had been the title of a well-known film of the seventies. They chortled in disbelief.

Castro had the atmosphere of a medieval town being dragged unwillingly into the twentieth century. Horses still limped along the waterfront, hauling carts piled high with potatoes or fish; but they now shared Castro's steep, narrow streets with juggernauts of the kind driven by Carlos and Mario. On the quayside, the town's famous *palafito* houses still jutted over the water, wobbling picturesquely if rather perilously on their spindly stilts. But Chiloé had begun to attract tourists from Santiago, and some of the *palafitos* had become fake-rustic restaurants, offering lobster and king crab at absurd prices to a clientele which, as far as the

Chilotes were concerned, might just as well have come from Mars.

In my pocket I had an introduction from a Santiago friend to Renato Cárdenas, a local historian and writer. I'm always a little wary of waving introductions on people's doorsteps, but Renato had been recommended so warmly that I asked in Castro if they recognized the name. They all did. *'Por supuesto, señor.* Don Renato lives *arriba* – up the hill.' I followed the directions of a dozen willing hands, and found myself climbing a broad street which gave way to a deeply rutted lane as it left the town.

Eventually the house came into view, a decaying two-storey structure built, like everything else, of wood. Renato answered my knock – a slight figure with deep-set, enquiring eyes under a shock of black hair. His goatee-bearded face was that of a 40-year-old, but the ripped sweater, baggy corduroys and carpet slippers hinted at someone more elderly. A picture flashed through my mind of a mad scientist having a day off. At first he stood framed by the doorway, momentarily nonplussed by his unexpected visitor, but then I mentioned the name of our mutual friend and his eyes lit up. 'Why, yes! Francisco Valiente's a good fellow. How is he? Do come in and have some tea!'

Renato already had several guests in his kitchen, and I found them earnestly discussing Chile's forthcoming general election, now less than two weeks away. Along with a great many other Chileans, they'd been looking forward to this moment for nearly 20 years.

I knew some of the background. In 1973, with help from the United States, the armed forces had ousted Marxist president Salvador Allende and installed in his place the Army chief, Augusto Pinochet. There followed a decade of violence un-equalled in Chile's history. Allende's supporters (real or imagined) were hunted down, arrested and interned. Many were subjected to the most brutal forms of torture, and 2,000 were never heard of again.

In 1988, after years of domestic and foreign pressure, Pinochet agreed to hold a plebiscite on the question of whether he would step down. Not surprisingly – except, apparently, to himself – the vote was resoundingly that he should. So now a new president was to be chosen and the campaign was in full swing. Chile's last general election had been so long ago that more than half the population had never voted before. I'd seen them listening on the hustings with a variety of expressions, ranging from curiosity through bewilderment to frank disbelief.

'When Pinochet agreed to the plebiscite,' said Renato, 'the door to democracy was opened a crack. Now it's been pushed ajar. But once his successor is installed it'll be thrown wide open, and the military bigwigs will be furious! What we're afraid of is that they'll slam the door shut again.'

'Don't forget Pinochet will still be in charge of the Army,' one of the others reminded him.

'And he's infiltrated the ministries with his henchmen,' chipped in a third. 'Whoever steps into his shoes is going to be surrounded by Judas Iscariots.'

'I simply don't trust that man,' declared Renato. 'I haven't forgotten 1984.'

'What happened in 1984?' I asked.

'Well, I suppose it was inevitable,' he said, sipping his tea reflectively. 'I've always kept my views fairly private, but on that occasion someone reported a remark I'd made in confidence, a sarcastic quip about the junta.' He grimaced. 'The *Investigaciones*, the secret police, came for me on Christmas Eve. At first I was really worried; I thought I was going to join the ranks of the disappeared. Then they explained that the comment hadn't been sufficiently subversive for that.' He smiled momentarily. 'I was simply to be put in "internal exile" for a bit.'

'Internal exile?'

'Yes. They had two camps for people they wanted out of the way for a while: one in the north of the country, one in the south. I was sent to Quillagua in the north. The name means "Place of the Moon" – quite appropriate really, as it's out in the desert. I spent several months there under a kind of open arrest. I could go for walks, but never very far, because I had to report twice a day to the camp commander. They also let me write to my family and friends. I sent dozens of letters, but it turned out to be an empty privilege because none of them ever arrived.'

I thought of the thousands who had been dispatched to such camps, never to return.

'I'm surprised you're still alive.'

'Yes,' he grinned. 'I suppose I should have been a bit more subversive.'

I knew that Renato had written several books. Had they contributed to his trouble with the secret police?

'I don't think so,' he replied. 'Most of my writing was about Indians and "unimportant" things like that. But I did do some political canvassing – very discreetly, of course – so that we'd be ready when democracy returned.' He looked towards the others. 'That reminds me. We must finish our posters!'

We trooped into another room, where a pasting board was covered with artwork in various stages of completion. The posters were asking people to attend a Communist Party rally. A silk screen stood in a corner. Now I began to see why Renato had been put into 'internal exile'. Considering that the Communists were arch enemies of both the junta and their North American backers, it was a miracle he hadn't been shot.

I visited Renato several times during my stay in Castro, helping with the posters and sharing many cups of tea. On the third day he asked, 'Would you like to see an old Chiloé tradition?'

'Of course!'

'It's called a *minga de tira de casa*. Many years ago, when a Chilote family wanted to move house, they did just that – they took their house with them. Being timber-framed, it would simply be jacked onto a kind of raft, and each farm in the neighbourhood would send a team of oxen to help pull it. The tradition has almost died out; but there's one happening tomorrow in San Juan, my home village.'

San Juan turned out to be a minuscule hamlet, set in a sheltered inlet on the east of the island. It was approached by a track so steep that only four-wheel-drive vehicles could reach it – we had to abandon our car and walk the last half mile. A dozen houses lined a makeshift street, giving on to a beach of coarse shingle. There were no shops or bars, but the community was not without a focus, for at its centre stood a towering wooden church. I looked inside and was surprised to find row upon row of dusty pews: clearly it had been designed to serve a congregation either larger or more devout than San Juan could muster today. The soaring roof echoed to the sound of rain dripping from gutters, and a few yards beyond the vestry I could hear waves breaking.

But then came a more distant noise. Waxing and waning on

the breeze, it was the unmistakable bellowing of oxen. The *tira de casa* had begun.

I raced along the shore, following my nose as much as my ears, for 20 sweating oxen assail all the senses. The house was lying at a drunken angle just above the waterline, and the beasts were being driven in bursts of 30 seconds or so, covering perhaps 20 yards at a time. Each pair of animals had a handler who goaded and whipped them at a signal from a foreman perched on the house's stoop. *Minga* means 'community job', and so it was; the few villagers not actually taking part were lining the route and cheering passionately. In between pulls, strong homemade cider was passed round in demijohns, and the men drank deeply from the bottles and wiped their mouths on their sleeves. The bulls, I noticed, were uncastrated. This would undoubtedly explain their prodigious strength, though it occurred to me that it would also make them pretty aggressive if encountered out in the fields. I made a mental note to beware of uncastrated bulls.

By tradition, the family whose house is being moved provides victuals for the handlers (though not for the bulls). This *tira* would be a long one – more than half a mile – so at midday the foreman called a halt. The men sprawled in a meadow, oblivious to the rain which had been falling in sheets since mid-morning. Soon the mother of the family arrived with a vast stewpot, followed by her daughters bearing tablecloths, loaves of bread and more demijohns.

Renato had gone back to San Juan to distribute posters, but his cousins the Bahamondes asked me to join them in their house by the beach. Here I found another stewpot waiting. The stew consisted mainly of a small fish called *pejerrey*, the staple diet of San Juan fishermen, which comes up by the hundred in every net. We piled our plates high, and I asked my hosts why it was that everyone I'd met in the village seemed to be called Bahamonde.

'Ah,' they replied. 'So you've noticed our little secret!'

For more than a century, they explained, Chiloé had suffered from inbreeding. On the remoter islands the practice had become almost a matter of necessity. With boats visiting only once a week, the opportunities for meeting potential marriage partners were rare. To stop the rural population dying out altogether, the Church had made hundreds of dispensations for

Chilotes to marry their first cousins, and there were even examples of nieces and nephews marrying uncles and aunts. On the island of Acuy this had led to mongolism. Another symptom, less publicized but equally common, was over-calcification of the joints.

A further difficulty was the one I'd noticed in San Juan: everybody ended up with the same name. In just two villages, for example, there were seven Juan Bahamonde Bahamondes – the first Bahamonde being the father's surname and the second one the mother's maiden name. To avoid total confusion the villagers had given them nicknames; the village liar was called Juan Bahamonde Bahamonde de la Verdad ('Honest J.B.B.'), and a seven-stone weakling had become Juan Bahamonde Bahamonde el Gordo ('J.B.B. the Fatty'). Later, I discovered that the problem was not limited to the villages. In the Castro telephone directory there was a Luis Cheuquepil Cheuquepil, a Felipe Bórquez Bórquez, and an Elías Segundo Gómez Gómez ('Elías Gómez Gómez the Second').

Eventually the *tira* got under way once more, and the house began to creep towards its newly prepared plot. When the job was nearly done, the demijohns started being refilled not with cider but with wine. The men struck up a *saloma*, an old ploughman's song, but some had become quite drunk by now and had difficulty remembering either the tune or the words. Later, the family whose house it was would throw a party for the whole village, with dancing till midnight. But the rain had soaked me to the skin, and I decided to leave San Juan. As I climbed the hill, the strains of inebriated yodelling wafted up through the drizzle, almost drowning the bellowing of the toiling bulls.

To get a better idea of what Chiloé's early settlers had faced, I decided to make a trip into the sparsely populated centre of the island, where streams had carved valleys deep into the Piuchue cordillera, its backbone ridge. Much of the area was virgin forest, but in 1947 a local woodsman had hacked a track through to the Pacific coast, and Renato thought it might still be passable. The morning after the *tira de casa*, I walked out of Castro and quickly left the fields and houses behind.

At first the path was wide – more like a road, really – and though it was still raining heavily I felt a surge of exhilaration at being on my own. This was one of the things that had drawn me to Patagonia: the endless opportunities to explore an uninhabited land. A tent, stove and sleeping bag lay deep in my rucksack, and in my pocket was a scribbled map, copied from one I'd discovered on the wall of Castro's forest service office. As the track began to climb, I looked back over the distant scattered farmsteads and felt my journey had begun.

In such a Welsh-looking landscape it seemed entirely appropriate that it should be pouring with rain. How many times had I squelched in identical conditions out of Old Radnor or Llandrindod Wells? Yet the downpour was also worrying, because it would be adding water to rivers already swollen by the previous day's rains. In Castro they'd warned me that 30 inches had fallen the previous week – more than London receives in a year.

My fears turned out to be well founded, for after a couple of hours I was brought to an abrupt halt by the River Puchabrán. I'd been assured that a fallen tree-trunk would provide a safe crossing, but now I saw 60 feet of brown, fast-moving water separating me from the opposite bank. The path led straight into the river. I cast about for several hundred yards upstream and downstream before resigning myself to the fact that the trunk must have been washed away. Indeed, quantities of other vegetation were bobbing past me. The rain was, if anything, getting worse, and I was about to go and find shelter when an old man shouted from away to my right.

'Caballero!'

I trudged over and he confirmed my fears. 'You mustn't try to cross today; the river's in a dangerous state. See how it's about to break its bank over there? Come, my house is on higher ground; you'll be able to dry your clothes, and perhaps cross tomorrow.' As an afterthought, he added matter-of-factly: 'I haven't seen it like this for 30 years.'

José Hemmelmann was a forester: wrinkled and slightly stooping, he looked every bit his 70 years. But his appearance was deceptive, because he outpaced me on the path to the house, and for most of the way seemed to talk without pausing for breath. He'd been born in Temuco, the son of a German labourer, but had lived on Chiloé since the Second World War.

'What brought you to Chiloé?' I gasped.

'I fell head over heels in love,' he replied, eyes twinkling. 'My

21

sweetheart was a Chilota – a Chiloé lass. Her name's Eliana; you'll meet her when we get home.'

We approached the house through a yard full of pigs and geese, rapidly becoming a quagmire under the onslaught of water from the heavens. Eliana was busy in the kitchen, entirely unconcerned by the deafening drumming on her corrugated iron roof – or, indeed, by the presence of two figures steaming and dripping all over her kitchen floor. She signalled me to take off my sodden outer layers, then continued at the stove.

Relaxing on a bench, I asked José about his work as a forester. He'd retired some years ago, but had spent much of his life working with the alerce, *Fitzroya cupressoides*. This magnificent, soaring tree, a relative of the sequoia, grows so slowly that even after 60 years its trunk measures only four inches across. It is one of the longest-living organisms on earth. Left alone, an alerce can live to 3,000 years or more before crashing down upon its neighbours. Unfortunately the rich, red wood is both durable and attractive, and demand for alerce panelling and furniture has become so great that the forest service recently imposed a nationwide ban. José thought this an idiotic idea, dreamed up by bureaucrats in faraway Santiago who knew nothing about the real situation. 'They say the alerce needs protecting, but I could show you hundreds of hectares of untouched alerce forest in this valley alone!'

I asked about that other mainstay of the Chiloé economy, fishing; but he saw little future in that either. 'It's been bumped off by the multinationals,' he lamented. 'Take the company Salmón Antártica, for instance. Since they brought their factory ships here, Castro's *chalupas* hardly go out any more. They catch so little, it's just not worth their while. After all, why should a young man get cold and wet in a Chilote fishing boat, when he can earn four times as much in Concepción or Santiago?'

I recalled that Carlos and Mario's lorry had had 'Salmón Antártica' emblazoned down the side. But before I could dwell on the connection between those amiable characters and such an evil business, José was rummaging angrily in the larder. 'And another thing,' he bellowed. 'You see this tin of sardines?' He jabbed a finger at the label. 'Do you know where it comes from? Iquique! I ask you! That's 2,000 miles north of here. They haven't caught a sardine in Iquique since the Book of Genesis. These are

Chiloé sardines, shipped up to Iquique to be tinned, then brought back for me to buy, at three times the price, in my local grocer's!'

I mentioned how, in the European Community, the people of Cheddar had to suffer the insult of eating Dutch and French Cheddar cheeses.

'These politicians, tschaa!' snorted José. 'I wouldn't give you ten pesos for any of them.'

But by now Eliana had laid a table for five. Their son and daughter-in-law had arrived from a neighbouring farm, and after a spirited introduction by José we sat down to vegetable and egg soup, a plate of mutton, a bowl of sweetened blancmange, and – as Christmas was approaching – a liqueur known as *cola de mono* ('monkey's tail'), which looked and tasted exactly like Irish Cream.

I'd been warned that some of Chiloé's out-of-the-way farmsteads were occupied by evangelists, who spent a great deal of time trying to convert those still ignorant of the joys of church-going. If such people existed, José Hemmelmann definitely wasn't among them. After the fifth *cola de mono* he announced that as well as cutting down alerce trees he'd once run a bar in Castro. He'd called it 'El Gringo'. He brought out a photograph album in which almost every picture showed him drinking heartily at formica-topped tables with robust Germanic men. Though the snapshots were old and faded, the flushed cheeks and merry eyes were the same as those before me. José Hemmelmann, I decided, had led a full and frolicsome life.

After a night curled up by the oven, I thanked the Hemmelmanns and took my leave. 'By the way,' José called after me. 'You remember you said your friend told you the path was cut through in 1947?'

'Yes?'

'Well, it was 1946. I know, because I was the one who cut it.'

The rain had died out overnight, but the Puchabrán was still running too high and fast to wade across, and with no sign of the tree-trunk I reluctantly turned east once more.

The walk back to Castro was a good deal easier than the walk out. Not only did I now know the way, but I soon had company as I marched along. The next day, 14th December, was the day of the long-awaited election. With voting compulsory for adults,

Chiloé's country folk were already setting out for the polling stations in the town. For those under the age of 40 it would be a new experience, and an air of expectancy hung over the ragged bands of pilgrims filtering in from the forest. Some were quite nervous at the prospect. 'They say it'll be a secret ballot, but how can we be sure?' The older ones feigned nonchalance. 'Oh, you just write crosses on the paper – you don't sign anything.' The youngsters looked doubtful, and I noticed that one or two of their elders did too. They'd heard too much about rigged elections, blackmail, intimidation and torture to treat the matter so lightly.

But despite the apprehensions, polling day in Castro passed off peacefully – almost disappointingly so. Canvassing was banned, a public holiday had been declared, the bars were shut and the main street was closed to traffic. Anyone who'd come along hoping for a carnival would have been disappointed, for the mood was solemn. Queues had been forming since early morning in front of the schools which were to be the polling stations – women at one, men at another – and now the voters filed into the buildings under the watchful gaze of navy cadets. Renato and his friends were there; and the Bahamondes from San Juan; and Carlos and Mario; and Pedro Bórquez the chocolate salesman; and at the back of the queue, dressed up to the nines, I even spotted old José Hemmelmann.

There were three votes to be cast: one for the president, and one each for a deputy and senator to represent Chiloé. Each voter was ushered into a classroom, where a dozen invigilators stood by the yellow, white and blue ballot boxes, watching gravely as the ballots were cast. To make sure no one tried to vote twice, everyone was required to have their thumbprints taken. With some 80,000 on the electoral roll in Chiloé alone, this struck me as rather a futile check, but the procedure itself looked intimidating enough to deter anyone from going through it twice. The voters I saw looked quite petrified.

Renato wanted me to stay for what he was sure would be a victory celebration. I was tempted, not so much by the promise of revelry as by the opportunity to spend more time with this unusual man. But Patagonia was calling and I could wait no longer. Early next morning, as Chiloé's votes were still being counted, I boarded a ferry back to the mainland.

The Carretera Austral

For Patagonia-bound travellers, Puerto Montt was until recently the end of the road. South of here the coastline changes dramatically. Some 2,000 miles of fjords and islands separate Puerto Montt from Cape Horn – the most convoluted coastline on earth. Inland, a tangle of beech forests sheltering an undergrowth of matted bamboo makes movement impossible without a machete. Puerto Montt used to be, therefore, where the civilized part of your journey came to an end. If you wanted to continue south – to Punta Arenas, Tierra del Fuego or the naval bases and Indian hamlets on the Beagle Channel shores – you had to take passage with the state shipping line, Empremar. This voyage had such a reputation for awfulness that many travellers would cross the Andes and make a wide detour through Argentina, rather than endure it.

In Patagonia they have a saying: 'Chile is God's way of keeping Argentina from the Pacific.' Ever since the first Europeans set foot on Patagonian soil, the two countries have disputed vast tracts of their southern territories, and four times in the last 100 years they've reached the brink of war. In 1833, when the *Beagle* was carrying out its now-famous survey of the Patagonian coastline, the area was considered as worthless as Alaska or Siberia – a wasteland fit only for Indians. Darwin described it as having the curse of sterility upon it. Even by 1870, more than 50 years after Chile and Argentina's leaders had wrested independence from Spain, they still hadn't fixed a frontier in the far south. After 100 years of wrangling, some aspects are still unresolved today.

When Latin America's Spanish colonies declared their independence, they generally kept the old colonial boundaries under a principle known as *uti possidetis* – the idea that what was good for the colonies was good for their successors. Both Chile and Argentina based their claims to Patagonia on this dictum. The Spanish had divided the continent using natural features such as deserts or mountain ranges, but with so much still unexplored they had no choice but to leave some of the frontiers vague. Once the independent states expanded into these remoter parts, clashes were inevitable.

In 1843, prompted by the voyages of the *Beagle* and by rumours that the French were also about to send an expeditionary force, the Chilean Government founded the colony of Fort Bulnes overlooking the Magellan Strait. Argentina protested, pointing out that the Spanish had placed Patagonia under the Viceroyalty of the River Plate. As successors to the Viceroyalty the Argentine Republic could justifiably claim all the land east of the Andes as far south as Cape Horn. Chile accepted this claim in principle but contested its boundary, especially in the all-important Magellan Strait. Proposals and counterproposals followed, until in 1881 the two governments agreed by treaty that the boundary 'shall run over the highest summits of the cordillera which divide the waters, and shall pass between the sources of streams flowing down to either side'.

I don't know if geographers were consulted on this wording, but for the next two decades it caused continual acrimony, which twice almost boiled over into war. The problem was that glaciation and river capture had shifted the watershed well east of the line of highest peaks. As surveyors tried to demarcate the frontier, politicians on both sides gradually became aware of what was at stake. Not unnaturally, Chile argued that the frontier should follow the watershed; Argentina that it should connect the highest peaks.

In 1896 they asked Queen Victoria to arbitrate on the matter – a move which seems strange in view of more recent events, but which reflected Britain's longstanding links with both countries, and also the British reputation for fair play. The Queen appointed a tribunal, which after some lengthy hearings dispatched a commission under a vice-president of the Royal Geographical Society, Sir Thomas Holdich, to look at the situation on the ground. This must have been a venture of the utmost delicacy. With the two countries on a virtual war footing, the five-man party spent the southern summer of 1901–2 examining 800 miles of the disputed frontier. In the event their recommendation, a masterful compromise which in the north favoured Argentina and in the south Chile, was accepted by both sides.

But this was not the end of the story. Beyond Tierra del Fuego the Andean chain disintegrated into a scatter of rugged islands, some of them uninhabited and unsurveyed. The 1881 treaty had awarded those east of Tierra del Fuego to Argentina, those west of Tierra del Fuego and south of the Beagle Channel to Chile. An unresolved bone of contention was the channel's course around three islands known as Picton, Nueva and Lennox. The Chileans maintained that it ran north of them as a logical eastward continuation of its main segment; this would give all three islands to Chile. The Argentines argued that it swung south of Picton and Nueva and possibly even west of Lennox, thus placing at least two of the islands within Argentina.

Funnily enough it was the Antarctic, several hundred miles to the south, that was to give the Beagle Channel dispute a new and lethal dimension. From the 1940s both Chile and Argentina claimed territory there, and after the Antarctic Treaty was signed in 1959 they quickly realized that what was now at stake was more than national pride. Whoever held Picton, Nueva and Lennox could, when the treaty came up for review, use the principle of extrapolating lines of longitude to consolidate their claim to a land of prodigious mineral wealth. There was economic promise closer to home too, since by now it was almost certain that the South Atlantic contained reserves of oil and gas. Picton, Nueva and Lennox held the key to mineral rights extending over 200 miles of sea bed.

The two countries seemed to be moving inexorably towards war. In 1965 an Argentine patrol shot dead a Chilean border guard near Punta Arenas, and the Chileans responded with massive troop manoeuvres. Then in 1968 the two navies and air forces confronted each other during exercises in the Beagle Channel. Three years later the governments appeared to pull back, and asked Queen Elizabeth to arbitrate on the basis of a decision made by the International Court of Justice. The Queen awarded the islands to Chile; but Argentina rejected the ruling, and in December 1978 there followed what came to be known as 'the six-day crisis'.

During those six days the armed forces of both sides deliberately violated each other's territory and airspace, as if determined to spark off a war. The Argentines announced that they no longer considered the Queen an acceptable mediator; but luckily, at the eleventh hour, Pope John Paul II stepped in. Hostilities were suspended. The Pope's mediation took six years, and his award, when it came, was a monument to diplomacy. He granted all three islands to Chile, but appeased the Argentines by confirming the so-called 'two-ocean' principle whereby a line drawn south from Cape Horn would be taken as the boundary for Chilean and Argentine claims to territorial waters and mineral rights within the 200-mile limit. Around the islands themselves Chilean sovereignty would be limited to twelve miles, and the Argentines would be guaranteed access to the port of Ushuaia. With this formula the Pope seemed to have succeeded where others had failed, and in 1985 both sides announced that they would abide by his decision.

But in Chile and Argentina political issues have a habit of resurfacing. The Argentines have never quite forgiven Chile for allegedly helping the British in the Falklands conflict. The Chileans, for their part, remain suspicious of Argentine intentions in the Antarctic. (It is still a capital offence in Argentina to publish a map of the country without including Antarctica and the Falklands.) In the 1980s both countries put great effort into their Antarctic activities, to consolidate their territorial claims in case for some reason the Antarctic Treaty was not renewed. Meanwhile army, navy and air force patrols maintained an unspoken tension in the Beagle Channel. According to a newspaper article I came across, the Argentines have another reason to hold on to their Patagonian territory. 'If the northern hemisphere were to suffer a more serious accident of the Chernobyl kind,' it ran, 'Patagonia might be one of the few places left radiation-free. We could well see a wave of immigration comparable with that of the early years of this century.'

In Chile, the poor communications between the heartland and the disputed territory have always irritated the military strategists, and after the 1978 crisis President Pinochet ordered the building of a road to open up its most isolated and vulnerable part. The £50 million, 900-mile Carretera Austral doesn't look like a military road; no tanks roll along its hastily laid surface, and civilians can use it without restriction. Officially its purpose is to make life easier for the communities which for 50 years relied on horses, flimsy river rafts, and more recently motor launches to receive their provisions and mail. But everyone in Chile knows that the Carretera Austral's message to the Argentines is: 'We won't be caught napping again.' No wonder, I thought, that my friends in both countries had been worried when I left for the far south. 'Be careful of the Argentines,' the Chileans had warned me. 'Be careful of the Chileans,' warned the Argentines.

The Spanish word *carreta* means 'cart', so *carretera* strictly means 'cart track' – an apt description for this single-track gravel road, which in Britain would be marked 'unsuitable for motor vehicles'. But its influence has been immense. From Puerto Montt to the deep blue waters of Lake General Carrera and the River Baker, it has transformed people's lives.

The wind screamed off Reloncaví Sound, as I stood nervously with my thumb out where the paved road ended on the edge of Puerto Montt. I needn't have been anxious; the first vehicle, a Land Rover full of sheep, took me fifteen miles, then I bounced along for the same distance in a bus. It was a public service, but the driver refused any payment. By late afternoon I'd travelled a full 70 miles, shared two family picnics, been shown round a timber yard, and received an invitation to spend Christmas in Coyhaique, 350 miles to the south.

Dusk overtook me at Hornopirén, a logging and fishing community at the head of a splendid fjord. In the village square, a pig looked up from its grazing and grunted suspiciously.

'Where are you going?' asked the village constable.

'I'm on my way to Chaitén,' I replied confidently, naming the next town southbound on the map.

'You've got a boat?'

'No; I'm hitchhiking.'

'Really?' The constable gave this a moment's thought. 'Well,' he said at last, 'I hope you can walk on water. The ferries won't start running till next year.'

I listened in disbelief, as he explained that the road ahead involved two ferry crossings which only operate in the high summer months of January and February. For the rest of the year, Chaitén-bound motorists take the direct ferry service from

Puerto Montt. He was amazed no one had told me this. I confessed that I hadn't bothered to ask.

Seeing my unhappiness, he led me gravely across the road to the police station, brewed some coffee, and disappeared for a few minutes. When he returned his countenance had taken a brighter turn.

'I thought as much! My friend who runs the village council is sailing for Chaitén tomorrow. I've told him you're going with him.'

I could hardly believe my luck. It's not every council boss who would take a complete stranger on an 80-mile voyage – even under pressure from the village bobby.

While I'd been on the road from Puerto Montt, the outcome of the election had filtered through. Patricio Aylwin, the 'grandfather of Chilean politics', had won a clear majority with the support of an alliance of parties including the previously banned and tortured Communists. He would head the new government from the following March. That evening, on the steps of the council offices, I stood alongside the constable and witnessed Hornopirén's contribution to the festivities which were taking place all over Chile. Aylwin's supporters (about 50 in all – i.e. most of the village) were holding a dashing victory parade. Horns bellowed dementedly, and a toy drum thumped out a gleeful rhythm as young and old marched round the square in full-throated celebration of Chile's hard-won democracy. Some of the lyrics about the outgoing President Pinochet were decidedly rude.

The constable was unruffled. He rocked back and forth on his black leather heels, surveying the square with a 'boys-will-be-boys' expression. 'I'm glad Aylwin's won,' he remarked affably. 'Now perhaps we'll have some peace and quiet.' I couldn't imagine quite what he meant. Even at the height of the revelry Hornopirén remained the most serene place imaginable. As the demonstrators made their final circuit of the square, the pig didn't even raise its head.

Next morning, promptly at the appointed time, the man from the council arrived at the slipway with half a dozen soldiers. He introduced himself as Oswaldo and handed me a statement to sign, absolving him of any responsibility for my safety. Was it this, or was it his fraying cardigan, which made it cross my mind that he was the very picture of a local government officer? The launch rode at anchor 50 yards offshore. From where I stood it looked extremely cramped and not a little rusty. I hoped the voyage wouldn't be a long one. Oswaldo hailed briefly, and a hand acknowledged him from the wheelhouse. A boy stepped sleepily into a dinghy and rowed ashore to collect us.

In the event, the launch turned out to be neither as cramped nor as rusty as I'd expected. During the eight-hour voyage the soldiers taught me the Spanish names for the seabirds wheeling about our antennae: elegant, ocean-going petrels and fulmars, as well as the more familiar gulls and geese. We steered a course close to the bamboo-clad shores. Cormorants bobbed in our wake, riding low in the water as if about to sink, and looking this way and that as if hopelessly lost.

The soldiers passed the time discussing politics and the price of whisky. Oswaldo looked weary and said little, but the soldiers were in higher spirits because they were about to go on leave. One of them had met another British traveller the previous year. 'Señor Kenteen Crayway, he was a writer like you. He drank with me in Chaitén, and one day I will drink with him in England!'

'Kenteen Crayway?'

'Yes – look!' And he showed me a business card from his wallet, on which was printed the name Quentin Crewe.

After a while the soldiers and Oswaldo slept; and the boy took the wheel, staring expressionlessly through the cracked wheelhouse window towards the grey horizon, just visible through the spray. Although no more than fifteen years old, he steered his course with the silent concentration of one who had spent a long lifetime at sea.

As we cleared the final headland before Chaitén, stormclouds threatened and a crosswind struck the little craft. Soon it was raining hard. Black islands drifted past, outliers of the archipelago that hugs Chiloé's eastern flank; but the launch heaved so violently that at one moment they seemed to tower above us, while the next they were lost beneath the waves. I turned nervously to my companions, but they continued to doze, and before my anxiety could turn to alarm the motion subsided as we entered the shelter of the bay. Within half an hour we were stepping onto a rain-sodden jetty; the voyage was over.

According to the notice in the tourist office window, Chaitén's summer holiday season had already begun, but both the office and the mock-Alpine Hostería Schilling opposite were firmly shuttered. The storm had gathered momentum, and telephone wires howled over my head. Some figures in ragged parkas and thick woollen hats appeared briefly before diving into a house. Taking refuge in the church on the square, I watched Father Félix give the bellrope a final tug for evensong and step across a polished pine altar to face his congregation of one. The church had been built to seat 200, indicating either a touching optimism on the part of Father Todesco, who built it, or a severe moral decline amongst the flock.

I found a corner shop, on whose door a notice read 'HIRMA LOPEZ – SUPERMERCADO ABIERTO'. Could Hirma López recommend anywhere to stay?

'Well, you could stay here if you like.'

She led me up creaking stairs to a first-floor bedroom and dusted it down apologetically. 'I'm afraid I'll have to make up the bed. You're the first visitor I've had this year.'

Hirma was a stout woman of 50, and in her ample but well-cut black dress she gave the appearance of a rich Spanish widow. She hated Chaitén. I could have told that just from her eyes, if she hadn't told me herself. She'd come ten years ago to be the postmistress, but they'd tried to send her to Coyhaique and she'd resigned in disgust. 'Coyhaique – I ask you!' she snorted. 'Goodness knows, Chaitén is in the back of beyond, but Coyhaique. . . .'

So Hirma had stayed in Chaitén, and had opened the town's only 'supermarket', and it had been a modest success, and in between customers she looked out at the rain and dreamed of her home on Chiloé. A long time ago, she hinted, there'd been a man; but he'd left for Tierra del Fuego and never came back.

From Chaitén, the Carretera Austral wound through a patchwork of forests, fields and bog. In 1930 a small band of men had hacked a horse trail through this difficult country, providing the first Pacific outlet for the rich pastures along the Argentine border. Like much of the far south, the area had previously depended for its supplies on Argentina; so the growing community intended this new path to be a statement that they wanted to be Chilean. It must have severely tested their loyalties.

The Welsh/Argentine village of Trevelin lay just a day's ride across the border; Chaitén, even with the new trail, remained a long week's journey away. In 1956, the Government made its first attempt to drive a road through to the main centre at Futaleufú; and in 1982, after several changes of heart and a change of route, it finally succeeded. It was this road that was now passing slowly beneath my boots.

Two men in a smart Japanese station wagon responded to my outstretched thumb. They were heading for an island on Lake Yelcho, where they explained that they'd bought some land and were now building a house. The driver, Otto, was depressed by the news from Santiago; for years he'd been devoting himself to the Pinochet cause, and now he felt his efforts would be undone. 'You know, the Marxists left the country in one hell of a mess,' he complained. 'Pinochet was getting us out of it. His monetarist policies were exactly what was needed; and we were just beginning to turn the corner.'

Despite his distress about the country's new direction, Otto seemed relaxed and self-assured. He lounged indolently in his seat, driving with one hand while the other languished round his friend's shoulder. Rosy-cheeked and tousle-haired, he wore well-cut slacks and expensive shoes; and beneath a discreetly open-necked shirt I glimpsed a gold chain.

'Gradually,' he continued, 'Pinochet built up confidence and prosperity again. It took a long time, and I know everyone says the middle classes bagged all the gains; but the truth is that we were heading for an economic miracle from which everyone would have benefited – despite the efforts of the subversives.'

Now, it seemed, the 'subversives' had voted out his hero and the new-found wealth was going to be lost. 'I blame democracy,' he said firmly. 'You can't trust common people to make sensible decisions. Mark my words – Chile will be ruined.'

His companion stared silently at the road ahead.

Otto then launched into a glowing description of the island idyll where they were planning to spend the next two weeks. 'Why don't you join us for the day?' he crooned. 'You could swim and sunbathe while we work. Then, this evening, we'll have an *asado* – a barbecue – and drink some wine.'

At this suggestion his friend's lips at last unbuttoned and showed the trace of a smile. He nodded encouragingly towards me. Despite Otto's arrogance I'd warmed to them both, and was tempted to accept the offer; but an inner voice made me say no. They let me out at the village of Amarillo, and as the vehicle receded I knew instinctively that I'd made the right choice. Maybe it was something coquettish in Otto's manner; maybe it was his unabashed failure to introduce his friend. Or maybe it was simply that I can never trust anyone who wears too much perfume.

There can't be many places in the Andes where you can bathe in an open pool, stark naked, and not get frozen to death. The sign by the roadside read 'Termas del Amarillo – 5 km'. I followed it eagerly, because *termas* means hot springs. An hour later I was up to my neck in a warm, slightly sulphurous pool, surrounded by flowering sorrel and looking up at a mountainside clothed in beech. Though several huts and cabins had been built around the place, they were all quite deserted, confirming once again that the visitor season hadn't yet begun. From a nearby bog came a croaking pit-a-pat, as if a bag of billiard balls were being gently shaken. I soaked in the steaming water, wondering what kind of creature might possibly make such an odd sound. As if to answer my question, from out of the weeds floated something which made my stomach turn. Upside down and with pale limbs outstretched, circling gently in the current, was a small dead frog.

Freshened and relaxed by my bathe, I sauntered southwards through ever-thickening forest. The beeches around Amarillo had now been joined by cypresses, their fluted trunks garlanded with old man's beard. The rain had begun again, and I welcomed the shelter of these grand old trees. For several hours there was no traffic, then the sound of a straining engine announced the approach of a car.

Ignacio and Gloria were in their sixties, the most elderly holidaymakers I was to meet on the Carretera Austral. A friend in their adopted town of Punta Arenas had drawn their attention to the road's recent opening, and now they were working their way with military precision through the points of interest set out in the latest edition of TurisTel, a guidebook produced (for some reason) by the national telephone company. Ignacio was clearly in charge. Steering with one hand and holding the book in the other, he read from it as if dictating to a secretary. When the book said look left, we looked left. When it said 'a good place to picnic' we stopped and picnicked. For the last eleven summers Ignacio and Gloria had chosen one of Chile's twelve regions and used their holiday to cover it in the same systematic way. 'After this year we'll really know our country!' Ignacio announced.

'Ignacio's a bank manager,' explained Gloria, implying that this might account for everything.

As we bounced along the twisting road, I noticed that Gloria did indeed act as a kind of secretary to Ignacio. If he felt cold, he would mutter 'window up', and she would close the window immediately. If thirsty, he had only to bark 'water' and she would produce it like a magician's assistant. Even when parked and picnicking, he issued orders like a sergeant-major. My initial amusement was beginning to turn to irritation, until I remembered that I was after all in Latin America. Outside the capital cities, the husband is still customarily the decision-maker in family affairs. He is also the protector of honour, and it's no coincidence that the Spanish for 'gentleman' is *caballero*, which literally translated means cavalier. Had I been tactless enough to ask Ignacio why he was treating Gloria in this 'cavalier' way, we might well have found each other's reasoning equally absurd.

The couple's slavish dependence on their guidebook reminded me of the enormous influence popular guides can have. Leafing through their copy, I read on its second page that 55,000 had been printed – an amazing quantity for an annually updated guide in a nation of only thirteen million people. If just ten buyers in a thousand used it on their journeys down the Carretera Austral, that would be more than 500 travellers per year looking at the region through TurisTel eyes.

It was many years ago that I first reflected on the impact of guidebooks, when I co-authored one for hikers with the writer and publisher Hilary Bradt. In our case the dilemma was more serious, since we were enthusing about parts of the Andes which in those days received relatively few visitors. We'd tremendously enjoyed our research, and wanted to share our discoveries so that others could follow us into the high valleys. The book was to be written in English and published simultaneously in Britain and the United States. What, we wondered, would be its effect on the people of those high valleys? Would they be drawn, however gradually, into the grip of a tourist economy? Would the children learn to beg? Throw stones? Steal? Would the paths become eroded and strewn with litter?

The adventure travel business was already growing quickly. By the 1970s there were few places that couldn't be visited – legally or otherwise – by a spirited and resourceful traveller; and as the developed world became more frenetic, so it seemed to spawn more and more individuals looking for adventure and escape. But for the first time, on that fact-finding trip, I found myself observing the situation through the eyes of an Andean peasant. With the arrival of outsiders, money would seem to appear almost for the taking – and in quantities scarcely credible – once the local people had understood and exploited the newcomers' peculiar needs. Would they be tempted to cast aside traditional values, and even leave crops and animals unattended, in the rush to open drink stalls and ramshackle hotels?

Anyone old enough to remember Cuzco before Kuoni (or, for that matter, Corfu before Club Méditerranée) is well aware of the damage that conventional tourism can do. But independent travellers like myself may be tempted to think we are a cut above the ordinary tourist. Surely we could never bring about such devastation?

Unfortunately, the evidence suggests that we could. Twenty years ago, only the occasional stalwart ventured off South America's well-trodden tourist circuits. Today, thanks to a proliferation of 'how-to-do-it' guidebooks, thousands do. Even if this new generation demands fewer creature comforts than the old, the pressure of numbers will continue to take its toll. Hilary and I hoped that those who had taken the trouble to read our book would think twice before leaving litter, abusing hospitality or spoiling children with unsuitable gifts. In our own experience, most hikers' behaviour was exemplary. Yet Peru's famous Inca Trail to Machu Picchu has deteriorated so badly that it was recently dubbed by John Barry, director of the UK-based Survival Club, as 'The Andrex Trail'. And on a smaller scale, I'm ashamed to say that a thoughtful and considerate woman who lives beside a certain Chilean lake is still cursing my name for suggesting that readers might camp on her lawn.

*

Ignacio dropped me at Puyuhuapi, 'a mist-swathed port at the head of a long sea inlet, worth a few minutes' pause'. It comprised a jetty, a single street, and a few gaily painted cottages lining the shore. With Ignacio and Gloria's departure the place seemed deserted, and I was about to continue down the road when suddenly a voice hailed me.

'Claus Hopperdietzel,' announced a tall bearded man, approaching with hand extended. 'I saw you arrive.'

We shook hands and I explained that I was on my way to Coyhaique. 'You might find it difficult to get a lift,' he warned. 'I don't think more than a couple of dozen vehicles have gone that way all week.' Then an idea occurred to him. 'My father's planning a trip to Coyhaique tomorrow. Why don't you come to lunch and meet him? We don't get many visitors here.' As if reading my mind, he added, 'They stop for a few minutes, consult their guidebook, and drive on.'

Claus's house near the jetty was square and heavy-timbered, with big shuttered windows and overhanging eaves. His father Walther gave me a boyish smile. He looked younger than his 79 years, but moved slowly and carefully, as if afraid of bumping into things. In 1935, he told me, he'd left Europe with three other young men with the idea of founding a colony amongst the Chilean fjords. 'Our home was in the Sudetenland,' he explained, eyes narrowing as he strained with distant recollections. 'After 1919 we were among three million Germans who found ourselves being ruled by the Czechs. The cold truth was that there was no future for us there. Puyuhuapi, we heard, had one of the highest fainfalls in Chile – more than 150 inches per year. A German called Hans Steffen had explored the valley in 1894 and thought it would be a good place to rear livestock; so we came. Our idea – innocent though it seems now – was that after a few years we might send home news of our success, so that others could join us to make a proper colony.'

'What went wrong?'

'Well, for the first four summers we were just working to survive. Parts of the forest we burned; other sections we felled with hatchets and our bare hands. Then came the war, and we lost touch with the Fatherland, and in the war's aftermath emigration was forbidden.' His eyes began to water. 'So, you see, the village has stayed as it was: the four original families,

37

our children and grandchildren, and a few Chileans who've thrown in their lot with us over the years.' He dried his eyes, threw back his head and laughed. 'We must be the smallest colony in the history of the world.'

A shelf against a wall bulged with dog-eared books in old German script, including an illustrated copy of Heinrich Harrer's classic *Seven Years in Tibet*. It seemed to me that Walther's life had had some parallels with Harrer's. Like Harrer, he'd been caught up in the whirlpool of Hitler's Germany, to be catapulted into a long exile. In Harrer's case the exile had lasted only until the end of the war; but Walther had invested much sweat in his new homeland. Almost single-handed, he'd cleared 700 acres of forest and founded a successful cattle-breeding business. His four sons knew no other home. 'Go back to Europe?' he asked in response to one of my questions. 'No, that would be out of the question. It's never even crossed my mind.'

We ate cod and sauerkraut, and I decided to try my luck on the Coyhaique road. If nothing came, Walther would pick me up the following day. 'Remind those who read your book,' he said when I came to leave, 'that we haven't forgotten how to give old-fashioned European hospitality.'

As Claus had predicted, nothing passed me that afternoon or evening. I camped miserably in a dripping forest. Christmas was approaching; and the thought prompted memories of the friends and loved ones I'd left behind in Britain. There are times on every trip when I seriously question my sanity. What is it that makes me take off from my safe, familiar surroundings, often for months at a time, to pit my wits against unknown perils – and foreign ones at that? Of course, the perils usually turn out to be mostly in my head. The real risks of hitchhiking through Patagonia, Africa or the Gobi Desert are much lower than those of an average car journey in Britain. But the emotional strain can be enormous; and for me, the worst part is when a significant date or a chance comment reminds me of friends back home. Then it makes no difference if I'm alone in my tent or surrounded by crowds in a city; I become lonely and miserable.

But rescue, as usual, was at hand. The following morning, I'd hardly been walking for an hour when an elderly lorry came coughing round the corner. It was Walther's. Smiling down from the cab, he motioned me to climb on the back. So it was from this vantage point that I witnessed our crossing of the River Simpson, a foaming torrent in a gorge, and our arrival a few minutes later in Coyhaique, the only settlement of any size between Puerto Montt and the far south.

The name of this town, pronounced 'Koy-aye-ke', showed that I was deep in one-time Indian country. The Mapuche word *coy*, meaning 'tree', crops up all over Patagonia; *haique* is a more local Huiliche term meaning 'place'. The Mapuche and Huiliche were just two of a score of tribes whose campfires lit up this part of the cordillera in the middle of the last century. Their cousins on the Atlantic coast had already brought themselves to Charles Darwin's attention in 1832:

When we came within hail, one of the four natives who were present advanced to receive us, and began to shout most vehemently, wishing to direct us where to land. When we were on shore the party looked rather alarmed, but continued talking and making gestures with great rapidity. It was without exception the most curious and interesting spectacle I ever beheld: I could not have believed how wide was the difference between savage and civilised man; it is greater than between a wild and domesticated animal, inasmuch as in man there is a greater power of improvement.

In 1858 another European gentleman – rather less distinguished than Darwin, though he would probably have disputed this – stepped ashore in northern Chile on a mission to unite the Patagonian Indians under one leader. He was Orllie Antoine de Tounens, a lawyer from the Dordogne, and his intention was that the leader should be him. He certainly cut an imposing figure. Flowing locks of jet-black hair tumbled from under his hat in the fashion of the day, framing a high forehead and dark, distant eyes. An ample beard sprouted from his chin; his tailored coat hid a large curved sabre at the waist; and in deference to his new Indian friends he strode about with a poncho tossed casually over the shoulder. At home he'd read avidly of the brutality of the Spanish *conquistadores*; now he was going to redress the balance. In 1860 he crossed the Bío-Bío and joined with the chief of the Araucanian Indians to proclaim a kingdom extending from the 42nd Parallel to the Horn.

Antoine was, if nothing else, a man of conviction. He drew up a constitution, a flag and a coat of arms for his new nation, and set about appointing a council of state and a supreme court. Among his French and Chilean friends he called his brainchild New France; in Indian circles he referred to it loftily as Araucania. By coincidence, a belief had been circulating among some of the tribes that the end of slavery and oppression would be signalled by the arrival of a bearded white stranger. Obviously the saviour had arrived! Thirty thousand Indians rallied enthusiastically, took up spears and stolen muskets, and converged on the banks of the Bío-Bío, hot-blooded for revenge.

But the campaign was short-lived. Antoine proved an uninspired leader in battle, and after a while the Indians turned their passion to settling differences amongst themselves. His half-caste interpreter betrayed him to the Chilean police, who arrested him as a menace to public order, and without their bearded saviour the Indians lost heart and drifted back to their camps. After some months Antoine was put on trial. He tried every ruse to escape sentence, from pretending he couldn't speak Spanish to insisting that one judge sitting at a wooden table had no authority to pass judgement on a king. The French Ambassador in Santiago suggested that the case be dropped as the defendant had clearly taken leave of his senses; but medical tests showed him to be quite sane, and he was sentenced to ten years in a squalid provincial jail. Here the unfortunate king contracted dysentery, causing all his magnificent hair to fall out – but at the same time attracting widespread sympathy among his Indian friends, who had by now heard of his plight. Fearing another uprising, the Government hurriedly packed him aboard a French warship bound for Brittany.

This might well have been the end of the Kingdom of Araucania. But back home, restored to health and with his locks and beard flowing again, Antoine renewed his efforts to drum up support. He wrote his memoirs and published a manifesto promising land, jobs and money for 'the disinterested people of Old Europe, whose intelligence and hands are inactive because they have no place in the sun'. In view of his experience of southern Chile's climate, the last few words of this statement seem odd to say the least.

The French knew a fraud when they saw one; and in almost

six years the exiled king received not a single letter of support. Embittered but still stubbornly holding court, he returned to Patagonia twice in the years following 1869, the second time sporting a huge pair of black spectacles and carrying a passport in the name of 'Jean Prat'. His luggage included a trunkful of copper coins bearing the Kingdom of Araucania's coat of arms. The disembarkation of a king at Bahía Blanca – especially a king by the name of Jean Prat – must have caused something of a stir, because the Argentine authorities packed both king and retinue on to the first ship back to France.

In a poignant sequel to the tale, Antoine found himself a job as a lamplighter in his native Dordogne, where he died alone, disillusioned and destitute, in 1878. His successor to the crown, a cousin by the name of Gustave Laviarde, held court for many years in Paris but wisely never visited his distant kingdom. A queen, two further kings and a prince were to follow. The last, a certain Philippe Boiry, was said to be still giving audiences near the Gare du Nord as recently as 1975.

Today you will find no Indians around Coyhaique, the 'place of trees'. The remaining scattered bands of Mapuche and Huiliche were killed or tamed by sheep and cattle ranchers in the first decades of this century. Nor will you find many trees. The region's great beech forests, which once extended far up every hillside, disappeared in flames during the wave of settlement which followed Chile's so-called Colonization Law of 1937. Until that year ranching had been mostly in the hands of state corporations or *sociedades* which, for all their devotion to exploiting the region, had at least left the forests alone. Not so the private ranchers! Lacking the machinery or manpower to fell trees to make pasture, they simply set them alight. The resulting *incendios* burned out of control, sometimes for months on end, and the smoke from hundreds of thousands of acres drifted across Argentina and out into the Atlantic. A quick way to clear pasture it may have been, but Chile's early *incendios* are now regarded as among South America's greatest environmental disasters. Only a fraction of the land 'cleaned' in this way was ever trodden by sheep or cattle; but Patagonia's short summers proved a severe hindrance to regeneration, and after half a century the new growth remains stunted. Gnarled rotting tree-trunks still litter the hillsides like spilt matches.

The town of Coyhaique was founded in 1929 to provide a centre for *sociedad* employees and private ranchers. Its recent expansion has been startling – during the 1980s the population doubled to 40,000 – and the pressure on space is beginning to show in the form of two- and even three-storey buildings. But in the suburbs I was pleased to see the huts and allotments of an era when land was in ample supply. In southern Chile it used to be understood that a plot could be claimed if a house appeared on it between sunset and sunrise. Like forest mushrooms, cottages would spring up overnight, and they became known as *casas brujas* or 'enchanted houses'. Years ago a similar law used to apply in the New Forest near my home. If a house was once built and roofed and a fire lit in its hearth, the landowner could not have it pulled down. By the end of the eighteenth century New Forest folk had perfected the art of achieving this under cover of a single winter's night; and the curl of smoke rising defiantly in a grey dawn was a signal that the squatter had triumphed and was there to stay. Many of the New Forest plots were later engulfed by development or became second homes for Londoners. But in Coyhaique they have simply acquired an extension here, an outhouse there, and these natural accumulations give the eye more pleasure than any architect could contrive.

It was the day before Christmas Eve, and the townsfolk had taken it upon themselves to celebrate the approaching holiday with the help of an electronic glockenspiel, which broadcast carols over the rooftops, complete with harmony and descant. It could be heard from miles away. I climbed Cerro MacKay, the basalt dome that towers above Coyhaique's eastern suburbs, and listened to 'Hark the Herald Angels Sing' booming across the cordillera.

In the nearby village of Los Torreones, a crowd had gathered to welcome the newly elected Deputy, Baldemar Carrasco. Or so I thought. On closer inspection the shindig in the village hall turned out to have been laid on by the Deputy himself. It was, he said, a thank-you gesture to his Coyhaique supporters and to the *campesinos* – peasants from the surrounding countryside – who were now approaching in cheerful anticipation from all points of the compass. I stepped in from the pouring rain and found myself in the grip of a mighty handshake.

'*Hola, bienvenidos, gracias por su vota!*' the Deputy greeted me above the din. I quickly explained that I was not a supporter, nor even a constituent – just a foreigner who was pleased to see democracy return to his country.

'Yes, yes, we have *la democracía* again,' he replied with a sweep of the hand. 'You see it here! Look around you! Have some wine!'

I watched his campaigners bustling with plates and glasses. A sheep had been slaughtered, and butchered hunks were popping and spitting over a grill by the back door. On a corner table, plastic bowls were piled high with lettuce. The wine must have been flowing for some time, for both guests and host already seemed quite drunk. A plump accordionist struck up a waltz; the Deputy chose a young girl, and, leading her to the centre of the hall, began to dance. She blushed with embarrassment. But soon other *campesinos* followed, their steps slow and clumsy and their partners held at arm's length under the banners and bright lights. A queer sort of democracy, I thought, but wooing voters this way was better by far than the terror tactics of countries further north. Would the peasants remember this beanfeast when the next election came? Would they vote for the candidate who promised the best victory blowout?

The Deputy swayed towards me, his face the colour of the *vino tinto* in his glass. '*Gracias por su vota!*' he called dreamily.

An hour later, the continuing downpour had turned the entrance to mud. Late arrivals were sliding about, clutching each other and giggling as they hurried to the feast. The accordionist was playing 'I Only Have Eyes For You'. I slipped out into the night, and glanced back to see the Deputy still thanking people for their vote, and the girls still blushing when he took their hands to dance.

'Scratch a Coyhaique man,' they told me, 'and you'll find a runaway.' One such was J.H. He was waiting for me in front of his house, a stooping figure under the shade of an ancient cypress. The house was old, protected from the elements by varnished shingles which hinted at a cultivated respectability, echoing the man's V-necked cardigan and carefully knotted tie.

J.H., it was said, knew more secrets about the Pinochet regime than anyone alive in Coyhaique. I wanted to extract as many of those secrets as I could.

J.H. and Salvador Allende hadn't been the best of friends. The man in front of me seemed possessed by an almost fanatical hatred for the Marxist who'd led his country for the three years before Pinochet's coup. J.H.'s career had been extraordinary. After learning English, French and German and completing a degree at the University of California, he'd spent three years doing odd jobs around Los Angeles and San Francisco before returning to Chile to take a job in the Army. It was 1972; there was much to be done, and promotion came quickly to an able boy. Allende's policies were beginning to strike at the middle classes who, as in many countries, provided the armed forces with most of their officers. J.H. found himself in the intelligence branch, developing clandestine contacts among politicians and civil servants and pinpointing those who believed most fervently in the Marxist cause.

'I also did psychological work within the Army itself,' he told me cryptically. 'The officers had to be made to see the damage Allende was doing – made to understand that the only solution was a coup.' He smiled, warming to the recollection. 'Most of them took little persuading. Many had lost land or property under the appropriation programmes. And, of course, there was the prospect of personal advancement – perhaps a role in the new government. Of course, the country's needs came first,' – his eyelids fluttered as if to acknowledge the lie – 'but these other considerations made my job – how shall I put it? – less unpleasant.'

His wife brought in buttered toast and cheesecake, introduced herself briefly, and scuttled back to the kitchen.

'What did your family think of your army work?' I asked.

'Oh, we lived a normal life,' he replied, sipping his tea. 'You must remember that I worked anonymously. Within the Army I was known as Commander González, but for my government work I used other pseudonyms. Checking on the civil servants was easy; they were so naïve. All I had to do was make sure I never used the same name twice. Also, I moved quickly from job to job; so by the time they suspected alias A, I was already using aliases D, E or F.'

Not even a dictator's henchman is without friends, and I wondered who J.H.'s were. 'Everyone says the Americans helped plan the coup,' I ventured.

'Absolute rubbish! No one outside Chile played any part in it. In fact the State Department in Washington tried to scuttle our plans. We confided in them a few days beforehand, and they ratted on us to Allende.' He waved his toast angrily. 'People should be warned about the State Department. It's full of lefties.'

'What happened to you after the coup?'

'I did some interrogating and troubleshooting. Not much. There wasn't any need; we already knew who the troublemakers were. But those years were difficult for me. Some of my contemporaries became insanely jealous of my success. I'd been earmarked for the job of Ambassador to Ecuador, but lies about me started circulating and the generals vetoed my appointment.' He became reflective. 'Then I worked for CORFO, a government development agency, winkling out corrupt elements. But that place was – how do you call it? – a can of worms. My superiors were the worst of the lot. I worked there for a year, achieving absolutely nothing. Eventually I left public service and took a job as a consultant in industry; then, five years ago, my wife and I decided to get out of Santiago for good.'

'So you came to Coyhaique?'

'Yes. It was for the children's sake, really. The drug culture was beginning to infiltrate the schools up north.'

I wanted to follow up this interesting comment, but our tea was finished and J.H. decided that it was time for me to go. Perhaps he felt he'd already said too much. But I was appalled, not so much by what he'd said as by what he'd obviously withheld. The secrets of the past weighed visibly in his resentful, heavy-lidded eyes – the paranoia stale now, but still nagging, like the woodworm in the beams of his old shingled house.

A newly arrived Coyhaique family invited me to join them for Christmas Eve – a gesture which, at this emotionally charged time of year, meant more to me than they could possibly have realized. Midnight brought a flurry of excitement as the children opened their presents; then the father announced, 'And now, bring on the Christmas dinner!' I already knew that Chileans tended to dine late, but this tradition was new to me. Adults and toddlers were still eating and playing party games when, at two in the morning, I finally put on my coat.

'But haven't you visited the Englishman?' they asked as I stepped out into the mild summer night. 'Oh, before you leave Coyhaique you must go and meet the Englishman!'

The 'Englishman' was called Johnnie MacLean. A mile beyond the southern suburbs, my directions led me a couple of days later up a gravel road hemmed in by six-foot lupins and marguerite daisies. It certainly looked like an English house, dark-timbered and surrounded by a vast garden from whose every nook sprouted fine-petalled poppies, squat pansies, roses, delphiniums and white jasmine; and along its borders the shiny dark leaves of rhododendron with splashes of flowering sweet briar. To the left was a menagerie of hens and rabbits; and at the rear I glimpsed neat rows of cabbages, carrots, asparagus and beans.

But Johnnie MacLean turned out to be not English at all. Born beside the Magellan Strait to a Scottish father and a Swiss mother, he spoke no English and had never travelled further than Argentina. 'I know they call me *El Inglés*,' he sighed. 'I've given up trying to explain the difference between English and Scottish.' An athletic 40-year-old, he lived with two arthritic old ladies who behaved like sisters, although one turned out to be his sister and the other their mother.

Over lunch beneath a wall map of Scotland, Johnnie recounted one of the hazards of being '*un inglés*' in South America.

'It was in 1982 – just after the Falklands War,' he began. 'I had an Argentine friend staying with me, quite an important man in the Government, when the British Ambassador and his wife arrived from Santiago to pay a visit. How was I to introduce them? What could I say? Luckily, my friend slipped away at that moment to look at the garden, and the Ambassador and his bodyguard passed no comment on the Argentine-registered car in the drive. But it was terribly embarrassing: like a scene from one of those comic films. I spent a whole hour trying to keep them in different rooms.'

Johnnie MacLean had the unusual distinction of having come to Coyhaique from the south; and compared with the unremittingly foul climate of his birthplace, he found Coyhaique relatively dry and mild. Not everyone shared his enthusiasm. A few days after Christmas I was continuing south in the company of

René Vásquez, who'd come from Santiago to teach in the village of Villa Castillo, founded in 1966 and now home to 500 souls. 'Today the sun's shining, so you'll probably wonder what I'm complaining about,' he told me as we drove through a gorge towards Cochrane. 'But when the cloud is down, as it usually is, I can't tell you how depressing Villa Castillo can be.'

We stopped at a bend, where the gorge narrowed almost to a slit. 'You like trout?' asked René. 'Follow me.' And taking his rod and line, he scrambled down to where the river thundered over a small waterfall into a pool. I'm always sceptical about fishermen's promises, but a few seconds after casting his line into the foaming water René did indeed pull forth a struggling foot-long trout. 'What did I tell you?' he grinned triumphantly. But his second cast snagged the hook on a rock. It took him 20 minutes to free it, and by the end he was so wet and bad-tempered that we agreed one trout was enough. We slung his prize in the back of the car and continued on our way.

Of all the names in my guidebook to the Carretera Austral, Cochrane stood out as the most peculiar. The town was so called in memory of a Scotsman, Thomas Cochrane, who rose to command the Chilean Navy during the war of independence with Spain. Chile's early history is full of foreign heroes. This one had been a British naval captain, and later a member of parliament, before being jailed for fraud. Meanwhile José de San Martín had liberated Argentina and was marching over the Andes to try and do the same for Chile. News of this campaign on the other side of the world somehow reached Cochrane's prison cell, and on his release he sailed to join the revolutionaries. The year was 1817. By 1820 he'd routed the Spanish in a courageous engagement at Valdivia, which proved to be the turning point of the war. Independence was declared soon after. Chileans always refer to Cochrane as *Lord* Cochrane, a mark of respect which, though touching, is massaging history a little, as his Chilean exploits ended almost a decade before he inherited his father's seat in the upper house.

Arriving in Cochrane, I noticed that its foundation date was 1954, more than a century after its namesake's death. The Carretera Austral reached this far south only in 1988. Until then Cochrane's few visitors had to endure many days in small boats coming round from Puerto Montt, or else risk the notorious

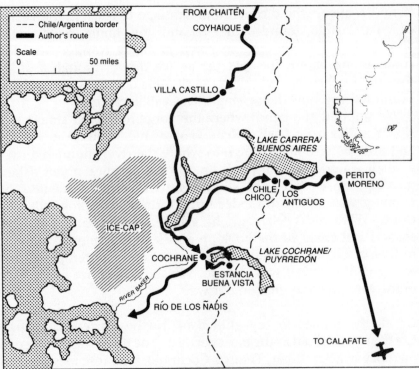

COYHAIQUE TO PERITO MORENO

Roballos Pass over the cordillera from Argentina. The embryo settlement had yet to come to terms with the fact that people could now drive direct from Santiago. Children played hopscotch in its unpaved streets, and gauchos raced horses round the square, dodging the occasional wide-eyed motorist as if vehicles were just another kind of horse. There was no petrol station and no hotel; but the general store had the most comprehensive stock of saddlery, fencing materials and veterinary products I'd ever seen. Clearly I was now in sheep country.

Chile's sheepfarms have always been somewhat overshadowed by the bigger and better-known ones of Argentina. Indeed, many of those around Cochrane were founded by Argentines. Until the 1960s they sold their wool on the Buenos Aires exchange and even looked to Argentina for their supplies. But today the owners and managers tend to be Chileans or Europeans, an independent breed who prefer to make their own buying and selling arrangements. Unlike their opposite numbers across the border, they still shear their flocks in the time-honoured way, with hand clippers. In Coyhaique I'd met a German named Gunter Schäfer who owned a farm on the far side of Lake Cochrane. 'Why don't you come and watch the shearing?' he'd suggested. Others had warned me that this would entail either a twelve-hour walk or a crossing of the deep and often stormy lake; but in Cochrane I found a boatman who was about to sail for the far shore with supplies for the gauchos. The weather held, and four hours later we bumped against a beach and I walked up a line of poplars to the farm known as Estancia Buena Vista.

Gunter was still in Coyhaique, but his Swiss wife Verena and their teenage son Niki greeted me on the porch of a small white-washed house. The building had been hidden from the lake, but I'd easily pinpointed it by the encircling poplars, planted to protect it from the unremitting wind which is every Patagonian's night-mare. Beyond the outbuildings, a vegetable garden followed the contours of a gentle slope for 200 yards; then a bluff soared up towards the cordillera. Other ridges advanced on either side, their ends truncated in vertical cliffs from which boulders tumbled occasionally into the lake. There was, Verena told me, a neighbour-ing farmstead beyond a headland, but otherwise the ranges were uninhabited. Buena Vista wasn't a farm for softies.

By a twist of luck the shearing team had arrived that very morning. The sheep stood bleating in corrals: 2,500 of them. I was just in time. Niki took me straight to the shearing shed, where seven animals lay trussed and panting. To one side, seven roughneck shearers stood sharpening Sheffield-made clippers on an oilstone. Niki, acting as foreman, took his place by the door as they began work on the colossal fleeces.

A good shearer can clip a sheep in twelve minutes. As the fleece comes off, the grey outer layer is peeled back to reveal a blanket of creamy-white curls, and by the time the animal is allowed to scramble back bleating to its pen it will have shed no less than five and a half pounds of wool. The work isn't clean; sheep secrete lanolin, a natural oil, and by the end of the day the shearers' jeans are shiny from the fleeces of up to 40 animals.

The men were paid by the fleece, and as each sheep was done Niki would gather up the wool and toss a token into the shearer's cup. The tokens would later be cashed for 600 pesos or £1.20 apiece – not bad by any standards for twelve minutes' work.

But how difficult it is, complained Niki, for the small farmer to make ends meet! This year the price of wool had plummeted to 80p per pound. After paying the shearers, the boatmen and the haulage company which would take the wool to market, they would be lucky to break even. It was a story I was to hear repeated many times on my journey south, with varying degrees of desperation.

Growing up in the Europe of the 1960s, Gunter and Verena had tasted the first fruits of postwar prosperity. After leaving school they'd spent long summers by the Mediterranean, experimenting with what we call today a hippie lifestyle. Oppressed by Europe's claustrophobia, and at the same time excited by the arrival of cheap travel, they packed a trunkful of leather waistcoats, gipsy skirts and Procul Harum cassettes and set out to see the world. One might have expected such a couple to follow their contemporaries to Goa or Kathmandu, but an independent streak made them turn in the opposite direction. They learned Spanish and spent five years in Colombia. Later, casting their fate to the winds again, they decided to try Chile; and now, 20 years on, they were sheepfarmers. Somehow they'd succeeded in combining this essentially pragmatic occupation with the best of their vagabonding life. Gunter still wore his blond hair shoulder-length, and Verena her gipsy dresses. Procul Harum still featured prominently in their cassette collection. More importantly, they spent long hours nurturing Buena Vista's vegetable garden so that as far as possible they remained self-sufficient. Appropriate technology had been introduced in the form of an ingenious hydroelectric plant, which as far as I could make out was constructed from a cartwheel and a couple of starter motors, but nevertheless produced enough power to run the hi-fi and lights.

Niki, one of two sons, was uncertain where he fitted into all this. He'd had the most carefree childhood imaginable – no school, no responsibilities, and for much of the time no clothes – and this had left him with a deep and intimate affection for his natural surroundings. Now, as he approached his 20th birthday, he still felt happiest riding through the spinifex and calafate bushes or watching from blustery hillsides as the shadows of scudding clouds turned Lake Cochrane's peacock-blue waters to indigo. But he'd never learned to read properly, and working out how much to pay the shearers was a nightmare. Also, he wanted to live in a town where he could meet girls.

You could see that these thoughts were troubling him, for he would often pass mealtimes in silence. His elder brother Tiel had already left home to live in Switzerland; but Niki wasn't sure if he had the drive or self-discipline to survive in the fiercely competitive society his mother had described. Like his father, he was good with his hands – the evidence was all round the house – and he could marry a local girl and make a living of sorts here at Buena Vista. He already had his eye on a pretty Coyhaique lass. . . . And yet; and yet. As he gathered up the smelly fleeces and tossed the tokens into the men's cups, Niki's quandary was written all over his face.

I walked back to Cochrane through the spinifex and calafate bushes, wondering how many other Patagonian youngsters shared Niki's dilemma.

Some offers are irresistible, and Rolando Wellmann's was one of these. His motorbike stood, with several bits missing, in the corner of a workshop on one of Cochrane's windblown side-streets. That afternoon he'd be riding 20 miles up a gravel track to Estancia Chacabuco, and after giving the matter some thought he agreed that I could go with him.

Having seen the spectacle of Buena Vista's sheepshearing, I very much wanted to witness the mechanized version. The Chacabuco farm, I'd been told, was larger and more up-to-date than Buena Vista – and its shearers used mechanical clippers. But the farm's agent in Cochrane warned me that shearing was due to finish the following day. After that the machines would go silent for another year; hence the significance of Rolando's offer.

Perhaps I accepted a bit too readily, for Rolando soon proved to be no ordinary motorcyclist. We launched ourselves onto the track as a bobsleigh team might begin the Cresta Run. Once clear of the town he put his foot down, and soon we were roaring along at 60 miles per hour, and still accelerating. The machine, being a somewhat stripped-down model, had nothing for me to cling to apart from a hot exhaust pipe or a revolving wheel. I envied Rolando his crash helmet and leathers; if anyone was going to need them, it would be me.

Rolando had explained that he was making this trip to visit his Chacabuco girlfriend; but even this, I felt, didn't excuse such indecent haste. Our wheels barely touched the gravel. Shouting at him was useless; either my shrieks weren't penetrating the crash helmet or his thoughts were concentrated totally on the evening ahead. They certainly didn't seem to be on the road. Eventually, to my relief, we stopped in a dip. I stepped down trembling, but Rolando was too busy to notice my unhappy state. In preparation for our arrival, he was combing his hair in the rear-view mirror.

'How much further is it?' I ventured as casually as I could.

'Just round the corner,' he replied, still preening himself. 'Sorry we took so long.'

At first Chacabuco seemed deserted – a collection of dismal huts and sheds scattered across the mouth of a broad valley. I sat on a fence and surveyed them. Rolando hurried away; but just as I was wondering if he'd brought me to the right spot, a rumble like distant thunder reached my ears. Turning, I saw a dustcloud approaching, and almost hidden within it were men on horseback – ten, twenty, it was impossible to tell. 'Hoo-yaa!' they yelled. *'Hoo-yaaaaah!'*

As the cavalcade came nearer, I began to see the outlines of hundreds of sheep. The thunder of hooves became deafening. 'Hoooo-yaaaaah!' called the gauchos again, and their dogs ran in circles round the flock, keeping it on the move. Eventually the surging woolly mass reached a corral behind the monolithic shearing shed. The dogs barked demonically, leaping forward, and each time they did so a hundred sheep lunged in the desired direction.

Eventually the last stragglers had been chased into the corral. The gauchos' foreman slammed the gate and came over to where I stood watching. 'Gerardo Praderas,' he said, wearily pushing back the beret on his head. Then he added in English, 'I heard you might be coming. You were nearly too late.'

This final batch of 2,000 animals was to be sheared the next day, and I'd be welcome to watch. The men would be pleased; they didn't often have spectators. Gerardo looked no different from the other gauchos, so I asked him where he'd learned English. 'Oh, I spent five years in California,' he replied casually. 'And last summer, I went over to New Zealand on a United Nations scholarship to learn a bit more about breeding techniques.' A frown crossed his face. 'Not that it'll do much good round here. These old Corriedales are past it; 25,000 of them we've got, with another 7,000 born every year. But the owner has gone to live in Europe; he isn't interested in improving the strain.' He sighed. 'With a bit of investment and some new breeds, I could double the income from this place.'

Gerardo then explained that Corriedale sheep, though hardy and good for mutton, don't produce the fine silky wool of the Merinos he'd seen in New Zealand. 'Merinos have always given good fleeces. Do you know, the Spanish used to be so proud of them that you could be executed for trying to smuggle them out of the country? There are 1,000 million sheep in the world, and almost 1,000 breeds; but one sheep in three is a Merino.' He made a face. 'And what do I get saddled with? Rotten old Corriedales.'

The huts were full of shearers, so I slept in my tent. Early next morning I awoke to an extraordinary sound. From Gerardo's open window came the over-amplified but just recognizable voice of John Denver. 'Thank God I'm a country boy,' he trilled. Over a breakfast of fatty mutton grilled directly on top of the stove, Gerardo explained that this was the only way he could get the shearers to start their shift at seven. They didn't understand the song's words, but apparently the voice of John Denver was sufficient to send them running for the shearing shed.

Where the Buena Vista shearers had worked silently, the Chacabuco ones laughed and sang their way through a fourteen-hour working day. The cacophony of merry voices, coupled with the roar of the 50-year-old Perkins diesel engine which drove the shears, made for a deafening workplace. The men held each animal with one strong arm, while with their free hand they passed the cutters across the woolly bellies in bold curving sweeps. Five minutes was sufficient to complete the job; some did it in three. During the morning one man found himself shearing a bisexual sheep, and he called me over to look at it. The unfortunate creature had both male and female organs; goodness knows what went on in its mind. Gerardo said there were usually half a dozen or so bisexuals on the farm at any one time, which I calculated to be about one in 4,000 – a high incidence, it seemed to me, for such a bizarre condition.

Gerardo also told me how shepherds castrate their lambs. Every farm keeps a stock of devices like cigar cutters for this purpose, but at lambing time they are often in short supply, and then the age-old method known as *la capa a diente* comes into play. The term is quite self-explanatory and Gerardo could have left it at that. But to make sure I understood – or perhaps to see my reaction – he explained that an experienced shepherd could bite his way through 200 lambs at a sitting. The penis was never swallowed: they always spat it out. And to guard against infection (so he said) the men would stop work every so often and take a swig of brandy. After a long session their mouths would be covered with blood. 'What a pity we haven't got any lambs at the moment,' said Gerardo with a genuine look of regret. 'I could have shown you!'

Estancia Chacabuco was founded at the beginning of the century by Lucas Bridges, an indefatigable Englishman who led an extraordinary life. Born in 1874 on the shores of the Beagle Channel, he befriended many of Tierra del Fuego's Ona Indians, and spent much of his early life helping them through the traumatic changes being wrought by the white man. His father, a missionary by the name of Thomas, had already built up a successful sheepfarming business on the island, and Lucas started looking for a way to expand the family interests without intruding further on the Onas' hunting ground. Chacabuco, with its wild empty grasslands, must have seemed ideal.

I knew that in Tierra del Fuego the Bridges were remembered with affection and respect, yet in Cochrane the name evoked a mixed response. Lucas had certainly spent several years in the area, working with two Falklanders called John Fletcher and John Glasson to put up fences and build cabins. He was also reportedly seen trying to buy animals in the town of Chile Chico. In those days Chacabuco, along with other newly established farms in the Baker Valley, still exported its wool via a long and gruelling route over the cordillera to Buenos Aires. Bridges left his administrator, Edward Lancaster, with the task of building a jetty at the mouth of the Baker so the wool could be shipped out by sea.

At this point the story becomes confused. Twice in Cochrane I was told a version that went as follows. One day, early in 1906, Lancaster set off down the Baker with materials for the jetty and several dozen labourers or 'peons'. Later that year he returned with only one. He insisted that the other peons had either died of scurvy or returned to their homes on Chiloé; but the word got round that he'd poisoned them. In those days many Patagonian farmworkers were harassing their employers for proper wages and decent living conditions; so it might have been convenient for both Bridges and Lancaster to have them out of the way. The sole survivor of this tragedy, an eighteen-year-old boy, refused to say a word about it until his dying day. The jetty never got built, but many years later, not far from where it was supposed to have been, some prospectors unearthed 40 shallow graves on an island which became known as the Island of the Dead. The bodies were too decomposed to pinpoint the cause of death; and despite continuing pressure from the peons' families, Lancaster was never made to face charges.

The tale seemed plausible, and later I recited it to some new acquaintances in Chile Chico. 'I've heard that story too,' said one of them, 'but I assure you it's not true.'

My informer had been doing some research into local history when, quite by accident, she'd come across Edward Lancaster's marriage certificate. Under 'Husband' had been written 'Born Liverpool, U.K., 20th October 1907'. Such a man, she argued, could hardly have been poisoning peons in 1906.

But how did the rumour come about? It would have sounded credible only to those who either had no idea of Lancaster's age – unlikely, since he continued to live in Cochrane till his death in 1973 – or were unaware of the date of the incident. It seems odd, too, that Lancaster didn't take steps to clear his name. Or could it be that the tale only resurfaced after his death, when dates had been forgotten and he was no longer there to defend himself? Though little more than a village, Cochrane struck me as easily big enough to harbour one or two vendettas.

The adventurer A.F. Tschiffely, who visited Chacabuco in 1938, reported a different version of the story in his 1940 book *This Way Southward*. According to Tschiffely, the leader of the work party was not Lancaster but a bullet-headed, blue-eyed Mancunian named William Norris. After heroically trying to save his peons (who Tschiffely calls 'Indians'), Norris was turned upon by the ungrateful savages and barely escaped with his life. Tschiffely's account is so brazenly one-sided that I'm inclined to dismiss it outright – but the possibility that the hero/villain was someone other than Edward Lancaster could be a starting point for anyone who dabbles further in this curious plot.

*

Before starting on the next stage of the journey, I wanted to see the point where the Carretera Austral ended, 25 miles south of Cochrane, at a wall of rock. Getting there was easy; the army engineers engaged in blasting the road through to its final destination on the splendidly named Lake O'Higgins were delighted to show me the fruits of their work. From the back of their lorry I glimpsed houses being built on plots freshly cleared from the wilderness: a foretaste of the ribbon of development which was bound to come. To see what the forests had been like before the road, I rooted out a horse trail and continued southwards on foot.

The trail followed the Río de los Ñadis, a tributary of the Baker down which Chacabuco's peons had made their fateful journey in 1906. The path had been cut by *campesinos* granted plots of land under Allende's expropriation programme. The setting was sensational – not only because of the sight of glaciers high up the tributary valleys, but also because of what I found underfoot. Spring had at last given way to high summer, and carpets of cranberries were swelling and showing a first hint of the purple which would indicate that they were ready to eat. In the spaces between them, white bell-shaped flowers with stamens of deep ochre thrust their way skywards. Crevices in the peaty soil harboured horn-shaped fungi: microscopic in size, the palest green in colour, and hard and crisp to the touch. Some were fringed in scarlet as if touched by a camelhair brush. I walked through meadows awash with violets and clover, and rested in shady beechwoods where frogs hopped blindly between my feet. The elder was already in full fruit, and hawthorn blossom gave off a sickly-sweet scent as I brushed against it. By the river, a hummingbird came out of nowhere and spent a couple of seconds motionless in the air alongside me, inspecting my surprised face. Two-inch dragonflies skimmed the surface of the water. And as evening approached, the horseflies and mosquitoes emerged, their rapacious appetite making it impossible to think of anything except escape.

At a bend in the river, where a notice by a footbridge read 'Maximum Weight Two Cows', I came across a low farmhouse, the first habitation for miles. Inside, a woman by the name of Clementina Ruíz was brewing maté, the lethally addictive herbal tea without which a Patagonian cannot get through the day.

Pronounced 'ma-tay', the infusion is sucked through a silver straw from a gourd which is refilled again and again as it passes from mouth to mouth. 'My maté is my soulmate,' a gaucho once told me. 'A companion when I'm lonely, a comforter when I'm troubled, and a devoted nurse when I'm sick.' Children clung to Clementina's dress or dashed into other rooms as she ushered me to a place by the stove. 'So you've walked from the *carretera*,' she said in surprise. 'What on earth brings you here?'

I explained that I was just wandering – seeing what the valley was like before the new road arrived.

'Ah, then perhaps you can tell me when that will be? I've talked to the people working up there, and they say it won't be long. I do hope so. Do you know how long it takes me to ride to Cochrane?'

I shook my head.

'Two days! Once a month for seventeen years I've made that journey – and each time it takes two days to get there and another two to come back!'

I saw her point. The destruction which would come with the road would take a back seat when compared with a journey like that.

'Which side of the river is the road going to go?' I asked.

She stared at me quizzically. 'I haven't the faintest idea. No one has told me anything; I'm just a peasant. Still, it doesn't really matter, does it? When the road comes everything will be different. Our lives will be so much better. There'll be opportunities for the children; I might even open a shop.'

I asked how many children she had.

'Ten,' she replied proudly; then hesitated a moment. 'No, wait – eleven. With me we're twelve round the dinner table, so it must be eleven.'

We passed the maté between us, and I stayed for an hour as child after child emerged from the woodwork of the little house to play with the stranger. Eventually, waving goodbye, I turned northwards again.

Later, back at the engineers' camp, I examined the plans for the road. It looked very much as if they were going to take it right through Clementina Ruiz's farmyard.

Argentine Detour

From the Río de los Ñadis, for the time being, you can go no further south in Chile. To continue to Punta Arenas and Tierra del Fuego you must either take to the water or cross over to Argentina, which many people do at the quaintly-named town of Chile Chico. Basking on the sunny southern shore of Lake Carrera, in a microclimate which yields such unlikely Patagonian crops as tomatoes, Chile Chico is completely cut off from the rest of the country. Most visitors arrive by lake ferry. For me, coming from Cochrane, this would have meant retracing 150 miles by road, so I cast about for a better plan. There was said to be a horse trail along the lake's precipitous southern shore, and if this were true it would cut my distance by more than 100 miles. Although I had no horse, I decided to give it a try.

Finding the beginning was easy: the track simply continued where the road gave out. For the first day it wound through rolling beechwoods, but on the second morning a headland, perhaps 1,000 feet high, hove into view. The track climbed, twisted and descended again, as if uncertain how to tackle this formidable obstacle. Finally it entered a gallery hewn out of the vertical rock, 300 feet above the lake, just wide and high enough to take a horse and rider. I passed through exhilarated and relieved.

After a further day of clambering over headlands and plunging towards the deep waters of the lake, I rounded a corner and quite suddenly left the cordillera behind. The lake continued onwards to the eastern horizon, but now it was flanked not by mountains but by bleached, powder-dry desert. Lying in the Andes' rain shadow, Argentine Patagonia supports little more than tussock grass and scrubby thorn bushes. Rains can be torrential but are widely spaced; and irrigation is needed to get the most from those pockets blessed with warm summers and mild winters, such as the one ahead of me now.

Chile Chico was first colonized in 1909, when a band of Argentine pioneers crossed the newly-established border along the River Jeinimeni and made primitive homesteads on the southern lakeshore. From its source high in the cordillera, the river provided a year-round water supply, and the settlers soon realized they'd hit upon a little paradise. Fruits ripened quickly, providing a welcome variant to their usual diet of mutton and beef. The Santiago government's attention was fully occupied by affairs in the heartland, and a colony which was only accessible across a stormy lake could be confident of being left in peace. So it came as a surprise when, in 1918, two gringos arrived on horseback flourishing official papers.

One was a German by the name of Karl von Flack. The other, an Englishman, is unnamed in the historical sources, but may have been Lucas Bridges from Chacabuco. To the settlers' horror and disbelief, von Flack's papers – which bore the seal of the Ministry of Colonization in Santiago – included the deeds to the entire southern lakeshore. He and his companion had simply come to buy up their animals before they threw them out.

The papers were certainly genuine; von Flack had a receipt to show that to conclude his deal he'd paid the Ministry 28,700 Chilean pesos – more than the settlers would earn in a lifetime. The civil servants in Santiago apparently hadn't known that parts of the land had already been occupied for the best part of ten years; that houses had been built, fences put up, tracks and even bridges installed. In fact their knowledge of the area was so poor that they thought they were giving von Flack the deeds to a mere 87 square miles, though a later survey showed the holding to be 1,250 – one of the best land bargains in Chilean history.

In a stunningly tactless move, von Flack offered the 200 settlers a derisory 20 pesos for each of their cattle, and one or two pesos for the sheep. Their reply came in the form of pointed, loaded rifles. Scared and incensed, he retreated to the safety of Argentina, where he holed up in a farm and telegraphed the Ministry in Santiago. A few weeks later the settlers looked out of their windows to see him approaching again, this time with a sergeant, five constables, and a government order that they get off the land forthwith.

The clash which followed was an object lesson for beleaguered small fry in the face of corporate muscle. It came to be known as the War of Chile Chico. The settlers were fighting for their livelihoods – and in some cases, towards the end, their lives. Von Flack, on the other hand, had paid over his money in good faith and regarded the land as legitimately his. As the conflict gathered momentum, there arose amongst the settlers a leader by the name of José Silva, who called the able-bodied men to arms. One day the inevitable happened. The police set fire to a couple of houses and the men retaliated. Under cover of darkness they hunted down the constables and their sergeant, and by morning three of the six lay dead.

Von Flack and the survivors retreated once more to Argentina, with the settlers in hot pursuit. The Argentine authorities, ever touchy about territorial matters, responded by sending their own force up from the coast. Meanwhile the Chilean sergeant had issued a desperate call for reinforcements from Santiago. Within three months a pair of mini-armies stood facing each other across the border, with von Flack maintaining a nervous line of communication between the soldiers and the settlers barricaded in their homes.

More people were to die, and a great deal of rancour was to be exchanged between the governments and settlers on either side, before the issue of who owned Chile Chico was finally resolved. Against all odds the settlers won. In 1921, worn down by their aggressive forays and receiving less and less help from a disinterested government, von Flack renounced his title to the land. Four years later the Ministry refunded his money. The 'guerrillas' of Chile Chico went back to farming their land, and in 1931, after more than a decade of lobbying, the authorities gave them the deeds to which they had been legally entitled all along.

Today Chile Chico's wide streets look like those of a much grander town. With government recognition it briefly prospered, and its apples and cherries appeared on streetstalls as far away as Santiago. But the problem of transport was never fully overcome, and trade barriers crushed any markets there might have been in Argentina. So the streets remain unpaved, and sulky waitresses in the half-dozen bars serve the sons and grandsons of José Silva's men. It strikes the visitor as a town of farmers and dreamers – of rumour upon rumour that so-and-so has struck gold or such-and-such a company has found oil. One day, perhaps, one of the dreams may come true. Meanwhile, for most of Chile Chico's citizens, the highlight of the week will remain late-night opening at the grocery store.

The evening before I left for Argentina, clouds burst over the tiny town, raising by several feet the level of the Jeinimeni River. The road between the two countries crosses this river by means of a ford, negotiable by four-wheel-drive vehicles and also, I was assured, by pedestrians. But one look at the swelling brown waters told me that neither jeeps nor pedestrians would be making the attempt today.

The frontier police confirmed my judgement. 'Don't try it,' they warned. 'You'll be swept into the lake.'

I'd resigned myself to returning to Chile Chico when a passing farmer noticed my predicament. 'Why don't you try the *pasarela*, the footbridge?' he asked. 'It's four kilometres upstream. A bit flimsy, but you could give it a try.'

Flimsy it certainly was; I walked past the footbridge three times before even spotting it. Makeshift cables swayed to within a few inches of the surging water, and as I stepped out over the river I heard them grating alarmingly in their anchorages; but they held, and I reached the opposite bank safe and dry.

The Argentine frontier guards regarded me with ill-concealed suspicion. 'You've come from Chile? How?'

I explained my unorthodox route; then spent half an hour explaining my unorthodox credentials, which consisted of two British passports – a Chilean exit stamp in one and an Argentine visa in the other. One of the privileges of being British abroad is that it's quite legal, under certain circumstances, to carry two passports. Frequent travellers find them vital when visiting the increasing number of countries whose consulates keep your passport for weeks while they ponder your application for a visa. They also, as I now found, enable you to skirt round tiresome regulations. The visa in my older passport was only valid for a 90-day visit, and I was expecting lengthy arguments when I came to renew it. To my surprise, however, the immigration officer not only offered but actually insisted on putting his stamp in the newer one. Months later, therefore, I was able to re-enter the country on the older passport with the visa apparently unused. I strode into the village of Los Antiguos with a smile on my face.

Passing from southern Chile to Argentina, the traveller is immediately struck by the change in materials and textures. In Chile Chico the houses had been entirely wooden, sparingly embellished but well protected by varnish or pitch. In Los Antiguos, less than five miles distant, they were of concrete, plaster and imitation brick, and had been adorned with the most extraordinary variety of bolt-on additions, from aluminium shutters and brass coachlamps to curly finials and even a plastic sundial. The absence of wood was understandable, for the eastern side of the Andes is almost treeless; but the materials which had replaced it owed nothing to the surrounding countryside. No desert-baked mudbricks, no cornerstones quarried from nearby barrancas: just concrete, plaster and imitation brick.

Another of my impressions on that first day was that Argentines preferred things shiny. It was evident in the chrome strips on their cars and the burnished anti-roll bars on their pickups. With the economy on the brink of bankruptcy, not many garish things could be afforded these days, so Los Antiguos was full of rusty chattels that must once have looked dazzling. It was something I was to notice again and again.

I dumped my rucksack on the edge of the village and gazed around. The road stretched to the eastern horizon, skirting the electric-blue waters of Lake Carrera, which I would now have to think of by its Argentine name of Lake Buenos Aires. There seemed to be plenty of traffic; so I put on a winning smile and let my thoughts wander ahead towards Perito Moreno, 40 miles to the east, where I would surely be by nightfall.

It was some time before I realized that there was something strange about the traffic of Los Antiguos. Vehicles would pass by, their drivers gesturing to indicate how heavily loaded they were, or how close to their destination, or some other reason why they couldn't take a hitchhiker to Perito Moreno. I'd wave my thanks and shield my eyes against the wheel dust. Then, ten minutes later, they'd come by again. The same gestures would be exchanged, to be repeated after a further ten minutes when they'd pass me yet again. After an hour of this I came to the conclusion that Los Antiguos had no normal traffic at all; the same vehicles simply went round in circles. I recalled the same thing happening in small towns of the American Midwest, where young boys would show off to young girls by cruising up and down the streets in their fathers' cars. In Los Antiguos cars were much too valuable to lend to sons, so it was the fathers who were doing the cruising. But the high-heeled and stretch-jeaned girls seemed much the same. Indeed, they might well have been the daughters of the cruising drivers; they certainly looked young enough.

An elderly man had been watching me from a house, and after a while he brought out his chair and sat down for a chat. It seemed that few people passed through Los Antiguos, and even fewer ended up standing by his garden gate. We shared a kettleful of maté while he plied me with questions about life in Britain, the United States and Chile Chico across the river – places which for him seemed equally remote. Eventually he returned indoors ('for my siesta', he explained), and one of the circulating drivers stopped and handed me a cold beer. He'd been home specially to collect it. He continued on his way, and two circuits later stopped again to pick up the empty bottle.

A taxi driver offered to take me to Perito Moreno for £12. 'You think I ask too much? Do you realize the tax I have to pay on this car? And the price of petrol these days – you wouldn't believe it! Besides, gringos have plenty of money, don't they?'

'Other gringos,' I said.

Finally, as dusk was approaching, a lorry stopped. I clambered gratefully onto the top, and as the sun fizzled into Lake Buenos Aires I stepped down at last in Perito Moreno. The tiny town seemed comatose. Not a shop was open; not a gaucho was on the street. In the window of the Hotel Belgrano, a plump man with a shock of black curly hair drew a curtain aside and beckoned to me, so I pushed my way through the swing doors. Now I understood the reason for the empty streets. In a bar crowded with tables, 50 people were smoking, drinking and watching a television set in the corner. Argentina was playing football.

The game of football has achieved what 175 years of successive Argentine governments have failed to do: it has united the people in a common cause. Surprisingly for a country with a military tradition, Argentina's national identity hinges not on its political clout (which is considerable), nor on its economic might (which has been in decline for as long as anyone can remember), but on the prowess of its national football team. With the fortunes of these eleven men goes the self-respect of 35 million people.

I stood at the back with the man who had beckoned. 'De Fuad Mattar,' he shouted above the noise. 'This is my hotel. You want room?'

My reply was drowned by an explosion of sound from the television. 'Goooooooooooalllllllllll!' Argentina had scored. In the bar the crowd rose and cheered as one. It took several minutes before order was restored. Win or lose, I thought, no one would be sleeping much in the Hotel Belgrano tonight.

De Fuad Mattar was Arabian, the son of Lebanese immigrants. After the Second World War, when the creation of Israel brought about the first of many crises in what we used to call the Levant, his mother and father had found themselves standing on the Buenos Aires quayside. They were completely penniless; but not without hope, for President Perón had been luring immigrants with the promise of a secure and even prosperous life. It was a time of confidence – the last, as it turned out, which Argentina would enjoy for nearly half a century. People were pouring off the steam packets – dark wiry Latins, rough-faced Anglo-Saxons – and jobs in the capital were becoming scarce. The Mattars headed south.

When Bruce Chatwin passed through Perito Moreno in 1975, he wrote that De Fuad kept a sprig of mint on the bar to remind him of a home he'd never seen. I saw no mint and found him not the slightest bit interested in his ancestral origins. Like all the other descendants of immigrants in the Hotel Belgrano that night, De Fuad was Argentine, and whooped and hooted the fact every time a goal was scored.

I slept by a lake, and in the morning was discovered by one of the founding fathers of Perito Moreno, a rheumy-eyed old-timer called Francisco Cant. He was walking his dog.

'Good morning, gringo! Tell me, from where do you come? Britain, eh? Aha, *un inglés*! And your name? Really! Age? Only 40? Is that so? Why, with your hair so white, I took you to be at least 55!'

I invited the old man to tell me something of his six decades in Perito Moreno, but he declined. 'It would take half a day,' he grinned through nicotined teeth, 'just to cover the first five years.' But he did tell me at some length about an affair he'd had in 1948. 'She was a Valdivian girl. Chilean women make so much better girlfriends than Argentines, don't you think? Good, simple fun, and no fuss.'

Partly because of his Argentine accent, partly because his false teeth didn't quite fit, I found Francisco Cant's discourse difficult to follow. Whenever I asked him to repeat something, he'd simply change the subject.

'Every year I see more gringos. Americans, Europeans, Japanese; on bicycles, in cars, on foot. Why do these people come to Patagonia?' he asked, jutting out his jaw. 'I'll tell you – they come to gloat!'

I assured him that this wasn't true, but he waved my appeal aside. 'What do you know?' he grunted, moist eyes gleaming. 'A mere 40-year-old.'

A little-known joy of travelling in southern Patagonia is the opportunity to fly with the Argentine Air Force. Planes seating 30 or so make weekly or even daily flights, using makeshift airstrips to serve communities which would otherwise have to rely on unmade roads across the plains. They are amongst the world's great travel bargains; for £14 I flew from Perito Moreno to Lake Argentino, 300 miles to the south.

The town of Calafate lies on the southern shore of this greatest and possibly bluest of all Argentina's lakes. Fed by glaciers spilling down from the Patagonian Ice-Cap, this broad, cold stretch of water was thought by its discoverer Francisco Moreno to be an arm of the Pacific. I'd visited Calafate briefly more than ten years previously on my way to the Moreno Glacier, at that time one of the few advancing glaciers in the world. Since then the town had doubled in size, and friends had warned me that the result wasn't pleasant. I'd argued to myself that it might not be too bad; that the new development would perhaps have dovetailed with the old rather than crushing it. As I walked the few hundred yards from the airstrip, I saw that my hope wasn't going to be fulfilled.

The main street had been paved since my earlier visit. The Hotel Ambato, where previously I'd huddled for warmth round an iron stove in a peeling room whose only furniture had been a half-collapsed bed, now boasted leather armchairs and accepted an array of credit cards. Señora Berberena's corner shop had become a supermarket. And on the pavements – now separated from the roadway by neatly cropped grass verges – the only pedestrians were tourists.

The pioneering spirit was maintained mainly through the medium of shortages, which left gaps on the shelves of the Berberena supermarket. It was difficult to establish why Tuesday's absence of sugar should become Wednesday's lack of cheese; or why the queues outside the filling station should form at 6 a.m. one day but not at all the next; or why the single bakery should close for two days without warning or explanation. But whatever the reasons, people accepted these inconveniences as perfectly normal. There were no complaints, and no expressions of exasperation or even surprise. The stoicism of the average Calafate citizen would have done justice to a Russian.

Strolling down a side-street, I came across a young man in a ditch. He was dressed in rags and he was weeping. At first I thought he must be hurt, but it soon became clear that he was drunk. We talked for a few minutes. He was a Salteño, from the far north of Argentina, where the tottering economy had led to mass unemployment. 'People there are hungry,' he told me through his sobs. 'I want to work. There's work here in the restaurants and hotels; I know there is. But no one will employ me.'

It was the usual story, common enough in London, Buenos Aires or a hundred other world capitals. But in this Patagonian ditch, surrounded by some of the finest scenery on earth, the man's misery seemed doubly poignant.

It was now the beginning of February – high summer – and for a week I put aside my pen and notebook and headed into the Fitzroy mountains. This extensive range lies at the north-west tip of Lake Viedma, that body of water which the vice-president of Chile's Society for History and Geography had thought might one day drain to the Pacific. Picture a set of giant's dentures, the lower and upper halves set side by side in a bed of undulating beech forest. Sprinkle the dentures liberally with snow. Add a couple of dozen aquamarine lagoons, and into them toss an assortment of small icebergs. Place the entire diorama under a velvet black sky studded with the shapes of strange constellations; transport the whole to a place 300 miles from the nearest town; and you have the Fitzroy range, Patagonia's answer to Yosemite.

Normally plagued by appalling weather, the mountains were enjoying a rare sunny spell, and I hurried to make the most of it. On my first afternoon I reached the base camp of Cerro Torre, a surreal granite needle whose faces are so sheer that blocks of snow breaking off the summit cornice fall intact for 6,000 feet before hitting the pediment below.

Cerro Torre and its flanking pinnacles were for many years thought to be unclimbable; and although the main summit was finally conquered in 1974, the mountain has claimed many lives. The number increased just as I arrived. An Italian husband-and-wife team, both experienced climbers, had set out to tackle Torre Egger, the second summit of the group. They'd established an 'advance base' in the form of a small tent in a remote spot at the foot of the face, so the alarm wasn't raised until they failed to show up at the main base camp on the day appointed for their return. It took a whole week to organize a search party, but less than two days for them to find the couple's advance base. The tent was intact but unoccupied. Clearly the pair had met with some misfortune on the face itself. Their chances of surviving such an accident would have been virtually nil, and the rescuers' mood was grim. The news was radioed down the valley to the Italian Consul who'd flown in from Buenos Aires. Nothing more could be done; and as the party silently dismantled the couple's base camp tent, I packed my own things and left.

Being so close to an incident like this brings home in the strongest way possible the dangers of mountaineering. I remembered having had the same sickening feeling a few years previously, when I was close to the scene of an accident in the Torridons of north-west Scotland. Climbers, like other adventurers, learn to be objective about the risks they take; but their mishaps tend be dramatic ones, leaving a lasting impression on rescuers and observers.

Walking, on the other hand, has always struck me as the perfect way to appreciate a mountain range. Moving steadily through the landscape, varying my pace with the pitch and fall of a mountain path, I have time to think and daydream as the views unfold. The imagination soars. Distractions are few; indeed, I sometimes find that on reaching a narrowing of the path or some other point that needs care, I'm jolted into consciousness from a kind of walking dream. On long level stretches the motion itself can induce hypnosis. Peaks and ridges are seen far ahead, then approach and are passed; and when I next turn my head they've been left far behind. The lure is all the more potent because my own muscles are producing the motion, without mechanical help.

Even now, at the height of summer, the Fitzroy range was all but deserted. Where else, I thought, could one roam in such splendid surroundings and meet no more than a score of other human beings in an entire week?

One of my rare encounters was with Ricardo Arbilla, a skinny ascetic who had made his home in the woods alongside the oddly named Electric River. Attempting, perhaps, to move with the times, Ricardo had converted his hut into a crude but pleasant lodge, offering a bed for the night together with omelettes, homemade bread, beer and even whisky for the few who beat a path to this isolated spot. He was alone when I knocked on the door. Flourishing a frying pan over the stove, he settled me in a corner seat and told the story of how he'd come to be the builder, owner and manager of Patagonia's remotest inn.

'I was always a city boy,' he began with a smirk. 'Grew up in Río Gallegos, down on the coast. But I hated town life, with its jealousies and petty rivalries. My uncle had some land up here, which he often talked about but had never even seen, so when he died I thought, "I could do something with that." It's mostly forest, you know; but I keep a few milking cows, and I'm starting up a beehive.' Ricardo took self-sufficiency only so far. 'I had a group of Japanese climbers here the other day,' he said. 'They drank me out of whisky. So I did a deal with them. I rounded up my horses and put their equipment in the saddlebags, and said, "I'll take you all down to the hotel at Chaltén, if you fill these bags with bottles of whisky!"'

I was heading for Chaltén myself, and asked Ricardo how far it was. 'Five leagues,' he replied mysteriously. Speculating on what a league might be, I recalled that the indomitable Lady Florence Dixie had come upon this problem in 1879:

'How far have we still to go?' was a question which was often on our lips, though from experience we might have known that, whatever answer we got from the guides, we should be no wiser than before. They would reply glibly enough, four or five leagues, as the case might be, but we had found that their ideas of a league were most elastic, appearing to vary daily, and to an extent which made it impossible for us to form any mean average even, to guide us to an approximate estimation of the value of their assertions. Thus a league might mean ten miles to-day, and to-morrow possibly only one.

English dictionaries define a league as an 'itinerant' measure of distance, varying in different countries but usually about three miles. William Halliday, the first settler at Río Gallegos, wrote that it was 'somewhere round about between four and eight miles', and a retired farmer in San Julián was later to tell me that it was precisely 3.1 miles. The Karten Dictionary, published in Buenos Aires, puts an Argentine league at '5,572 metres and 7 decimetres, or 3.4627 miles' – but I would defy anyone to measure with such accuracy in the wastes of Patagonia.

Not having a pedometer, I never found out what Ricardo considered to be a league. But after what seemed rather less than a fifteen-mile walk, I found myself next day at the hotel where he had so unexpectedly replenished his whisky.

Late that evening I returned to Calafate to find it in the grip of canine howls. It was the night of the full moon, and the town's dogs whined and bayed as if the world were in danger of imminent demise. Not one of Calafate's 20,000 citizens could possibly have enjoyed a wink of sleep. The contrast with the previous week's tranquillity couldn't have been greater.

The eastern flanks of the Andes include some of the finest sheep country on the continent, and before leaving Calafate I wanted to visit one of the old estancias. I'd been thinking of paying a call on La Anita, showpiece of the sheepfarming mogul José Menéndez, which had been the scene of a massacre of peons in the troubled year of 1921. But a travel agent warned me that La Anita nowadays gets visitors by the coachload; I'd be unlikely to see much of estancia life. An aeroplane pilot called Alfredo Boillat had a better idea. Two Canadians had booked to fly with him to an estancia called Cristina on a northern arm of Lake Argentino, one of the loneliest farms in all Patagonia. I knew that it lay somewhere near where the towering Upsala Glacier tumbled from the Patagonia Ice-Cap into the lake. In 1961 this mountain haven, run by a good-natured English couple, had been the goal of Eric Shipton's celebrated 52-day crossing of the ice-cap from the Baker Channel. The only practicable approach, Shipton had written, was by launch – and then only when the weather was calm. Now I was being offered a half-hour flight in a spare seat on Alfredo's plane. How could I refuse?

The plane was tiny but comfortable, and I was soon infected with the anticipation of my fellow passengers. After a surprisingly short time we spied the estancia, nestling at the head of an inlet sheltered by steep ridges. In Shipton's day these airy uplands would have been dotted with sheep; but now the estate had been incorporated in Los Glaciares National Park, and the Government had decided that in the interests of conservation sheepfarming should be banned. With the sheep gone, some parts of the range had been invaded by the guanaco, that elegant cousin of the llama; others had simply returned to scrub.

Landing on the beach, we tumbled out of the plane and soon spotted the estancia's present owner waiting for us at the garden gate. Janet Masters was not what you might expect of someone who bore title to several thousand of the most stunning acres on earth. Her slight girlish figure was dwarfed by the house with its corrugated iron roof and soaring radio aerial; only a strong chin and a glint of stubbornness in her eye suggested the spirit which was evident from her background. Alfredo had already told me something of this remarkable woman, born near Edinburgh but brought up from early childhood on one of Tierra del Fuego's Menéndez farms. After two long marriages to Anglo-Argentine farmers, she'd lived alone at Cristina for the last few years, self-sufficient in everything except sugar and maté. Remembering this, I looked with interest at the diminutive 80-year-old who stood before me. 'Well now,' she greeted us in sweet Midlothian tones. 'If you've come all the way from Calafate in that contraption, you'd better come in and have a cup of tea.'

We were ushered into a drawing room that could have been a stage-set for *The Boyfriend*. Deep armchairs and a sofa were arranged in an arc facing a broad bay window, through which could be seen the southernmost peaks of the Fitzroy range. In a corner, whisky bottles lined a panelled bar. On the back wall hung a framed portrait of Janet's father, still young when it was painted, gazing sternly from behind a cravatted wing collar offset by a jaunty peaked cap. On the coffee table lay copies of the *Illustrated London News*, most of them at least 20 years old.

The farm had been founded in the early years of this century by Percy Masters, a Southampton man. As a youngster he'd run away to sea, but after marrying a Hampshire girl named Jessie he decided this was no life for a family man. In 1900 the couple took a passage to Patagonia, where Percy spent four years as a farm labourer before setting about the task of building a home. Initially they based themselves south of Lake Argentino, but their flock there was decimated by puma, and after two further heartbreaking false starts they finally established the present farm. They named it Cristina after their first daughter, who died as a child soon after they arrived.

Despite having their own launch – an ex-lifeboat salvaged from a wreck in the Magellan Strait, and brought up by bullock-cart – Percy and Jessie Masters lived in almost total isolation. Their son Percy wrote to a friend in the 1950s, 'Visits are rare: and time slips by with no alternative in an incredible solitude in this world of rapid communications.'

But in 1989, with parents and children now long dead, a company called Patagonia Wilderness approached Percy's widow Janet with the proposition that it be opened up to paying guests. A resident manager would handle the arrangements and look after the visitors; Janet could, if she wished, move from the main house to a smaller one nearby, where she'd be able to maintain the privacy so central to her life. After deliberating at some length on this offer, she decided that in her 79th year it was time to allow others to take on the farm's burdens; and so reluctantly agreed. My Canadian companions were to be the first guests. Janet was clearly worried about having so much company all of a sudden, and expressed her anxiety in a way that I now realized was typically Patagonian. 'I don't know why people make such a fuss about Cristina,' she insisted. 'It's just an ordinary farm.'

But the truth was that the farm wasn't ordinary at all. Encircled on three sides by rock and ice and on the fourth by a deep and turbulent lake, for six months of the year it was all but cut off from the outside world. Things which couldn't be stockpiled or home-produced had to be foregone. The new manager, a baby-faced fellow from Buenos Aires, rolled his blue eyes despairingly as he described the task of making the farm suitable for visitors. 'I take our little boat across the lake – a four-hour journey if the weather's fine – and then I drive for six hours to Río Gallegos. There I look for fencing wire, cement, plumbing, fittings and a hundred other things. Half of what I want is never in stock; so I argue all day, then take what they have and ferry it back across the lake. Often this takes two trips; sometimes three. I tell you, it's a nightmare!'

A manager's nightmare it may have been, but to me Cristina was paradise. I was deeply envious of the Canadians, who were booked in for a week. But Alfredo was already warming up his engines for our return to Calafate, and Janet was once more watching from the gate. She looked impossibly fragile to have survived so long in this awesome setting. With almost indecent haste, we taxied across the foreshore and were aloft once more, the shadowy crevasses of the Upsala Glacier receding under our wings as we rose southward into the dusk.

With a swiftness that is the privilege and curse of our generation, I passed from the wilderness of Estancia Cristina to the squalor of Argentina's southern oilfields. Petroleum was discovered in Patagonia as early as 1907, but the reserves fringing the Magellan Strait remained unexploited until the 1940s. I don't suppose oil installations can ever be attractive, but these struck me as particularly repulsive ones. Nodding donkeys and storage tanks stood amid acres of rusting metallic debris. Where the desert thorn bushes had been allowed to remain standing, they were festooned with discarded plastic of every shape, size and colour. Their stems sprang from a bed of detergent bottles, food cans, broken glass, oildrums and old boots. Pipes, girders and even burnt-out vehicles littered the roadside.

I was well placed to appreciate the full horror of the scene, riding in the cab of a brightly-painted articulated lorry bound for Tierra del Fuego. Emilio the driver was from the north – a revolutionary, he said, who'd be in the front line when his people rose against the government reactionaries, as they surely would. 'Carlos Menem lied to us; he told us he was a Peronist, but as

SOUTHERN PATAGONIA

soon as we voted him into the presidency he started making concessions to the rich. What kind of Peronism is that? What help did he give the jobless, the starving, the sick? Why, none! Now he's paying his debts by selling off government enterprises – the telephones, the railways, the services that hold the country together – and the shares are being snapped up by foreigners.' Emilio snorted. 'Soon there'll be nothing left to sell, and how will he pay his lackeys then? The rich will have cut and run to Zurich; and the poor, if inflation doesn't come down – well, the poor will be at their wits' end. That's when the fun will start; that's when the people will rise up, rich and poor together. Just wait and see.'

His words had a familiar ring. Looking out at the desert, I imagined myself in the cab of a British lorry, crawling in three lanes of traffic on the M1. Our inflation rate might be one hundredth that of Argentina; but the complaint would have been much the same, and possibly the remedy too. I said as much, and Emilio gave an amused smile.

'But in Britain you'd be wise to lie low. Señora Thatcher, she has something our president lacks. It's what in Argentina we call *huevos*. She's got balls!'

73

We crossed into Chile and reached a fork in the road. Emilio's route turned south to the Magellan Strait; mine continued west towards Punta Arenas. As he set me down I saw his eyes flash and then twinkle. 'The revolution will come, you know,' he assured me. 'It may not come as soon as we would wish, but it will come. *Adiós, amigo.*'

On the road to Punta Arenas, not 50 yards from the shores of the Strait, I found the oldest estancia in Chilean Patagonia. For 90 years San Gregorio had been a Menéndez farm, but in 1971 its 220,000 acres were a sitting target for appropriation under Allende's reforms. The land was parcelled up and sold, and now the cavernous shearing shed echoed only to the scrabbling of rats and the moan of the wind.

San Gregorio's buildings, abandoned though they were now, testified to a supreme and unshakeable confidence in the market for Patagonian wool. In the 1880s wool prices began to soar, and the pioneer farmers, cocky from earlier successes, saw the potential of the endless ranges. They invested heavily and didn't skimp. Twenty thousand finely bred Merinos passed through San Gregorio's pens each summer, and 50 tons of fleeces were baled up and hauled across the wharf to be shipped to Punta Arenas in the Menéndez's ironclad *Amadeo*. Smithy, peons' quarters, kitchens and warehouses were designed by the company's own architects and raised by Santiago craftsmen using the best materials south of Concepción. More than a century later, the finely wrought doors of a workshop still boasted the letters 'S.G.', picked out in the company cream. But I saw that this and other buildings also carried evidence of less halcyon times, in the form of unadorned grills thrown up hurriedly over the windows to combat sabotage when, in 1921, the peons rose with their compatriots at La Anita to protest at their miserable lot.

On the foreshore opposite the shearing shed, the *Amadeo* lay beached like an emaciated whale. Its funnel and iron mast were still upright, but the bridge was a skeleton of buckled metal and splintered, rotting timber. On what remained of the lower decks, piles of chain had rusted into solid lumps. A propeller and half a rudder hung drunkenly in the water. The hull cladding had long since gone, and those ribs that remained were so corroded that some were no more than strands of rust, swelling and shrinking in the spray that came in with the breeze.

Anywhere else in the world, such a wreck would have been towed to a museum or at least looted for scrap; but in Patagonia shipwrecks are too common for anyone to take much notice. If the weather can be stormy inland, it can be truly tempestuous out at sea. Off Cape Froward, in the western Magellan Strait, gales of Force Eight or more are recorded on 80 days of the year, compared with only 32 days in the infamous western approaches to the English Channel.

The first reports of these appalling conditions reached Europe via the sixteenth-century navigators Ferdinand Magellan, Thomas Cavendish and Sir Francis Drake. Halfway through his second voyage of 1591–2, Cavendish wrote: 'Our shroudes were all rotten, not having a running rope whereto we may trust, and being provided only of one shift of sails all worne, our top sails not able to abide any stress of weather, neither have we any pitch, tarre, nail, nor any store for supplying of those wantes.' The ships' crews suffered miserably. 'Their sinews were stiff and their flesh dead, and many of them, which is lamentable to be reported, were so eaten with lice, as that in their flesh did lie great clusters of lice, as big as peasons, yea, and some as big as beanes.'

Not surprisingly, some were driven to mutiny. In the Argentine port of San Julián, Magellan hanged the ringleaders of one such plot, and 50 years later, at almost the same spot, Drake executed his friend Thomas Doughty. The epitaph on Doughty's grave read: 'That it might be better understood by all that should come after us.'

The stresses of navigating a safe passage through such difficult waters affected the officers too. Perhaps the most famous victim was the *Beagle's* one-time captain, Pringle Stokes. The vessel was scarcely 100 feet in length at the waterline, and hardly looked sturdy enough to cross the Thames Estuary, let alone the Atlantic. Stokes and his crew had spent several months charting the Chilean coastline for the British Admiralty, when the winter of 1828–9 overtook them in the aptly named Gulf of Troubles. Despite heavy seas they were coping well, when suddenly a hurricane struck the tiny ship. They sought shelter in the lee of a small unnamed island, and for a full two weeks rode out the storm before nosing gingerly down the Baker Channel to continue the survey. No sooner had they reached the open sea than they were hit by a ferocious squall. The vessel all but capsized; waves swamped the deck, and the crew prepared to abandon ship. Though listing badly the *Beagle* didn't sink. The squall subsided and they limped slowly to the shelter of Port Otway.

At this point, apparently, Stokes suffered a mental collapse. His entries in the ship's log became incoherent, his mood hopelessly despondent. Today we would diagnose the condition as a nervous breakdown. It fell to his second-in-command, Lieutenant Skyring, to supervise emergency repairs and steer the ship southward and round Cape Froward to the expedition base at Port Famine.

The coast of Patagonia is studded with sinister names. 'Useless Bay', 'Desolation Island', 'Gulf of Troubles', 'Last Hope Sound' and Port Famine itself leave us in no doubt as to the early navigators' wretchedness and despair. Port Famine had been so christened by Cavendish in 1587, after he found an abandoned Spanish colony containing more than 200 human skeletons. But for Stokes the tiny haven held a fate worse than hunger. After arriving his state of mind deteriorated further, and five days later he shot himself. On a brambly hillside overlooking the bay, a plain beechwood cross over the grave reads:

IN MEMORY OF
COMMANDER PRINGLE STOKES R.N.
H.M.S. BEAGLE
Who died from the effects of the anxieties
and hardships incurred
While surveying the western shores of Tierra del Fuego

Ironically, it was Stokes' suicide and his replacement by Robert Fitzroy that led to the eventual boarding of the *Beagle*'s most famous passenger, Charles Darwin.

Fifty years were to pass, and many ships to founder, before the Admiralty survey was complete. As on some of Britain's rockier shores, looting shipwrecks became a popular local pastime, though by 1887 the Magellan Strait chart could advise sailors:

In the event of a vessel being wrecked or abandoned westward of Cape Horn, the best course to Ushuwaia is eastward of False Cape Horn and through Ponsonby Sound, where Natives would be ready to pilot any shipwrecked man to Ushuwaia. . . . A great change has been affected in the character of the Natives generally, and the Yaghan Natives from Cape San Diego to Cape Horn and thence round to Brecknock Peninsula can be trusted.

Despite the new charts, ships continued to go down. One of many which foundered in the Magellan Strait's western approaches was the New Zealand packet steamer *Mataura*, under the captaincy of an Englishman, Charley Milward. In 1898 she hit rocks on Desolation Island, and only after a three-day struggle in one of the ship's boats was Milward able to lead his passengers and crew round Cape Froward to the safety of Punta Arenas. Choosing to ignore his heroic role in the rescue and an unblemished record spanning 20 years, the shipping company held Milward responsible for the wreck and sacked him in accordance with company rules. Unable to get another command, he gave up the sea and settled in Punta Arenas, where he started a foundry, became a modestly successful businessman, was appointed British Vice-Consul and is still fondly remembered in and around the town. So began a chain of events which, 76 years later, would inspire a grandson of one of Milward's English cousins to take off on his own Patagonian adventure. The grandson was Bruce Chatwin.

With the opening in 1914 of the Panama Canal, steam packets no longer called at Punta Arenas to take on coal, or square-riggers to replace mutinous crew. Nowadays its jetty is crowded with fishery protection ships and a jumble of brightly coloured vessels supporting the offshore oil platforms. But the world's southernmost city is still said to welcome drifters, adventurers and a ragbag of castaways – many of them, like Charley Milward, on the run from an overbearing world.

As I rode into Punta Arenas on the back of a stinking sheep lorry, I had time to speculate on the fact that I was about to add to their number.

Port Famine to Last Hope Sound

'I suppose there may possibly be drearier places,' wrote the crinoline-clad Florence Dixie in 1879, 'but I do not think it is probable; and as we walked over the sand-covered beach in front of the settlement, and surveyed the gloomy rows of miserable wooden huts . . . we all agreed that the epithet of "God-forsaken hole" was the only description that did justice to the merits of this desolate place.'

Punta Arenas in Dixie's time was certainly no Venice.

Today the wooden huts have given way to a mishmash of sandstone, concrete and brick. In characteristic New World fashion the town's grid layout pays no attention to topography, and streets continue straight up the hill behind the main square, giving way to steps where the gradient becomes too steep. On the stylish Avenida España, houses of the well-to-do sit smugly behind privet hedges: mock-Lutyens 'Bayko' styles cheek by jowl with Spanish haciendas, mid-European chalets, modernist Bauhaus blocks and Californian picture-windowed ranches. In the square itself more solemn Edwardian styles prevail, their dignity preserved in lemon-tinged stonework as yet unsullied by pigeon droppings. The feeling somehow combines the exotic promise of Dar-es-Salaam with the dourness of Aberdeen.

Its citizens struck me as sober, hardworking folk, in sharp contrast to the flamboyant Río Gallegans across the Argentine border. I was not the first to notice this. Michael Mason, the flinty English yachtsman who moored his chartered steam launch to the jetty in the autumn of 1930, wrote:

It would startle many employers of English labour to see the quietness, efficiency and speed with which . . . Chileans work. They seem a thoroughly good type all round – industrious, virile and cheery. The

78

middle-class Chileans are not so attractive, to my way of thinking; they seem to talk of little else but food and the cost of it. But we have not got to know any of them well enough to size them up fairly. And one gathers that when their determinations are thoroughly aroused they can show a brilliance and ruthless energy that leave one gasping with admiration.

Unlike Mason, I found it difficult to make out much of a class structure in Punta Arenas. There was certainly a distinction between the ramshackle suburbs to the north and the fine houses up the hill; but almost everyone seemed adequately fed and clothed, and I was not harassed by beggars. As yet, the growing town boasted few of the trappings of consumerism that I'd become used to in Europe, but I noticed that its teenagers were more smartly dressed than their counterparts in, say, Manchester or Glasgow. Punta Arenas mothers still took very seriously the ironing of shirts.

A hundred and forty years ago, outfits would have been of a more Spartan pattern, because from 1848 until 1877 the settlement enjoyed the status of a penal colony. By all accounts it was not exactly an orderly one. President Bulnes had modelled it on the open prisons he'd heard of in Australia – so, like Botany Bay, Punta Arenas was a 'prison without bars'. The strategy was perhaps too far ahead of its time, for the temptation to make trouble proved irresistible. In 1851 the prisoners and soldiers rioted, joining forces to murder the Governor, the priest, an unknown number of civilians, and three foreigners who had the misfortune to be on ships anchored offshore. Then, in 1877, the Artillery Regiment burst from their barracks and sacked the town, setting fire to public buildings and pillaging the houses of leading citizens. This was too much for the Government in Santiago, which promptly decreed that the colony be wound up. Prisoners would in future be interned on uninhabited islands, where they and their custodians could do less harm.

At this point the history of Punta Arenas might well have come to a full stop; but by chance a new raison d'être quickly took the place of the convicts. The newcomers were more easily regimented, and considerably less likely to raze things to the ground, for they were sheep. An Englishman by the name of Henry

Reynard is usually credited with being Patagonia's first sheep-farmer. He arrived by way of the Falklands, and to guard against rustling by Indians installed himself on a large island in the Magellan Strait, where his flock found rich grazing.

Through the expatriate grapevine, news of Reynard's success soon reached the ears of other émigrés: a few of them Spanish, but mostly Falklanders of English or Scottish stock. Some of the newcomers were said to have settled the problem of the Indians by having them discreetly shot: £1 per head, and no questions asked. Not unnaturally this is hotly disputed by the British community, but whether by design or disease the Indians were soon dispatched to their graves. Unmolested now by rustlers, the settlers spread boldly from their island bases, north to the mainland and south to Tierra del Fuego, fencing 1,000 acres at a time. By the turn of the century they'd turned the region into the third largest wool producer in the world. The British made full use of their contacts, and shipped machines, materials, manpower and stud rams from the Falklands or from Britain.

In the whole province of Magallanes, the jetty at Punta Arenas was the only place where ocean-going ships could tie up, and with the help of this monopoly the town began to flourish once more. British companies with names like Broom and Blanchard opened branches or agencies, and the British Navy increasingly paid courtesy calls, so that by 1900 it was said that more English than Spanish could be heard in the streets. Prices were quoted in sterling; traffic drove on the left; and the Honorary British Vice-Consul was second in status only to the Governor. Ballantine's whisky was freely available at five shillings a bottle.

The British community is still thriving today. Bruce Chatwin met some of them in 1975 but was not impressed:

The 'Englishman' took me to the races. . . . 'Day at the races, eh? Nothing like a good race-meeting. Come along with me now. Come along. Come into the VIP's box.'

'I'm not dressed properly.'

'I *know* you're not dressed properly. Never mind. They're quite broad-minded. Come along. Must introduce you to the Intendente.'

But the Intendente took no notice. . . . So we talked to a naval captain who stared out to sea.

'Ever hear the one about the Queen of Spain?' the 'Englishman' asked, trying to liven up the conversation. '. . . I'll try and remember it:

> *A moment of pleasure*
> *Nine months of pain*
> *Three months of leisure*
> *Then at it again.'*

'You are speaking of the Spanish Royal Family?' The Captain inclined his head.

The 'Englishman' said he had read history at Oxford.

I wondered how cameos like this might appear to a Patagonian. Undoubtedly the person best qualified to judge was Mateo Martinič, founder and director of the Patagonian Institute, a Chilean-born Yugoslav who in 20 years had written no fewer than eighteen books on local history. 'I should be delighted to talk,' he boomed down the telephone from his office. 'Why don't you come this afternoon?'

The Institute lay a little way out of town. It consisted of a series of huts surrounded by an astonishing collection of old reapers, harvesters, traction engines, railway engines and even a Model T Ford. Martinič, an indefatigable workaholic, was sitting at his typewriter surrounded by files.

'Regrettably Señor Chatwin didn't come and see me,' he thundered when I showed him the passage. 'Had he done so, I could perhaps have corrected some of his worst misconceptions. His story-telling may be excellent, but I'm afraid that in Patagonia his book lacks – how do you call it? – credibility. You know, there are people here who were extremely angry when it arrived in our bookshops. He'd called on them and they'd taken him in. Sometimes he stayed for days. They gave him hospitality in the Patagonian tradition, and enjoyed doing so. But after making pleasant conversation to their faces, he went home and wrote unkind things, *unfair* things, about them.'

I asked for examples.

'I'm not going to name names,' he replied briskly. 'But you'll find these people if you look hard. Why, some of them live not two miles from this office!'

But the soft-spoken Hebridean lady I met that evening had no recollection of Chatwin. She greeted me in her flat near the

81

Salesian church, fed me mutton casserole and talked about land. Although now widowed, Peggy Fell had been married for many years to a Falklander named John who farmed 40,000 acres on the Argentine border. Like others with an eye to the future, John's grandfather had squatted on this prime sheepfarming land and then bought the deeds for eight cents an acre. Even by Patagonian standards the farm was a remote one, 130 miles from Punta Arenas by rutted track, and in his spare moments John had taken to exploring the nearby Chico River, from whose *brazo norte* or 'north fork' the farm took its name. A cave he discovered there is still known as Fell's Cave. The couple raised six children at Brazo Norte, in more or less total isolation from the outside world. But then, in 1970, came Allende and the spectre of appropriation. 'I had a long talk with the lawyer who was administering the reforms in Magallanes,' said Peggy with the ghost of a smile. 'And do you know, by the time he got round to studying our case, the Government had been overthrown!'

I asked about other farms, like San Gregorio. 'Oh, we knew the San Gregorio people well. It was terrible to see! Allende gave the land to the peons, but without someone to watch them nothing ever seemed to get done. Sheep were left unsheared, carcasses rotted in the slaughterhouses; the farm just went down and down. And then towards the end came the shortages. We needed to buy shoes, but there weren't any for sale in the whole of Magallanes. The shop assistants here in town just hung around playing cards. Sometimes the food queues went right round the block and the tail got mixed up with the head. It was all such a waste of time.'

'But then came Pinochet?'

'Yes, and he was our salvation. Do you know, a month after Pinochet took office, you could go to the supermarket and buy anything you wanted!'

No one in Punta Arenas seemed to have a good word to say for Salvador Allende. An Anglo-Scottish woman, Margaret Harper, remembered his presidency with disgust. 'On the big farm at Cerro Castillo, the peasants let pigs into the kitchen garden. They weren't interested in gardening. The pigs ate the vegetables while they bought their own vegetables in town.'

Again I sought comparisons with Pinochet.

'I really don't understand why that man had such a bad press in Europe and America,' she replied. 'He was just what we needed. They said there were atrocities, but I never heard of any atrocities here.'

But Margaret must have been hard of hearing. At Dawson Island, just 65 miles from her house, Pinochet's opponents were being steadily tortured to death throughout the 1970s, as the whole world now knows.

One unusually fine Sunday, Peggy Fell's daughter Helen invited me to the rodeo. The arena overlooked the Strait, and the tang of horse manure joined forces with whiffs of seaweed from the kelp beds. Spectators scoffed empanadas and swigged Pepsi-Cola on rough benches, separated from the ring by a heavy stockade. Among them, in Oxford bags and ribbons, were Ignacio and Gloria from the Carretera Austral.

'*Señores y señoras!*' crackled the ringmaster. 'I give you, from Río Penitente, the Brothers Fernández!'

A pair of 'gentlemen gauchos' in thick ponchos and wide-brimmed hats emerged from a corral astride strutting creole thoroughbreds, and approached a young bull. At first it bucked, but working together they eventually forced the animal to run and turn at their will, finally cornering it against some stuffed sacking to a murmur of appreciation from the crowd. It was a good display, but Ignacio was deprecating. 'They're not real horsemen, you know. You should see the rodeos up north. Now those gauchos, they really know how to ride!'

It's a sad fact that many of Punta Arenas's most celebrated citizens now reside in the cemetery, and on a blustery morning I visited them. Tom Jones, who was British Consul in the 1950s, used to claim that walking out to the cemetery to pay last respects to departed Britons was about the only exercise he had. Certainly I found a good number of Anglo-Saxon names among the Gonzálezes and Sánchezes, but their memorials were humble compared with the Spanish ones, some of which were the size of a house. The richest families had their own vaults, with neatly labelled niches lining the walls like drawers in a filing cabinet. Those of more modest means were cared for by mutual burial societies; while the army, navy and police looked after their departed ones in cavernous underground catacombs. Several of

the British names were a result of accidents at sea. 'ERECTED BY
THE MASTER, OFFICERS & CREW OF THE S.S. "CHARLTON HALL" OF
LIVERPOOL,' announced one small granite cross, 'TO THE MEMORY
OF APPRENTICE TOM ARCHIBALD, AGED 15 YEARS, OF ABERDEEN,
SCOTLAND, WHO MET HIS DEATH BY ACCIDENT ON BOARD WHILE
DOING HIS DUTY, MAY 18TH 1908.'

Back in the main square, I chanced upon Chile's first ever
demonstration in support of the ozone layer. A hundred scouts
and guides were holding aloft a banner which read, in Spanish
and English, 'Help Us Help Ozone!' Others were handing out
leaflets which argued that the Magallanes province had been
more severely affected by the ozone hole than anywhere else on
earth. This struck me as an improbable claim; so the following
morning I tracked down one of the march's organizers, a Yugoslav by the name of Bedřich Magaš, in his office at the university.

'Do you realize,' he told me, 'that some parts of southern
Patagonia have had hardly any rain for five years? The water
table's falling; farmers are cutting their grazing densities by 10
per cent, 20 per cent, even 40 per cent in some cases over in
Argentina. And the bushfires! Go to the Torres del Paine and see
what a bushfire can do.'

'But haven't there been droughts before? How do you know
this one's being caused by the ozone hole?'

'You've got a point – this isn't the first dry spell we've had. But
those other droughts were limited to certain areas: Tierra del
Fuego, the Magellan shores, or Argentina's Atlantic seaboard.
This time it's total. Maybe it's my suspicious nature, but I can't
help noticing that this drought has exactly coincided with the
most serious case of ozone depletion outside the Antarctic.'

I resolved to keep an eye open for evidence – and to stop
buying aerosols.

For almost 90 years the English-speaking community has maintained a school in Punta Arenas. Known originally as St James's
College, now simply as the British School, it was started by
Anglican missionaries with the idea of providing a sound education for the children of British settlers. Some observers have also
detected an underlying evangelical streak. The headmaster, a
devout and devoted man called Peter Dooley, denied this hotly
when I put the suggestion, and pointed out that the parents of his
720 pupils – mostly aspiring Chilean families – would certainly not

want to see their fees spent on too much religious instruction. A recent visitor had accused the school of functioning on 'snob value', and Peter Dooley reluctantly admitted that there was some truth in this. The upshot of this snobbery was that more than 700 Punta Arenas schoolchildren, most of whom could trace no British parentage whatsoever, went through the daily ritual of reciting the Lord's Prayer in English, followed by a rendering of 'God Save the Queen'. Human ambitions can take the strangest forms.

In the winter of 1843, when Punta Arenas was still a deserted sandspit and most of Patagonia belonged to the Indians, some dramatic events began to unfold near Port Famine, where fifteen years previously Pringle Stokes had died so tragically. In 1837 the French navigator Dumont d'Urville had reconnoitred the Magellan Strait and seen the potential of its shores. His enthusiasm had infected the Paris government, and after some initial hesitation they dispatched the warship *Phaeton* to claim possession for France. The delay was sufficient for news of their intentions to reach President Bulnes in Santiago, who sent the 30-ton schooner *Ancud* to claim the land for Chile. There followed one of the most thrilling races in the history of colonization. The *Ancud*'s captain, a Bristolian by the name of John Williams, urged the tiny craft on a three-month dash through the southern fjords, and succeeded in raising the Chilean flag on a prominent headland near Port Famine just one day before the French arrived.

Wisely, the little band threw up a stockade on the promontory, which they named Fort Bulnes after their president. The accommodation was rudimentary in the extreme. Living quarters were in one-room huts, thrown together from whatever timber was available and caulked by turf against the incessant wind. Good drinking water proved elusive. After battling with these miserable conditions for five winters, the colonists moved to the more agreeable site where Punta Arenas now stands.

On a beautiful summer's day I inspected a cleverly reconstructed replica of the original stockade, trying in vain to visualize the settlers' hardships. Eventually I gave up and lay back to sun myself against a wall.

A foreign tourist strode across the close-cropped grass. He was in his mid-forties, muscular, and very tall. Beige slacks peeped from under a flapping fawn raincoat. On his feet he wore white sneakers; on his head a peaked cap which, for some unfathomable reason, bore the word 'CATERPILLAR'. But it was the man's actions, rather than his appearance, that made me take notice. He'd stepped down with perhaps a dozen others from a minibus which had just pulled into the car park. While the rest milled about, peered towards the fort or headed for the public toilets, he marched swiftly up the slope towards the stockade. In a bold sweep he skirted it and made for a vantage point beyond. There he stopped, put a camera to his eye, took a photograph of the fort, another of the Strait, and a third of his companions still swarming across the grassy slope. This done, he put the camera back in his pocket and returned to the waiting bus.

How easy it is to mock the antics of tourists! And how tempting to think that *we* would never behave so grossly. As a bird of passage, of course, no traveller can expect the kind of insight which Jan Morris, for instance, gave readers of her book on Venice. She'd lived there for years before she felt ready to write about it; whilst others, after half a lifetime, would admit that they still don't know much about their home town. As I sprawled against the warm stones of the wall, these thoughts led me to wonder if travel writing is perhaps a doomed discipline. Can the traveller – flitting here and there like a distracted butterfly – ever really come to grips with anything? Even if the long-term resident may ultimately recognize the true essence of a place, surely the only essence a traveller is likely to stumble on – literally or figuratively – is that of other travellers?

I believe Bruce Chatwin knew very well, as he wandered through Patagonia in early 1975, that he was not going to give its residents a fair hearing. Indeed, having met them superficially he may have been afraid to delve too deeply, suspecting that underneath they might be rather dull. To liven up the narrative of *In Patagonia* he focused his attention on an array of larger-than-life characters – Patagonians, to be sure, but extraordinary ones – and where details were missing he made them up.

In this he was not alone. Victorian travel writers went to astonishing lengths to give their public 'a good read'. As the modern writer Philip Glazebrook has observed, their crags all beetled, cliffs frowned, heights were invariably dizzy, chasms yawned and rivers became cataracts. Impossible dangers were triumphantly surmounted. Some of these texts were further embellished by engraved illustrations from the pens of Allom, Bartlett or Edward Lear, showing savages and werewolves at every turn.

The new century and the austere interwar years brought a fresh honesty to travel writing. Travelling still remained a cherished luxury, but more people aspired to it, and faithful reporting now took precedence over entertainment. This was the age of Freya Stark and Evelyn Waugh, of *News from Tartary* and *The Road to Oxiana*, and it survived well into the 1950s. Humour was permissible – as Eric Newby showed in his 1958 classic, *A Short Walk in the Hindu Kush* – but not at the expense of accuracy or fair play.

Recently, I've noticed a move back towards 'writing to impress', with a late twentieth-century twist. Take for instance the rash of books and magazine articles recounting hair-raising escapades by snowmobile, microlight, dogsled, mountainbike or simply on foot. Some of these are genuine adventure stories; others leave me with the feeling that the authors were writing more for their own benefit than for mine. One such work, taken at random from my bookshelf, includes a graph showing the author's consumption of chocolate during a 7,000-mile walk. The quantity was prodigious, and I'm sure the information will help anyone planning to follow in his steps; but I suspect that few readers will gain much from books of this kind. Nevertheless titles continue to multiply, encouraged perhaps by publishers trying every ploy to maintain their share in a diminishing market.

So is good travel writing impossible? I would argue not. For one thing, the traveller has one great faculty at his or her disposal: the power to compare. The lifelong inhabitants of, say, Punta Arenas won't be in a position to pass judgement on their town if they've never experienced anywhere else. A visitor from Britain, on the other hand, might be struck by similarities between the concerns of Punta Arenas and the preoccupations of a Cotswold village; while a Central Asian tourist – if such exist – might observe an obscure link with the gossip of Kirghiz nomads.

A second skill at the disposal of the observant traveller is the ability to pick out vital details from a welter of irrelevances. Again, natives of a place aren't likely to have much success in this. They'll be too familiar with some aspects, too distant from others; it would be like asking a fisherman to judge sheep.

Ultimately, of course, none of this may matter; for travelling is essentially a personal thing, more important in the doing than in the telling. Whether for ideas, inspiration or just vicarious pleasure, people will continue to enjoy reading about faraway places, and a visit to any bookshop will confirm that travel writing is here to stay. But I suspect that fewer travellers in future will join the ranks of great writers. And of course by the time a book reaches the reader's lap it is already history anyway; for as John Fowles has pointed out, the printed word is only the spoor, the trace of an animal that has once passed by but is now somewhere else in the forest.

'But haven't you seen the penguins?'

The voice was that of Sergio Krumenacker, an out-of-work ski instructor. He leaned against the wing of his 1973 Buick, buffing it absently with a piece of waste. 'Listen, they breed on Otway Sound – only a couple of hours' drive from here. If you pay for my petrol, I'll take you there. You can't leave Magallanes without seeing the penguins!'

Sergio was a rubbery little man, with a dark football of a head and a podgy belly – a most unlikely ski instructor, I thought, though he talked convincingly about the pistes up the hill, apparently the only ones in the world where you can ski in sight of the sea. Demand for his services wasn't sufficient to make a living, so Sergio spent much of his time doing odd jobs for the oil companies, hanging round the employment agencies, and polishing the wings of his Buick.

I asked how he came to have such an unusual surname.

'It comes from Schleswig-Holstein,' he explained. 'My grandfather emigrated before the First World War. But my grandmother, my mother and most of my cousins are Turks. What does that make me? I don't know. My father says I'm German, but my wife insists I'm a Turk.'

He certainly looked more Turkish than German. When he spoke, his brown eyes darted furtively from left to right as though he were afraid of eavesdroppers. I stole a glance at his moustache and noticed that, like his belly, it boasted an appreciable droop. Even his car had a trace of the Turkish *dolmuş* about it – too old to be fashionably modern but too new to be fashionably old. As we bounced over the rough track towards Otway Sound,

I stretched back luxuriously in the soft leather and listened to his chatter. He was nothing if not an amiable guide. He told me first what it was like to work at the world's most southerly ski school ('too little snow, too many skiers, too few women'); then about the new coal mine – actually a gaping opencast working – which we passed at Pecket; and finally about how an acquaintance of his had once brought dogs along this very road to bait the penguins. 'He was an evil man – quite deranged, if you ask me. He didn't intend to eat the birds, or even sell them; I think he just enjoyed watching them die.'

We arrived to find the penguins sunning themselves outside their burrows. It was one of those rare Patagonian days when the air was quite still. Otway Sound mirrored the low mountains to north and south, and the reflections were undisturbed by waves. We approached softly, and small black and white heads peered anxiously at us from behind grassy hummocks, twisting this way and that to get a better view. These were Magellanic penguins, also known as Jackasses because of their donkey-like braying. They are amongst the smallest of the species, the adults reaching a height of hardly more than two feet, and they are the only ones to breed regularly on the South American mainland. Early navigators thought they embodied the souls of drowned seamen. A friend who has seen hundreds of Jackass penguins in the Falklands says that when alarmed they run on all fours, using their flippers as front legs and achieving remarkable speeds. The Falkland ones are apparently quite highly-strung; but those in front of me simply wriggled backwards into their burrows, to glare crossly out of first one eye and then the other until I retreated out of range.

At the water's edge, a gaggle of 30 or more were taking advantage of the unusually calm weather, waddling along the shingly strand like geriatric holidaymakers. Offshore, a dozen penguin heads broke the surface, calling squeakily to their friends on the beach before disappearing again. The penguin is said to have been so named more than 400 years ago, by a Welshman on Thomas Cavendish's expedition who observed them in the water at Port Desire. *Pen gwyn*, in Welsh, means 'white head'. As I watched the promenaders paddling clumsily out to join those in the water, I couldn't imagine anyone, however deranged, wanting to molest such bumbling, comical birds.

*

Back in Punta Arenas, dramatic news was waiting. Two hundred miles north, in the Torres del Paine massif, 16th February 1990 had dawned cloudless and bright. By 9.00 a.m. the glaciers of Chile's 'showcase' national park were already shimmering in the heat haze. On the plains below, guanaco were moving listlessly among the thorny scrub. For the sixth day running, temperatures in the eighties seemed likely – a rare event at these latitudes – and they would be tempered only slightly by the breeze coming in from the west.

At a campsite by Lake Pehoé, 42-year-old Californian Thomas Whight felt the call of nature. He took his roll of toilet paper and found a secluded spot. Afterwards, not wanting to foul the place more than necessary, he put a match to the used paper, and stood by ready to stamp out the embers. To his horror, a gust carried the tiny flame into the adjacent grass, and within seconds several square feet were alight. Despite the frantic efforts of Whight and his fellow campers, the whole hillside was burning by sundown.

Patagonia has always been susceptible to bushfires. Apart from those started deliberately by the early colonizers – whose results I'd seen around Coyhaique – spontaneous *incendios* over the years have destroyed many millions of acres. In the southernmost regions, including the Torres del Paine, the brief growing season provides no chance for the vegetation to recover. The Paine park rangers were said to be fighting a losing battle; and with the number of visitors to this park alone doubling every fifteen years, it seemed to me that the problem of the careless tourist was potentially a lethal one. I decided to go and see the damage.

The so-called 'Towers of Paine' form the southern tip of the cordillera where, a month previously, I'd been admiring Mount Fitzroy and Cerro Torre. Like those Argentine peaks, the pinkish granite Paine monoliths have attracted many climbers and claimed many lives. Like the Fitzroy range, too, the Paine massif is a walker's paradise. Since 1959, when the park was originally established under the name of Lago Grey, it has featured in more and more holiday brochures. Hilary Bradt, the travel writer and publisher, who has more experience of hiking in South America than anyone else I know, still calls it her favourite place on earth.

'The trouble is,' chief ranger Jovito González told me when I arrived, 'almost all our visitors come in the summer months when the fire risk is at its highest. With each fresh year of drought, the potential for disaster gets worse. Fire prevention is our number one priority.'

Jovito González's resources looked pitiful to a European eye. To patrol nearly half a million acres he had just thirteen rangers, a couple of dozen horses, a motorboat and a jeep. It looked as if the park – declared by UNESCO to be a reserve of international importance – was being run on not even a shoestring.

There had long been talk of making visitors pay for more effective protection in irreplaceable areas such as this. Jovito González showed me the results of a survey which had shown that 19 out of every 20 visitors came from the world's 20 richest countries; yet to enter the park I'd been charged, like everyone else, a paltry 65p. I mentioned that some African parks were now charging visitors as much as £30. 'Well,' he replied, 'we do get some help from the Government in Santiago; but that has to cover trail maintenance and bridge repairs, as well as the rangers' wages. For firefighting we need much more. When things got out of hand during Thomas Whight's fire, my only consolation was that our Argentine colleagues across the border are even worse off than we are. Sometimes, for lack of equipment, they have to stand by and watch their prize landscapes go up in flames.'

I spent a week walking the park's famous 'circuit', an 85-mile loop encompassing the very best it has to offer. The first part was through golden grasslands, where guanaco took up heraldic poses on rocky outcrops, scrutinizing my progress inquisitively, while ostrich-like rheas broke cover noisily and scattered in frenzy. The guanaco's grace and dignity are breathtaking, and it's difficult to believe that until 20 years ago most Patagonians regarded them as vermin. Pointed, white-tipped ears stand proud above enormous brown eyes, which blink at newcomers in an expression of permanent surprise. They move in small herds, led by a male who chooses each grazing ground, occasionally raising his giraffe-like neck to watch for puma and other dangers.

The rhea, by contrast, is a skittish creature, unable to tell friend from foe. Like its distant cousins the ostrich and the kiwi, it's a cowardly bird, and if Patagonia had more sand I'm sure the rhea would spend much of its time with its head in it. Its mottled grey plumage blends in well with its scrubland haunts, so that the rhea's first response to approaching danger is to freeze. When it can bear the tension no longer, it bursts from cover and dashes squawking across the plain. This frenzied fleeing used to make it vulnerable to Indian hunters, who would bring it down easily with their *bolas* – a device made up of three hide-wrapped stones strung together, which if thrown skilfully could be made to entangle first the neck and then the feet of a running bird. The British explorer George Musters was one of the few Europeans to master this primitive weapon, and in 1869 he put it to good use. 'I observed an ostrich coming straight towards me,' he wrote later. 'I galloped to the cover of a friendly bush, and when he was within a short distance dashed out, and discharging the bolas, had the satisfaction of seeing him turn a somersault and lie with outstretched wings, stunned.'

From the meadows, I climbed through ancient beechwoods towards a pass which, though hardly more than 5,000 feet in altitude, was snow-covered even on this late summer's day. The top rewarded me with what must surely be one of the finest views in South America. At my feet the ground dropped abruptly to the dwarf outliers of another beech forest. Below and far beyond, the Grey glacier swept in from the north-west, a contorted tongue of ice so long and grotesque that it gave the impression of originating in an altogether different world. Belying its name, the ice was a splendid steely-blue, reflecting the sun with dazzling intensity. Following its course with my eyes, I strained to see where it parted from the distant ice-cap; but it merged seamlessly with the sky. Somewhere behind me the Torres lay swathed in cloud. I could make out some of their outlying steeples, but could only guess the shapes of the loftier peaks, which would later be casting their bulky shadows over my tent.

Although hikers were warned to carry their own shelter, the park did in fact have a number of rough timber refuges, some of which stood by glacial lakes where they enjoyed dramatic views and a supply of chilly but drinkable water. These huts, though equipped mostly with little more than a stove, were understandably popular and would usually be full by early afternoon. At one such place I came across a task force from the London-based Operation Raleigh, working hard to rebuild a refuge which had been destroyed by fire. This was just one of the ways in which individuals from a dozen or more countries were helping Jovito González to cope with his torrent of visitors. Another Operation Raleigh team was building a suspension bridge across a glacial stream, at a point where floods had nearly claimed several lives. The cheerful people involved in these projects included students, unemployed youngsters and the occasional office worker on sabbatical leave. As well as the actual building work, each team had been responsible for designing the structures and carrying in the materials. I couldn't imagine a more constructive use of their energies and time.

Many of my fellow-hikers felt they hadn't been sufficiently warned of the fire risk. On entering the park, most had received a list of do's and don'ts printed in Spanish and English. One or two had been asked to take special precautions. But on several evenings I met merry groups gathered round campfires in the forest, who either didn't understand the danger or didn't seem to care.

Thomas Whight's fire burned for ten days and destroyed more than 1,000 acres of prime park landscape. 'That was a small one,' said Carlos Bahamóndez, head of the team that eventually put it out. 'In 1985 we lost 45,000 acres in a single week.'

It has to be said that the Torres del Paine takes a certain toll on its visitors. After two weeks of clambering over tree-trunks and pushing through tangled calafate bushes, my legs were a welter of scratches, my clothes hung in tatters and my food supply was down to some strands of tagliatelle that had somehow escaped consumption. It was time, as Robert Fitzroy would have said, to put in for victualling and refitting.

The nearest settlement was the small fishing and wool port of Puerto Natales, 75 miles south on a windward shore of Last Hope Sound. This great sea loch was so named by Fitzroy's lieutenants Skyring and Kirke, who hoped it would provide a desperately needed outlet to the north-west. It didn't. After luring them for 30 miles in the right direction, the channel ended abruptly and brutally at the foot of Mount Balmaceda.

A generous passer-by called Alfredo took me to Puerto Natales, along with several other wayside waifs, whom he piled one by one onto the back of his pickup until it resembled a charabanc in a Heath Robinson cartoon. Some of his passengers had spent more than a month in the park; all of us were hungry as wolves and filthy beyond belief. As we headed for showers and restaurants, I reflected that life's essential experiences hadn't changed much since Florence Dixie's day:

We handled our knives and forks very awkwardly at first; it required almost an effort to eat in a civilized manner, and, accustomed of late to take our meals in a recumbent position, we by no means felt comfortable in our chairs. . . . The men of our party, particularly, were unpleasant to look at. Their hair had grown long and elfin; their faces were tanned to a dark red-brown, which the dust and the smoke from the camp-fires had deepened into – well – black; and their unshaven chins were disfigured by a profuse growth of coarse stubble. Our clothes did not bear close inspection, the blood of many a guanaco, the grease of many an ostrich-dinner, the thorn of many a califaté bush, had left their marks; and, altogether, a more ruffianly, disreputable lot than we looked it would be hard to imagine.

But on this particular morning, Puerto Natales probably wouldn't have noticed if Butch Cassidy himself had ridden into town. It was the newly elected Chilean Government's inauguration day, and the population had taken to the streets, either parading with flags and banners or following behind in cars. 'BIENVENIDOS DEMOCRACIA', read a placard held aloft by a group of teenagers. I'd have been interested to hear what they understood by the second word, as Chile's last democratic government must have fallen at about the time they were born.

On Calle Bulnes, in the Restaurante Central, Fernando the fisherman was on his third bottle of Austral beer. 'Don't talk to me about democracy,' he warned me. 'What's democracy going to do for me? For 20 years I ran my own boat, then along came an outfit called Pesca Chile and took all the concessions worth having. They put me out of business overnight. What's democracy going to do about that, eh?'

I'd heard similar complaints all down the coast. The outgoing junta had passed a law requiring fishing enterprises large and small to compete for concessions to fish. Pesca Chile, the largest operator in Magallanes, had been in a prime position to lobby for the richest waters; independent fishermen didn't stand a chance. Pesca Chile had also, it was rumoured, managed to get itself exempted from key restrictions on inshore fishing, so further monopolizing the available catch. People like Fernando were simply being pushed out.

Hoping to cheer him up, I ventured that the new government could do plenty to help him if it chose. Wouldn't he vote for a president who promised to restore the rights of the small fisherman?

'Now why would he do that?' he muttered. 'And even supposing he did promise something in his manifesto, the Pesca Chile people would nobble him long before he took any action. No – I don't vote for anyone,' he concluded, addressing the creamy-brown ceiling. 'What's the point?'

Fernando was 37 years old; at the time of Chile's last election he'd have been seventeen – just too young to vote. After coming down a different political road, I found myself identifying closely with his feelings about the impotence of the individual, and said as much.

'But my friend,' replied Fernando with a wink. 'I've read about your *Mujer de Hierro*, the Iron Lady. Think about it carefully. Have our two countries' roads really been so different?'

On a nearby street corner, outside another bar, another fisherman stood talking to his Alsatian. It was 3.00 p.m., the hour when serious drinkers began to think about going home for lunch; but this man simply stood there, swaying slightly. '*Mi camarada*,' he slurred. '*Mi amigo único*.' The dog looked up at him with big forgiving eyes; but his workmates on an opposite corner shook their heads. '*Es alcohólico*,' they told me, turning away. 'He's just a drunkard.'

That evening, with two of my fellow vagrants from Alfredo's pickup, I enjoyed a memorable meal of sea trout, an indulgence marred only by the memory of the *alcohólico* and the spectre of Florence Dixie frowning her disapproval. Puerto Natales was a younger, smaller and less solidly built community than Punta Arenas; most of its houses had a temporary air. They seemed to consist largely of sheet metal, painted in thin, watery colours and braced by battens against the salty breeze which blew permanently off the sound. Coats of paint faded quickly, peeling and merging with rust patches to form intricate patterns in a thousand pastel shades, so that the older houses looked as if they'd been gift-wrapped by Laura Ashley.

Some friends had invited me to meet their family, and I found them next day having tea. At the head of the table was a formidable woman who introduced herself as Aunt América. She'd just returned to Chile after spending three years in Río Gallegos, and had some strong opinions on the subject of Argentines.

'There's no getting away from it – they're bone idle,' she assured me, offering a large plate of cake. 'You should see the coal miners at Río Turbio! Half the workforce is Chilean, and puts in a normal day's work. The other half is Argentine, and do you know what they do? Why, they sneak off home at lunchtime!' I nodded through mouthfuls of cake and she continued, warming to her theme. 'And then, when they get home, they find the most enormous lunches waiting for them. Tables groaning with food! It's no wonder they can't work in the afternoon. So when eventually the bills come in, of course they can't pay them because they've only earned half a weekly wage. The electricity company, the telephone company, all Argentina's companies are going bankrupt, because no one ever pays their bills.'

I asked Aunt América if she saw a solution to the Argentine condition, but she shook her head. 'They always look to other people to solve their problems, but the problem is up here.' She tapped her head pointedly, before reaching for another slice of cake.

Aunt América's father was half-Scottish. He smiled conspiratorially across the table and changed the subject. 'If you want to know more about Puerto Natales, you ought to meet my cousin Roderick MacLean Cameron,' he told me. 'He's the butcher.'

The name over the butcher's shop on Calle O'Higgins announced in bold red letters: 'CARNICERIA ROTISERIA MAC-LEAN'. I looked at it for some time before it struck me what was wrong. Patagonians, unable to grasp the typographical subtlety of the prefix 'Mac', often split Scottish surnames into two. But the hyphenated variation was new to me. I stepped inside and asked for Don Roderick 'Mac-Lean'.

If his sign seemed out of place in Puerto Natales, the man who greeted me looked even more so. At 82, Roderick Mac-Lean had long ago hung up his butcher's smock, but the well-worn tweed jacket, buttoned cardigan, blue eyes, ruddy face and shock of white hair spoke of Scotland as clearly as if he'd been wearing a kilt. His assistants busied themselves around the shop, pretending not to listen, as he answered my questions about the early days.

'Yes, I remember them clearly. Puerto Natales hadn't even been founded when I was born here.' He waved his arm up the street. 'All this was countryside. Of course, there was the abattoir, and a few houses along the beach; but nothing you could call a town. No, that came later, after the Great War.'

Suddenly he thumped the table. 'The strikes of 1921 were the turning point, you know – a real boost to trade. The Communists had taken over the abattoir and production was at a standstill. Some of them went to join their Argentine co-conspirators and were wiped out by the Army; others tried to set fire to the freezing plant. But it all came to nothing, absolutely nothing; the ringleaders were arrested and the rest went back to work like lambs. With the subversives in prison or dead, the farmers built a new abattoir and things have never looked back.'

His assistants continued to busy themselves, all ears. I asked about his family, wondering if Johnnie MacLean in Coyhaique might be related in some way. In Patagonia anything was possible.

'Well, you may not believe this, but I had six brothers and six sisters. In those days families were families. Let me see now. I've got brothers and cousins still living in Punta Arenas, in Tierra del Fuego, even in Puerto Montt. But Johnnie, you say? Coyhaique? No, I don't think he was one of us. Might have been, but I don't think so.'

I raised the subject of Allende and the land reforms. The old man choked, turned a shade ruddier and frothed a little.

'Oh, what a thief that man was. A common thief! Took away everything, turned it over to the peasants, and then expected the economy to roll along just as before. But you see, the peasants had no discipline. That's what was missing – discipline. It was only after Pinochet took over that we saw any discipline.'

I said that Chileans seemed quite disciplined to me.

'And how do you think we became like this? Sixteen years of firm government, that's how! If you ask me we could do with sixteen more.'

His assistants flew about the shop, feigning indifference as if their lives depended on it. Two pigs' heads gazed at us from a slab. I commented that many people were expressing confidence in the new president.

'We shall see,' said the old man. 'But I warn you: this new government is not to be trusted. It contains Communists!'

The assistants scrubbed away at a counter they'd already scrubbed three times.

During our conversation Roderick Mac-Lean had let slip a curious fact. Puerto Natales had been so named because it was founded on the *día natal* or birthday of Dorothy Eberhard. Dorothy's father, a German sea captain by the name of Hermann, had been the first settler on the shores of Last Hope Sound. It was Hermann who, in 1895, had discovered the putrefying heap of skin and bones which had so intrigued me in the museum in Santiago.

I was by no means the first to have been excited by the idea of the Giant Ground Sloth. A year after its discovery, the Swedish explorer Otto Nordenskjöld came to cart off bits to the Uppsala Museum, and the year after that the Argentine Francisco Moreno did the same for his own country's natural history museum at La Plata. As so often happened in those imperial days, Moreno's piece of skin fell into the hands of the British Museum. It sparked off such interest that in 1900 the *Daily Express* sent the zoologist Hesketh Prichard to find a living specimen of the extraordinary creature. Although he failed in this somewhat starry-eyed quest, Prichard's tale of his nine-month adventure provided Conan Doyle with many of his ideas for *The Lost World*.

The cave where Eberhard made the find was just fourteen miles up the coast of Last Hope Sound. Set in a limestone barranca with a sweeping view of the channel, it looked from a distance to be the stuff of dreams. Bruce Chatwin had described its mouth as 400 feet wide, and though I'd by now learned to be cautious of his facts and figures, I was nonetheless disappointed to find it spanning no more than 100. In the fourteen years since his visit the cave had acquired some new features, including a flagstoned path with explanatory notices, and a full-scale fibre-glass sloth which bade visitors farewell as they re-emerged blinking from their underground guided stroll. But I was relieved to see that the inevitable soft-drink stand had at least been kept at a distance, over by the entrance kiosk and car park. Thankful for small mercies, I weaved between an Italian family and a group of Japanese and sat down in an inner recess.

I felt unaccountably let down. This cave, which had attracted expeditions from halfway round the world, which had helped to inspire a great novel, and which had played a central part in one of the most acclaimed travel books of our time, was no more than a cheap and tawdry tourist trap. I'd fondly imagined it to be reached only after an arduous journey by horse or on foot; yet the Puerto Natales travel agents were offering half-day trips in air-conditioned minibuses. My immediate reaction was to blame the Italians and Japanese who, as I sat, were testing out the echo by shrieking like chimpanzees; or Chatwin, who described so much as it might have been rather than as it actually was; or myself, for travelling in the slipstream of others instead of trusting my own instincts. But then I recalled that my disappointments had so far been mostly superficial ones; a little delving had usually shown the substance of Patagonia to have survived.

On an impulse I dug my fingers into the sandy soil of the cave's floor – at first without much enthusiasm, then more eagerly as I realized the significance of the search. Eventually I found what I was looking for: a peaty brown layer with half-digested bits of straw sticking out at angles. My heart beat faster. To be quite sure, I carved a slice and carried it to the daylight. There could be no doubt about it! Crumbly, evil-smelling and 11,000 years old, the brown clod in my hand was nothing less than a sample of Giant Ground Sloth-shit.

Fireland

'You're in luck,' said the farmer, as he picked me up on the road back to Punta Arenas. 'I'm on my way there now. Everyone else went this morning for the Livestock Show.'

Though Patagonia-born, Robert McDonald was deeply proud of his Scottish blood. In 1908 his father, one of the Ross-shire McDonalds, had seen an advertisement in a Scottish newspaper: 'WANTED – SHEPHERDS'. The advertiser was the Sociedad Explotadora de Tierra del Fuego – 'Tierra del Fuego Development Company' – at that time the biggest sheepfarming enterprise in the world. The successful applicants were to present themselves,

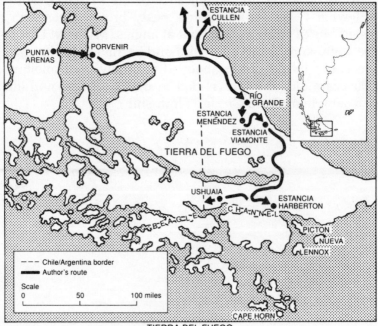

TIERRA DEL FUEGO

each with a pair of sheepdogs, at Liverpool's Rock Ferry terminal on a certain day.

Robert McDonald, father of the man beside me now, knew nothing about either the company or Tierra del Fuego. But he had a nose for adventure. The choice before him was between a lifetime of shepherding on the familiar Scottish fells, or trying his luck on this island on the other side of the world. He answered the advertisement and was accepted. In Liverpool he met the others – 39 lads from all over the British Isles. They came from widely varying backgrounds but had one thing in common. Not a single one possessed a sheepdog.

The contracts specified two dogs each, so on their last night the boys raided a butcher's coldstore and set out into the Liverpudlian streets. With hunks of raw meat they lured dog after dog, and each was hurriedly bound, muzzled and bundled off to the ship. By dawn 80 mongrels had been laid howling in the hold. The contracts were fulfilled and the ship sailed on the morning tide. Some of these 'forty thieves' later rose to become managers of the company's vast farms on Tierra del Fuego and the Patagonian mainland. Others acquired farms of their own. The dogs were not so lucky; apparently fewer than a dozen survived the voyage.

Half of Punta Arenas seemed to be at the show. They'd been pouring in all day from every direction – the country people in old station wagons, the townsfolk on foot – and the atmosphere was expectant. Marquees and bunting flapped in the rising wind. A tannoy summoned competitors to the gymkhana ring. Side-stalls offered organic marrows and Cooper's sheep dip; or, if you preferred, you could have your ears pierced or your fortune told.

In the Women's Institute tea tent I was introduced to an auctioneer. He wore a theatrical-looking handlebar moustache, carried a bowler and cane, and presented me with a visiting card which read 'Vicente Gómez Echeverría, Public Hammerman'. 'Come with me,' he ordered in a voice to match his calling. We ducked out of the tent and entered a shed in which the stink of straw mingled with the sweat of 50 prize sheep. At first I hardly recognized them: they bore no resemblance whatsoever to the creatures I had seen scraping a living amongst the thorn bushes of Chacabuco and Buena Vista. These were Chile's best – Poll Merinos, Romney Marshes, Hampshire and Suffolk Downs and

Corriedales – all panting like prize fighters as they waited their turn in the ring. The animals had been groomed from birth for such occasions, and knew what was expected of them. They allowed me to plunge my hands through a full twelve inches of greased and combed fleece to the 300 pounds of body flesh below. The finest already carried rosettes, and would earn their owners a silver chalice.

Vicente Gómez had auctioned hundreds of such creatures over the years, for clients with names like Morrison and Saunders. 'You could always tell the British farms by their fences,' he declared. 'Not a post out of true. The Scots were the best managers, but the English had an eye for a good animal. When they turned up at my auctions I could recognize my English customers, even from the platform. It was the way they sniffed.'

The tannoy was calling competitors for the prizegiving and we all crowded into the main building. A television news presenter – recently fired, they told me, because of the change of government – took the stage and joked about not being used to the spotlight. Then the Governor of Magallanes spoke about his plans to develop the region. A woodchip mill was to be built on Tierra del Fuego. Applause. Help would be on hand for farmers wanting to clear land for cultivation. More applause. Remote parts of the region, especially in Last Hope province, would be opened up by new roads. Cheers. It seemed to me that large chunks of Magallanes' remaining wilderness were being given their notice, and the people most affected were hailing every move.

It was a September afternoon in 1871 when Tierra del Fuego's first European settlers set eyes on the island. A young couple stood on the deck of the topsail schooner *Allen Gardiner*, running up the Beagle Channel before a fresh easterly. The husband, a lean, black-bearded Nottinghamshire man, was the latest in a number of clergymen sent by the Patagonian Missionary Society to convert the Fuegian Indians. His wife, after weeks of seasickness in the South Atlantic, had lost the rosy cheeks of her Devonshire childhood and was too frail to stand without support. As they surveyed the sombre forests rising into grey-bellied clouds, she turned to her companion and said, 'Dearest, you have brought me to this country, and here I must remain, for I can never, never face that ocean voyage again.'

Thomas and Mary Bridges had met only two years previously, at a schoolteachers' gathering in Bristol. Thomas had already spent several years with his missionary father in the Falklands, making occasional forays to Tierra del Fuego; but for Mary the journey was truly into the unknown. Her husband's faith and dedication to his mission must have been equalled if not surpassed by her less trumpeted qualities during the 27 years they spent together on the island. Despite her vow, she did return to England after his death, and many years later fulfilled her wish to be buried in an English country churchyard.

With introductions in my pocket to several of the Bridges' descendants, I embarked for the island whose name, 'Land of Fire', recalls the campfires of the Indians Thomas tried to convert. The Magellan Strait was indigo and mirror-calm, but I knew that crossings were rarely so smooth. Bolted to the upper deck of the landing craft *Melinka*, which was serving as a car ferry, I found an illuminated shrine to the Virgin Mary. The vessel was crowded with farmers on their way home from the Punta Arenas show, and the familiar smell of sheep hung on the breeze. Approaching the island, I counted scores of cormorants on the shore, drying their wings in the weak autumn sun like supplicants at a festival of Druids.

Porvenir, the Tierra del Fuego landfall, was a town of dusty streets and rusty shops, seemingly without inhabitants. The farmers leaped into their station wagons and sped off to distant estancias. No one seemed to share my destination on the Argentine side of the island – no one, that was, until I met Gonzalo.

Gonzalo was a cobbler by trade, but made a few extra pesos running a taxi service in his old Renault. He'd found two other ferry passengers heading for Argentina, so it wasn't difficult for us to strike a deal. My companions, a pair of merry Chiloé women, collapsed into the back seat and I helped Gonzalo pile their numerous parcels on top of them. As we pitched and bucketed towards the border they kept up a stream of gossip over our shoulders, and Gonzalo joined in enthusiastically – despite the fact that our combined fares would hardly pay for his fuel.

Skirting the prophetically named Useless Bay, we came to

within a few miles of the Argentine border post and Gonzalo stopped to fix something in the boot. On getting out to help I suddenly understood why he'd agreed to such a reasonable fare. The boot was crammed with clothes, groceries and other consumer items which, though compact, would no doubt fetch a handsome premium in Argentina. Our role as passengers was evidently to distract the customs men. 'Just some presents for my Argentine friends,' he winked.

But at customs and immigration they were busy dismantling a Chilean container lorry, and paid no attention whatsoever to a car carrying three routine travellers from the Porvenir ferry. As we passed through the barrier and accelerated away, Gonzalo's composure remained exactly as before. Here, I thought, is a smuggler to be reckoned with.

Tierra del Fuego's largest settlement, Río Grande, possessed about as much character as an army camp. Indeed, part of it was just that, though the military presence had declined since my visit eleven years previously. In the intervening period an electronics industry had sprung up and failed. During its brief existence several thousand families had arrived to swell the town's population, and many had become trapped there, jobless and without any means of returning north. Beyond Avenida San Martín, the cheapskate version of Sunset Boulevard that passed for a main street, the shanties of these unfortunates stretched away to the horizon. Beach-pebble roads pitted with giant potholes served the sad suburbs, planned so recently but now decaying before they were even half-built. The town symbolized perfectly the enigma of Argentina – an inability to realize her potential, to see her projects through. No one has been able to explain how a nation with such a wealth of natural and human resources could, in less than 50 years, drop from 7th to 79th in the world's league table of rich nations. Yet this dubious honour is Argentina's.

At a kiosk a young boy sold me a newspaper. There was something wrong with his eye. I looked again and saw a scar, straight and neat, stretching diagonally across his forehead and through the eye, finishing on the side of his nose. The scar had almost healed but the eye was mashed to bits: a gruesome legacy of a streetfight. Mass unemployment has the same dreadful human consequences, I thought, whether it's on Tierra del Fuego or Tyneside.

Across the river stood an abattoir which had once been the pride of the island. Built in 1903 by the sheep mogul José Menéndez, it started life as a meat-salting and tallow-making works serving just two farms. In 1916 Menéndez transformed the place into a giant *frigorífico* or freezing plant, and put an Englishman, John Goodall, in charge. The scale of operations was awesome: in one year they slaughtered 100,000 sheep from one farm alone.

For 60 years the *frigorífico* was Río Grande's main source of employment. Many of the workers were Chilean migrants, whose idea of home was an uncured sheepskin thrown over a plank bed, and even as late as 1938 the visitor A.F. Tschiffely described Río Grande as nothing more than the packing house, some tin shacks, and corrals full of sheep. In those days, during the season, between 3,000 and 5,000 animals were being slaughtered daily. 'The few men who do the actual killing are so fond of taking life,' reported Tschiffely, 'that on Sundays, when they are free, they take a "bus-man's holiday". It takes the form of a sadistic perversion. Armed with their knives, they set out to a land point near the settlement, and there pass the Sabbath competing as to who can cut the throats of the greatest number of harmless seals. Having enjoyed the slaughter, they leave the dead animals to be eaten by the birds, and return home, happy and satisfied, ready for another week's throat-cutting of sheep.'

Not surprisingly, seals are hardly to be seen near Río Grande nowadays. Perhaps in retribution, the navigable estuary which was the reason for locating the works there has silted to no more than a creek, and the butchered carcasses are now shipped out by lorry.

I walked out of the growing/decaying town and started hitchhiking towards the Beagle Channel port of Ushuaia. A Hungarian took me ten miles to a police post, from where he assured me I'd find a lift. But it was one of those days when no one seemed willing to stop, and at nightfall I bade farewell to the kindly, bored policemen and followed their directions to Estanica José Menéndez. 'Say we sent you because there was no room in the jail,' they laughed.

The estancia buildings were a mile from the road, visible through a gap in the hills. This was Menéndez's third farmstead on the island. Its land once stretched from the Atlantic to the Chilean border – 300,000 acres of the finest grazing south of the Magellan Strait. By the 1920s the list of employees ran to more than 200, and the wool clip was so heavy that they built a railway to take it down to the coast. It was along this long-dismantled line that I now approached the neat rows of red-roofed buildings.

In the manager's house an old man was warming his back against a well-primed log fire. He had greying, slicked-back hair, a protruding jaw, and the heaviest pair of spectacles I've ever seen. To my request for permission to camp, he replied '*Sí, por supuesto*'; but as I was following his directions he called me back. 'Looks a wee bit like rain,' he remarked in English, grinning broadly. 'It's silly to camp when we've got a perfectly good spare room.'

Angus Murdo, the last in a long line of Scottish managers on the Menéndez payroll, was taking things easy on the orders of his doctor. Taking things easy didn't come easily to him. 'After my heart attack they tried to stop me working altogether!' he declared indignantly. 'Ridiculous, eh? A man needs to work or he dies.'

Stepping indoors, I apologized for my filthy state, covered in dust from the road.

'Ach, don't worry,' he replied. 'The filth round here's quite clean.'

As the evening wore on, a succession of visitors came to drink Angus's whisky and bask beside his generous fire. A sheep lorry had got bogged down in mud nearby, and the driver came in to have a shower. The estancia accountant arrived from the radio room and reported another slump on the Buenos Aires wool market. Some 37,000 fleeces, still stacked in the shearing shed two months after parting company with their original owners, would have to stay there for another two months at least. The current price wouldn't even cover the cost of shipping them to the capital.

The night brought winds and heavy rain, and sleep was made impossible by a combination of rattling windows and staccato drumming on the corrugated iron roof. I lay in my cot bed, wondering about the remarkable family firm of which the estancia was a part. Patagonian sheepfarming may have owed its origins to the British, but it was the shrewdness of Spaniards like José Menéndez that turned it into big business. As early as 1884 he bought his first 75,000 acres in Chile, paying just a few pence per acre. In 1896, with earnings from that first operation, he crossed the newly-agreed border and started buying concessions on the Argentine side. One of his five sons, Josecito, was packed off to study sheepfarming in Australia, and came back to direct further acquisitions. Such an ambitious family might well have felt threatened by some of their more successful British neighbours, but the Menéndezes saw the strengths of the British and decided to harness them. By the time of the Great War several million Menéndez sheep had been bred, shorn and slaughtered on the instruction of British farm managers.

'Do you see much of your boss?' I asked Angus over breakfast.

'Not nowadays. At one time the whole family lived in Patagonia, on one farm or another, but the youngsters seem to prefer the razzmatazz of Buenos Aires.'

'Don't they ever visit?'

'Only at shearing time.' He allowed himself the hint of a smile. 'Look, why don't you wander over and have a look round Don José's house, the *casa patronal*? It's quite empty, but the caretaker will let you in. The house will explain more than I can.'

I'd spotted the house from the main road – a double-bayed black-and-white structure set on a slight rise. Approaching between stunted conifers up the long drive, I reflected that not even Río Grande's electronics factories could have been less in keeping with the gaunt Patagonian landscape. A small forest had been planted to shelter the stately pile, but after 70 years in a bitter Fuegian climate the trees had attained a height of barely 20 feet.

I stood on a doormat inscribed 'MENENDEZ BEHETY' and knocked hard. The sound echoed through empty rooms. Eventually a sleepy-eyed girl came and opened the door a fraction. Yes, of course I could look round; I could inspect it all. The only condition was that I shouldn't take photographs. The girl was most insistent about this. Don José – no doubt fearing covetous eyes from Buenos Aires – expressly forbade photography in his house.

I padded from room to room, and soon began to see the reason for the ban. It was not that the place was unduly luxurious. The chandeliers were of glass; the silver well-worn; the paintings, as far as I could tell, by unknown artists. But with its eight bedrooms, four bathrooms, two drawing rooms and fully equipped billiard room – not to mention its convenient proximity to the Río Grande air base – such a house might offer tempting booty to some future general.

In the back drawing room I leafed through an album of fading family photographs. By the time the house was built in 1916, Don José had clearly passed well beyond his prime. In one print his sons, frock-coated and already middle-aged, stared imperiously at the photographer from a landscape not yet softened by trees. A Model T Ford stood at a white-painted gate, the chauffeur standing by. Another scene, dating from the 1920s, showed an elderly José addressing a conference of Buenos Aires businessmen. The audience was affluent and cocksure. The photographs spoke eloquently of Argentina's golden years, when the wool clip would never have lain languishing for want of an acceptable price.

Back at the manager's house, Angus was talking earnestly to one of the policemen with whom I'd spent the previous afternoon. The officer had come to collect some beef which Angus had promised him in exchange for a favour. A peon had been sent to round up a young bull calf, and after a while we spotted him riding towards us with the animal lassoed on a long rope. It was a lively beast, and three horsemen were needed to control it while the rope was passed through a steel ring beside the slaughtering pen. This achieved, it was an easy matter for a rider to back away with the rope until the animal was pinned.

On a large estancia death is a daily occurrence, and the peon cut the bull's throat as if he were swatting a fly. Blood spurted across the concrete. The bull sank to its knees, eyes popping, then rolled over into the rapidly growing pool of its own steaming blood. Within minutes the constable had skinned the carcass and was eagerly slicing through the still warm flesh. When dogs came over to drink the blood, I felt my stomach heave. It was time to continue southwards.

Back at the main road, the new day brought fresh luck. A young man called Oscar was driving south in his lorry, and seemed pleased to have a companion. The vehicle was 20 years old – exactly the same age as himself – and he informed me proudly that it had been three times round the clock. On right-hand bends he had to hang on to his door to keep it from swinging open and depositing him in the road; on left-hand bends I did the same with mine. In this fashion we motored sedately across the treeless plains of northern Tierra del Fuego, stopping for the occasional herd of guanaco to cross the road, or for Oscar to tinker lovingly with his cherished engine.

A new road was being built, and one day it would run all the way to Ushuaia, but for the time being the Government's money had run out and work had been abandoned – in spite of the fact that it was all but complete. After eight months in office President Menem could no longer afford to pay his own employees, let alone contractors, and there had been no choice but to freeze public works contracts nationwide. Meanwhile, anticipating the new road, repair crews had given up maintaining the old one, which was now in a dreadful state. We banged noisily through ruts and potholes and I feared for Oscar's lorry.

After many hours Oscar dropped me by Lake Fagnano, a sheet of royal-blue water set between cliffs of white shale. A bus then carried me over the Garibaldi Pass, named in memory not of the Italian campaigner, nor even of the famous biscuit, but of a local road engineer. As we climbed, the land became forested once more, and through the bus's cracked windows I gazed on hillsides of golden beech rising above swathes of red sphagnum.

This pass, which provides Ushuaia's only access overland, was for many years the scourge of horsemen and lorry drivers. Although only 1,420 feet above sea level, it takes the brunt of westerly storms, and in the old days used to remain snowbound for months on end. But in 1970 a new road was cut, with gentler gradients, and only in the worst midwinter months do today's juggernauts get stuck.

At Rancho Hambre ('Hunger Shack') the bus driver set me down, brushed off my attempts to pay for the 20-mile lift, and pointed to a track which wound through the woods towards Estancia Harberton. Although far from the main road, this was possibly one of the best-known farms in Patagonia, and the detour would, I was sure, be worth while. After camping in an abandoned sawmill I found myself ambling lazily through slant-ing sunlight towards the Beagle Channel. The morning was perfect. From beaver ponds beside the track, a mist rose gently in curls. In the silent beechwoods, shafts of light fell on clumps of wild gentian and on coral-red fungi which seemed to have sprung up overnight. Despite a heavy frost still lingering in the shadows, the sun warmed my hands and face and made the beech leaves dance. As morning turned to afternoon, I thought how well-timed had been my arrival in Patagonia's southernmost forests. The Fuegian autumn rivals that of New England in the loveliness of its reds and golds; but you need the luck of the gods to catch it.

Emerging from the woods, I found myself quite without warning beside the channel. A gale was whipping up white horses beneath the shadows of racing clouds. On the opposite shore, less than five miles away, the Chilean naval base of Puerto Williams appeared briefly through the spray. In the forest I'd hardly noticed the wind; now I could barely stand up. Sheltering in a shed beside the track, I examined my map and was dismayed to see I still had twelve miles to go.

Someone once said that Patagonia without wind would be like Hell without the Devil. Preparing myself for the walk ahead, I reflected grimly on this. After three months in Patagonia, instead of growing used to the occasional fury of the elements, I seemed to find such storms more debilitating than ever. I waited for perhaps half an hour until the gusts battering the shed eased a little, then hauled myself reluctantly to my feet.

Oh the joy of fears unfounded! Once under way I discovered that the wind was mostly on my back; far from hindering me, it bowled me along at a fine pace. Twigs and branches whirled overhead, but I covered the twelve miles without incident, and three hours later spotted my goal. Estancia Harberton, so named to remind Mary Bridges of the Devon village of her childhood, had been home to her descendants for more than 100 years. The little huddle of buildings was said to be a veritable museum of Fuegian history.

Thomas and Mary's great-grandson Tommy Goodall was in the workshop, busily engaged in welding rails. A tall, lean man with a straggling beard and distant eyes, he looked uncannily like the photos of his Victorian great-grandfather. He squinted up irritably as I peered in.

'Mr Goodall?'

'Yes.'

'I've come from Punta Arenas. I've got a package for your mother, Clarita.'

The package was a gift from a family friend. I'd hoped it might break the ice, but Tommy said simply, 'My mother doesn't live here any more.' Disappointed and embarrassed, I mumbled my apologies and promised to return when he was not so busy. 'Fine,' said Tommy, and turned back to his welding.

I strolled over to the house, wondering how to interpret this cold reception. I'd already been warned that Tommy didn't care for casual visitors, especially those who pestered him. Unfortunately the farm's popularity was growing fast. His wife Natalie, a tireless naturalist and historian, lectured widely about Tierra del Fuego and had even written a bilingual guidebook to it, inspiring a stream of foreign journalists, radio and television reporters and curious tourists to make the long journey to the Goodalls' front door. During her frequent absences, the task of showing them round would fall to Tommy. No wonder he sometimes felt testy.

Up the track I found a neatly painted sign which in my eagerness I'd overlooked. It read: 'TEA ROOM – GUIDED TOURS AT 11, 13, 15 AND 17 HOURS – MONDAY CLOSED'. Perhaps at one of the appointed hours I might have better luck.

To pass the time, I wandered out along a bay which was a carbon copy of one I knew on the Isle of Skye. The farm buildings hugged the shore, their freshly whitewashed walls supporting rust-red roofs. Behind each house was a large, neatly-hoed vegetable plot. Beyond the closest hills, sheep pastures could be seen rising to the foot of a golden mountain which my map labelled Cerro Almirante Brown ('Admiral Brown's Hill') – the diminutive *cerro* doing little justice to the grand snowy crags which formed its summit.

I chatted to some farmworkers building a wall. Mrs Goodall, they said, was away in Ushuaia; Don Tómas was on his own today. His mother Clarita, to whom I'd hoped to deliver the package, had lived for the last few years on the family's other farm at Viamonte, 100 miles to the north.

As we talked, I toyed absent-mindedly with one of the bricks the men were using. It was the colour of oatmeal, well-worn and oddly familiar. I hadn't seen any brickwork since leaving Chile. What was it doing here? Turning it over I found, embossed in its inner hollow, a small clue in the form of the well-rubbed letters 'BLAEN . . .' Could it possibly be Welsh?*

At five o'clock I returned to the workshop, and having now seen most of the estancia I spared Tommy the task of giving me the guided tour. Though still a little reserved, he was more welcoming this time, and willingly agreed that I could camp nearby. 'You won't bother the sheep,' he told me, 'but try not to frighten the birds.' I smiled at the thought that six months of travelling had left me looking like a scarecrow. That evening, relaxing by candlelight in my tent, I picked up a book Tommy had thoughtfully lent me. Written by his great-grandfather Thomas, it was intriguing not so much for what it was but for the extraordinary way in which it had come into being. The manuscript had been produced in the kitchen of the house just visible through my tentflaps – much of it by the light of a candle similar to my own. Its curious title was *Yamana–English: A Dictionary of the Speech of Tierra del Fuego*.

Thomas Bridges had become familiar with the language of Tierra del Fuego's Indians while growing up in the Falklands. Several of them had joined the so-called 'kelpers' at his adopted father's Anglican mission there, and while the elder men taught them the strange tenets of Christianity, the youngster picked up the equally strange subtleties of what he soon realized was a sophisticated tongue. By the age of 22 he knew what his life's work would be. 'Although I am improving in my knowledge of their language,' he wrote, 'my progress is slow and I am yet far from perfectly knowing it. To thoroughly acquire it, reduce it to writing and to form a dictionary and grammar is my longing desire, and I shall be very happy when I shall be able to tell them, to my satisfaction and their conviction, of the love of Jesus.'

---

* Months later, following up the clue in Wales, I was led to an entry in a turn-of-the-century Kelly's Directory: 'Colliery Owners and Fireclay Goods Manufacturers – Blaendare Co. Ltd, Pontypool, Monmouthshire'. In Lucas Bridges' autobiography, *Uttermost Part of the Earth*, there is evidence that bricks may have formed part of a shipment dispatched from Bristol on the orders of his father in 1893. Putting two and two together, it seems likely that the brick in my hand that day by the Beagle Channel was from a Pontypool kiln. Had it occurred to me at the time, I might have been surprised at the thought that I could have come so far in Patagonia before encountering anything Welsh.

The language provided rich clues to the Indians' understanding of their world. As Bruce Chatwin was later to comment:

What shall we think of a people who defined 'monotony' as 'an absence of male friends'? Or, for 'depression', used the word that described the vulnerable phase in a crab's seasonal cycle, when it has sloughed off its old shell and waits for another to grow? Or who derived 'lazy' from the Jackass Penguin? Or 'adulterous' from the hobby, a small hawk that flits here and there, hovering motionless over its next victim?

But when it came to spiritual matters, Thomas Bridges found the language 'a very poor means of educating them for a higher life, as it is sadly wanting in definite terms for ideas which the natives have never entertained'. They might have verbs meaning 'to moor one's canoe to a streamer of kelp', or 'to sleep in a floating canoe', or 'to hurl one's spear into a shoal of fish without aiming for a particular one'; but they had no way of talking about the Gospel.

But Bridges persevered, both in compiling his dictionary and in converting his new friends. In 1871 he founded a mission at Ushuaia, and sixteen years later, after the first of several measles epidemics decimated his little community of converts, moved 40 miles east to Harberton. Here he continued to work on the dictionary, often sitting with the Indians until late into the night. 'It is utterly impossible at first to get hold correctly of the pronunciation of a new language from the lips of a savage,' he complained. 'Often have I, until I was ashamed, made the Indians pronounce words so repeatedly that they have called me deaf, being unable to satisfy my mind as to whether I had it correctly, and after all being compelled to write it down when dissatisfied with my pronunciation, and consequently with my spelling of the word.'

Despite its imperfections, the dictionary boasted 32,000 entries by the time Bridges died in 1898. His son Lucas entrusted the manuscript – in those days, an only copy – to a Belgian explorer by the name of Frederick Cook, who promised to have it published in Europe. Several years later this charming charlatan was to achieve notoriety by claiming a bogus ascent of Alaska's Mount McKinley and an equally phoney journey to the North

Pole. In 1911, having long given up hope of seeing the manuscript again, Lucas received the astonishing news that Cook was preparing to publish it under his own name. Outraged, he took the first available passage to Belgium and persuaded the publishers that it was in fact the work of his own father. But the Great War was looming in Europe, and before the manuscript reached the printers it disappeared in occupied Belgium.

Again, Lucas resigned himself to the loss of his father's work. Then, in 1929, there arrived a letter from a Dr Ferdinand Hestermann of the University of Münster, who'd come upon the manuscript and was keen to have it published. Hestermann himself had no resources to do this, but the Bridges family decided to put up the money for a limited edition. Four years later, 300 copies came off a press near Vienna and were circulated to the world's main universities and libraries. Once again, however, the original was destined to be lost. On the outbreak of the Second World War both Dr Hestermann and the manuscript disappeared.

The doctor had last been heard of in Hamburg, and when news reached the Bridges of the Allied bombing of that city they decided that the manuscript really must be lost for good. Here the story might have ended, had it not been for an English friend of theirs by the name of William Barclay, whose interest had been aroused by the wandering dictionary. As soon as the war was over Barclay asked the Allied occupation forces to try and trace it, and after a while an officer in the 21st Army Group wrote him the following letter:

Dear Sir,

The MS of the Yamana Dictionary of the Rev. Thomas Bridges has now been discovered, as the result of a search put in train from your letters to Sir Leonard Woolley and the Control Commission. It is held in safe custody by the Military Government Authorities.

I may add that Dr Hestermann was discovered by a Military Government Officer and led by him to the kitchen cupboard of a farmhouse where the manuscript was kept. Dr Hestermann was apparently only too glad to hand it over into safe keeping. . . .

In view of its previous misfortunes, the Bridges decided that the safest place for the manuscript would be the British Museum.

In 1946 its journey – begun almost 100 years earlier in a wind-swept Falkland farmhouse – ended on an equally blustery winter's day in Bloomsbury. It can still be seen, by anyone with time to root it out, in the British Library's Department of Manuscripts.

My journey back to the main road was rather quicker than my approach. After only an hour a car stopped. Sergio and Liliana Beccaría were on an excursion from Ushuaia, looking for a spot to set up holiday cabins and possibly a teashop. It would be the first such venture on this part of the island, and they chatted excitedly about their plans. Rising to their enthusiasm, I pointed to a grassy riverside meadow I'd noticed on my walk in. Would that be suitable? Sergio stopped the car and sauntered over to it. 'Well, we could put a road in through those trees,' he reflected, pointing towards some gold-leaved southern beech.

Away from the track, the spot was more enchanting than I'd realized. For a few moments I stood listening to the river bubbling over its pebbly bed. Suddenly holiday cabins and a teashop became a hideous thought. I wished profoundly that I hadn't mentioned the place. Maybe, if I'd kept him diverted, Sergio would have driven straight on past. I tried to think of objections to such a scheme. Drainage? Subsoil? Finally I asked lamely, 'But what about the beavers? Won't their dams be likely to flood the land?'

'Oh, the beavers won't bother us,' replied Sergio briskly. 'If they give us any trouble, we'll poison them.'

I asked if he'd need permission to build in the forest, and he smiled indulgently. 'This is Argentina, my friend. You build first – *then* ask permission.'

He tossed an empty cigarette packet proprietorially into the meadow and we drove away.

Ushuaia, the southernmost town in the world, is hated by residents and visitors alike. Seldom have I heard a good word said about it. The neat gardens of Thomas Bridges' waterside mission have given way to a dense scatter of shacks, bungalows and apartment blocks sprawling far up the mountains which back the town. It's as if the town fathers had set out wantonly to destroy anything worth keeping. The explanation usually given is that the mushrooming population of the 1980s had somehow to be housed. Certainly its growth rate has been impressive: in the eleven years since my previous visit the population had risen from 7,000 to 35,000 – a fifth of them unemployed.

Ushuaia's greatest attraction nowadays is its setting. To the north the Martial Mountains, snow-clad for much of the year, offer a picture-postcard backdrop. To the south, the Beagle Channel's dark waters provide an element of romance. And when relations with Chile are tense, as they often are, the sight of the Chilean island of Navarino rising not ten miles from Ushuaia's waterfront is sufficient to provoke a sense of drama and confrontation in even the most phlegmatic Argentine hearts.

The world's southernmost town is also one of its most peculiar. The streets running parallel to the waterfront are fairly level, but those at right angles climb steeply up the hillside. This has given rise to an unusual traffic regulation which decrees that in summer vehicles on the horizontal streets have right of way, but in winter, because of the difficulty of braking on icy gradients, the priority is switched. Heaven help the innocent visitor on changeover days! Another, more sensible, rule is that one street is closed throughout the winter so that children can use it for sledging.

The *South American Handbook*, a bible for serious travellers on the continent, describes the Hospedaje Ona on Ushuaia's waterfront as 'used by lorry drivers, difficult to get into'. I had no trouble getting in. However I did have great difficulty getting out, mainly because the Hospedaje Ona occupies one of Ushuaia's oldest buildings, a wooden structure which is slowly collapsing into the Beagle Channel. Rooms overlooking the water slope downwards at a perilous one in ten; those at the back do the opposite. Approaching my door down an undulating corridor, I felt as if I'd walked into a Magritte painting, an effect enhanced by the snaking, hissing water pipes along the peeling walls. Lighting came from a ten-watt bulb at the far end, so excursions to the bathroom took the form of minor expeditions.

By an old gas heater outside my bedroom, a pallid man sat brooding over his maté kettle. He looked older than his 35 years. In 1982 he'd been a ground mechanic in a proud air force, supporting the pilots in their assaults on the British task force off the Falklands. Now, laid off by a state no longer able to pay its

ove: Viewed in a February dawn, the Torres del Paine
esent their 4,000-foot east faces to the morning sun.

ght and below: Two thousand Corriedales arrive for
e last day of the 1990 shearing at Estancia
acabuco.

Top: Tommy and Edwar[d]
Davies — Chubut Valle[y]
farmers since the days [of]
the Indians.
Above: The housemovin[g]
at San Juan on Chiloé, '[I]
made a mental note to
beware of uncastrated
bulls.'
Left: Guanaco in the
Torres del Paine.

Above left: Cabbages and seaweed for sale on Chiloé.
Above: Maurice Lewis outside his Santa Cruz cottage.
Left: Claus and Walther Hopperdietzel in their kitchen at Puyuhuapi.
Below: Phillis Kemp.

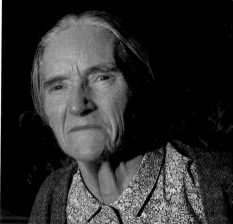

Above: Patagonian jalopy.

Left: The congregation at St David's in the Chubut Valley.

Below: A relic of the 'six-day crisis' of 1978, when Chile and Argentina came close to war.

Of the hundreds of bridges John Wilkington crossed, the best one (*above*) carried the Carretera Austral over the River Baker. The worst (*right*) linked Chile and Argentina near Chile Chico. Neither country seemed responsible for its repair.

bottom right: The Magellan Strait shore is littered with wrecks.

Antarctica: the last unspoilt continent. Or is it?

Above: Discarded fuel drums on King George Island.

Left: The Soviet Bellingshausen base was one of the worst environmental offenders.

Below left and right: Elephant seal and Chinstrap penguin.

'Patagonia without wind would be like Hell without the Devil.'

Dried-up lake bed near San Julián. 'When you've hit rock-bottom you can't sink lower,' said one drought-stricken farmer.

Jorge Parker o etc.
Usa distintos nombres.

Top: Aladín Sepúlveda shows John
Pilkington the cabin of the *Yanquis*.
Inset: Its builder, Butch Cassidy,
pictured on the 'Wanted' poster of 1906
Left: Chilean welcome.
Below: The Old Patagonian Express.

staff, he was taking whatever work he could: cleaning windows, driving taxis, fixing the diesel engines on the long-distance lorries from Buenos Aires. There wasn't much work to be had in Ushuaia – or anywhere in Argentina, for that matter. So for much of the time he simply sat sipping his maté, nursing memories of a futile war.

Ushuaia had been a front-line town in the conflict. From a jetty not 200 yards from where we sat, the *General Belgrano* had set sail on its final voyage. The ex-mechanic took me to see a handbeaten copper plaque in memory of those who'd died, and I was touched both by its simplicity and by its lack of belligerence. Whatever the rights and wrongs of Argentina's claim to the Falklands, I'd found it impossible not to be irritated by some of the monumental roadside signs proclaiming that the islands belonged to Argentina. This was the first memorial I'd seen that dwelt simply on the tragedy of lives pointlessly lost.

'How long do you think it'll be before your government sees reason?' asked the ex-mechanic.

I didn't have the heart to reply.

Back in the Hospedaje Ona, a little group had gathered round the gas heater. Four men sat hunched in a circle, each in his fifties, each with the telltale face of long-term despair. They were explaining to each other what they would do with their next pay cheques. One had decided to buy a car; another had in mind a new stereo system ('not one of those ghettoblasters, mind you – a proper set-up, with speakers round the walls'). A third was going to blow the money on his girlfriend in Buenos Aires. The others laughed at that; they knew he had no girlfriend, in Buenos Aires or anywhere else.

The fourth man sipped his maté in silence. Perhaps he recognized that there would be no pay cheques for any of them.

During my time in Ushuaia the weather deteriorated dramatically, a reminder that Patagonia's summer, so keenly awaited and so briefly enjoyed, was now long gone. One day I returned to the Hospedaje Ona to find a pane missing from my window and the room full of snow. At first I assumed that someone must have forced their way in; but nothing was missing, so I examined the broken pane on the floor. Several of the pieces were joined by Scotch tape. The pane must have fallen out of its own accord, and probably not for the first time. I swept the debris into a corner and blocked the hole with a blanket.

The snow was still falling when I walked out along the road which leads south-west towards Lapataia Bay. For many travellers there comes a point where the thrill of the outward journey is overtaken by the call of home – where the craving for new encounters gives way to a more powerful urge to consolidate what has been achieved. Now, after four months in Patagonia, I needed to take stock. I still had much to see – more, in fact, than I could ever have guessed. But the evidence was all around me, in the biting wind and steadily falling snow, that it was time to move north. Patagonians themselves regard winter as a time of hibernation, and faced with blocked roads and paralysed public transport I could now see why. Unless I was prepared to don skis, charter a boat or do a lot of bushwhacking, I'd come as far on the continent as it was possible to go. Apart from Navarino, home to a few settlers and a detachment of the Chilean Navy, the islands between here and Cape Horn were all but deserted.

The road to Lapataia wound over low hills, the Beagle Channel bobbing in and out of view. There was no traffic. Overhead, skuas and geese flew in wide circles, screeching petulantly as they prepared for their own long journey north. I passed a snowbound farm entrance, then what looked like a sphagnum bog, its spiky tufts sprouting like dozing hedgehogs from the soggy snow. I was close to the Chilean border now, and a frontier guard on horseback warned me not to stray far from the road. 'It's not that we mind,' he lied, 'but the Chileans wouldn't take kindly to you crossing without papers.'

A gaucho came by in a pickup and offered me a lift, but after a mile we became stuck in the deepening snow. Abandoning the vehicle with a kick and a curse, he walked with me as far as a plank bridge, after which I continued alone to where the road gave out at the water's edge. With a suitable air of finality, a rough sign announced: 'END OF ROUTE 3. FEDERAL CAPITAL 3242 KM.' Across the bay, the Lapataia Peninsula allowed only a most restricted view of the channel itself; and with black clouds almost merging with the black water there would have been little to see anyway. This was the scene which had greeted Darwin as he clung to the pitching deck of the *Beagle* in 1832. 'The climate was certainly wretched,' he wrote glumly. 'The summer solstice was now passed, yet every day snow fell on the hills, and in the valleys there was rain, accompanied by sleet. The thermometer generally stood about 45°, but in the night fell to 38° or 40°. From the damp and boisterous state of the atmosphere, not cheered by a gleam of sunshine, one fancied the climate even worse than it really was.'

I sat hunched under a bush, thinking of the many who have been shipwrecked in similar conditions or worse. On a foul January day in 1930 the Argentine steamship *Monte Cervantes* was trying to make Ushuaia when she struck rocks on one of the Eclaireurs Islands. Luckily she was carrying lifeboats, and the 200 passengers were safely delivered to the mainland, though not before some had felt the Beagle Channel's unfriendly waters closing over their heads. Earlier seafarers didn't always have such an easy escape. In his autobiography, Lucas Bridges recalled how one midwinter's morning in 1883 the villagers of Ushuaia were greatly excited to see three longboats approaching from the east. The eight-year-old Lucas, full of romantic notions about the sea, hoped they might be pirates, but the 22 exhausted, injured and frostbitten occupants turned out to be crew from the German brig *Erwin*. Bound for San Francisco from Liverpool with a cargo of coal, the 1,300-ton vessel had caught fire and exploded after rounding the Horn. The survivors had spent ten wretched days at sea.

An even more dramatic event took place on the island's east coast in 1907. Again, Lucas Bridges was involved. One day in July, his dogs' frantic barking told him that strangers were approaching, and soon, out of the mist, appeared one of his Indian friends with a couple of haggard-looking Irishmen. They were among 26 survivors from the cargo ship *Glen Cairn*. Guided by smoke signals from the shore, they'd found one of the few safe landfalls on that wild coast. When all had disembarked, the Indian leader, a man called Halimink, had taken the captain's pocket-book and made some curious scribbles, before handing it back with gestures which the captain took to mean that he was expected to sign his name below Halimink's scrawl. When Lucas Bridges heard this story he was much amused:

Halimink had not, in fact, been collecting autographs, nor had he been trying to trick the captain into signing an I.O.U. It had merely been his way of indicating that the captain should write me a letter giving details of the wreck, which he had then intended sending me by a swift runner. The suspicious master had misunderstood his intention and refused to have anything to do with it, so other steps had had to be taken. The second mate, whose energies had not abated in spite of his ordeal on the wreck, had offered to go in search of assistance with an Indian guide, and had duly set off. . . .

Bridges and the Indians later guided the entire party back to his farm at Viamonte near Río Grande, from where, after further adventures, they returned to Britain. This second of the Bridges' farms was now the home of Tommy Goodall's mother, Clarita, whose package still lay in my rucksack. I decided it was time to deliver it.

Juan Perón once commented that the Argentine military don't do much, but what they do, they do early in the morning. Much of Ushuaia's traffic seemed to consist of army or navy vehicles, so well before dawn I left the Hospedaje Ona for the last time and trudged off into the darkness, heading north. Sure enough, within 20 minutes I was bouncing along in an army lorry, and two hours later was standing once more on the Garibaldi Pass. A foot of snow had fallen since my previous crossing, so I was relieved when the very next vehicle skidded to a halt. As we descended through beechwoods towards the Atlantic grazing grounds, the driver turned casually to introduce himself. 'I'm the Governor of Ushuaia. How did you like my town?'

I stared at him in horror. What could I say? I'd seen worse places, it was true, but despite its fabulous setting Ushuaia was – well – ugly. I stumbled for the right word, and eventually found one which I hoped would encompass my feelings without causing offence. '*Es bárbaro*,' I suggested brightly. The Governor could interpret this to mean 'crude', 'barbaric' or 'splendid'; and to my great relief, he didn't ask which.

Though lacking its Beagle Channel setting, the farmhouse at Viamonte was grander than the one at Harberton. Through a window from the shady garden I spied easy chairs, piles of familiar magazines, a caged canary, and a grandfather clock engraved with the words 'Maple & Co. Ltd, London'. An elderly Englishman answered my knock. He accepted Clarita's package and the message that accompanied it, but made no move to invite me in. I was about to take my leave when Clarita herself appeared at the door. 'Don't go – come and talk,' she insisted, gently brushing the old man aside. 'How are my friends in Punta Arenas?'

Both Clarita and the old man – whom she introduced as her brother Len – were well into their eighties. While he dozed, she talked, displaying an impressive memory for people and events from her past, and also an eager curiosity about my own journey and impressions. 'So you camped at Harberton?' she asked with an amused smile. 'You must have made a good impression. Tommy usually sends people packing after the guided tour.'

Clarita struck me as an iron-willed woman from an age long ago. She imposed on her household an Edwardian discipline in perfect harmony with the furnishings, wiring and plumbing. At mealtimes a handbell was rung (by the cook, to announce that the food was on the table, and by Clarita to call for each subsequent course). For the rest of the day the servants tiptoed unseen.

Over a supper of mutton and chocolate pudding, we talked of sheep, shipwrecks, and Viamonte's many distinguished visitors over the years. Apart from seafarers and Argentine dignitaries, the visitors' book included a number of familiar signatures. I asked Clarita about Bruce Chatwin, who had written about her subsequently in his book.

'Yes, I remember him quite well. I was living at Harberton in those days. He was a strange young man – hardly said a word.'

I handed her the book, and pointed to Chatwin's photograph of the room in which we were sitting. In the fifteen intervening years nothing whatsoever had changed. Clarita smiled. 'We live cautiously in Patagonia, don't we?' Then she read the caption, 'English estancia', and her smile faded. 'He shouldn't have called it that. We're Argentines. For three generations the family has held Argentine passports; this is an Argentine estancia and our loyalties are Argentine. We don't like it when people call us English.'

I asked how the book had been received in Patagonia, and in answer Clarita handed me a magazine. 'This will tell you what Patagonians think of Bruce Chatwin.'

The magazine was called *The Bulletin*, a monthly journal published by the British Community Council of Argentina. The copy was dated December 1989. A review of Chatwin's book *The Songlines* had provoked the following letter:

I would warn any reader of [Chatwin's] books to be very wary of accepting as accurate that which he describes – if the book he wrote on Patagonia is anything to go by. I speak from first hand knowledge as I was born in Punta Arenas. The remarks he made about my father-in-law (Ernest W. Hobbs), one of the kindest and most Christian of men, are so untrue that one of his daughters (who lives in England) endeavoured to take legal action – only to be advised that the laws of libel cannot be applied in the case of someone already dead. So there was nothing to be done. Chatwin's cousin was a bridesmaid of mine – in those far-off Punta Arenas days – and in a letter to me a few years ago she referred to Chatwin as 'my cousin, of whom I am not proud'.

– DAPHNE HOBBS

Ernest Hobbs had already been long dead when Chatwin visited his farm, Gente Grande, in the Chilean part of Tierra del Fuego. But he knew that his forebear Charley Milward had spent some time there in 1900. Using this as his basis, he drew an engaging little sketch of the beleaguered sheepfarmer:

'Tell me, Hobbs,' Charley said. 'What do you propose to do about the Indians? Now they've killed two sailors, they'll get too big for their boots and someone else'll suffer. Your homestead's handy, and what with your wife and children and nurses and servants, I think you'll be next to be honoured with their attentions.'

'I don't quite know what to do,' Hobbs said. 'The Government's so horribly nasty nowadays if you kill an Indian, even in self-defence. I'll have to wait and see what can be done.'

A few months later, Chatwin tells us, Charley visited Hobbs again and found a human skull on top of the pigsty. As he'd predicted, the Indians had been giving Hobbs some sleepless nights, stealing his sheep and harassing one of his shepherds. Eventually, in desperation, Hobbs had equipped his 'tame' Indians with old guns and revolvers and asked them to join him on a guanaco-hunting expedition. When they sighted the camp of the 'wild' Indians, he sent his own to ask them where the guanaco were. The wild ones took one look at the newcomers, saw they were armed, and let fly with arrows. The tame ones retaliated with their guns. After the skirmish, Hobbs found to his satisfaction that the wild Indians had been beaten and the man who'd killed the sailors was among the dead. 'That's his skull on the pigsty,' Hobbs told Charley.

This account of the exchanges between the two men shows perfectly Chatwin's skill in livening up narratives with imagined details. It's true that in 1900 the Chilean warship *Errázuriz* lost two sailors in an Indian attack, and that a month or so later Charley paid a call on Hobbs. Their conversation would certainly have centred on the possibility of further incidents. The technique of elaborating on known events has a long pedigree in the historical novel, and Chatwin used it copiously. 'Facts shimmer on the edge of fiction, and fiction reads like fact,' commented an admiring Colin Thubron. 'They defy category.' Thubron thought Chatwin's literary model might have been the French novelist and playwright Gustave Flaubert, whose cool classicism and love of the bizarre reached its climax in *Trois Contes*. Like Flaubert, Chatwin never tired of exploring the Aladdin's Cave of theatrical possibilities which life offered up. He seemed to define the world not by its wisps of reason but by its potential as melodrama.

Chatwin had a running battle over whether *The Songlines* should be classified as fiction or non-fiction. 'Fiction,' he insisted. 'I made it up.' But both *In Patagonia* and *The Songlines* continue to crop up on the travel shelves, and his obituary in *The Times* described him as 'a writer of travel books – albeit travel books of a highly eccentric sort'. Only in Spain, apparently, did his readers fully appreciate what he was trying to do. The works in question were not *libros de viaje* but *novelas de viaje* – 'travel novels'. A nation brought up on *Don Quixote* understood the distinction perfectly.

I think what set the fur flying in Patagonia was that he played his cards so close to his chest. Imagining that few copies of this, his first book, would find their way back to the isolated communities in which it was set, he gave his creativity free rein. In no edition have I found the hint of a disclaimer or other clue that some bits are fiction; on the contrary, the impression of a travel book is strengthened by photographs of real scenes cross-referenced to the text.

These tantalizing ambiguities are for many readers one of the great joys of Chatwin's 'travel' writing. You never know quite what to believe. He researched passionately but also trusted his instinct. As one reviewer commented after his death, 'the unknown land which most fascinated him remained, as it had been since childhood, his own imagination'.

The Hobbs family weren't the first to misinterpret this unusual style. Always aware of the risks, Chatwin avoided naming characters if he thought his descriptions were genuinely unkind. But in Hobbs' case he obviously felt the portrait wasn't such an unflattering one. Indeed, by comparison with men such as Río Grande's 'Red Pig' – a Scotsman so brutal that none of Patagonia's historians has ever dared give his real name – Hobbs comes across as almost saintly. In Punta Arenas I was told of an Englishman, still alive, who admits to having burned farm records which contained incriminating evidence of the slaughtering of Indians. In Argentina the matter made national headlines in 1928, after a well-known journalist published a book accusing some of Patagonia's most influential sheepfarmers of genocide. Within a few weeks it had mysteriously disappeared from the shops, and the talk on the farms was that the whole edition had been snapped up by the families of the accused. In a fitting twist of fate, however, the resulting publicity brought about a demand for several reprints. Although it has never been translated into English, I found recently-printed Spanish-language copies still on sale in Ushuaia. But perhaps Patagonians, like us, have a penchant for exposés.

'Go safely,' urged Clarita, as I made my way out to the road. The morning sun had dispersed a heavy overnight frost. From the Atlantic a stiff wind was blowing, bringing with it bursts of sea-spray and a whiff of kelp as I trudged towards a distant promontory, the only feature in a panorama that boasted not even a hut.

A Salesian priest took me north, on his way to hold mass at an oil production plant beyond San Sebastián Bay. This was a stroke of luck, because the nearby farm known as Estancia Cullen had, 100 years ago, been the site of perhaps the oddest undertaking in

Tierra del Fuego's history. Even today the story is one of Patagonia's best kept secrets – for it involves gold.

The priest protested innocence of such worldly matters, but nonetheless went several miles out of his way to help me find the estancia. Following a dirt road across the darkened plain, we were guided, Magellan-like, by ghostly flames in the night – in our case not Indian campfires but the flares of oil and gas installations. Eventually the priest dropped me at a coastguard station whose three young incumbents, though surprised at their late-night visitor – or, indeed, any visitor – spared no effort to make me comfortable. Their prefabricated hut was trying to tear itself from its foundations in the teeth of a vicious gale. I gratefully accepted their invitation to join in a spaghetti supper and sleep in a spare bed. It wasn't a night for camping.

Next morning the coastguards pointed me in the direction of Estancia Cullen, six miles into the wind across a bare plateau. For the first mile I followed a fence, then struck off in the direction they'd indicated. A sheep's carcass lay festering, and as I drew closer I saw that I wasn't the first to have spotted it. Almost invisible against the grey plain, a grey fox was scavenging the grey remains. It looked up at my approach and circled warily, before returning to finish its meal.

The farm buildings stood at the foot of a bluff, splashes of red and white in the endless grey. The coastguards had telephoned to warn of my arrival, so for once I was expected. Naomi O'Byrne was in the middle of her weekly wash. 'Come in,' she beckoned briskly with soapy hands. 'Put your rucksack in the kitchen while I finish this basinful. You will stay the night, won't you?'

Naomi and her husband Pat were consummate Patagonians. Generous, hardworking, and with a good humour quite at odds with the realities of their gruelling life, they combined an instinctive farmers' expediency with the fortitude of pioneers. Between them, they were either related to or acquainted with many of the people whose paths I'd crossed since arriving in Patagonia. Pat's Irish blood made him a rousing drinking companion during my several long evenings on the farm; while Naomi's English ancestry was perhaps responsible for the rich and filling stews with which she indulged me twice a day.

Like many of the big estancias, Cullen gave the impression of being not so much a farm as a small nation-state. Though not quite large enough to justify the shops, health clinics and visiting magistrates which some boasted, it did make use of an invention attributed to the early British managers – it kept its own time. In summer the farm clocks were set an hour behind national time, in winter two hours. The idea owed its origin to the gauchos' insistence on having their midday break at midday: intolerable to efficiency-minded owners who wanted to get the most from their employees. In the far south the winter sun doesn't struggle above the horizon until ten o'clock in the morning; in summer, on the other hand, it stays light until eleven at night. By the device of 'estancia time', these extremes were painlessly moderated and farmworkers could get in a full morning's work before they heard the call of the dinner bell.

The farm lay close up against the Chilean border, and Pat and Naomi told me the chilling story of their involvement in the 'six-day crisis' of 1978. 'It was more than just sabre-rattling, you know,' said Pat. 'Río Grande was under blackout orders, with twice-weekly air raid drills and anti-aircraft guns being set up in people's back gardens. Work came to a halt. Troops arrived by the hundred, commandeering lorries, pickups, anything that could move, and their instructions were clear. "*Al Pacífico!*" was the rallying call – "To the Pacific!"'

'When the Pope agreed to mediate, we could hardly believe our luck,' added Naomi. 'We knew they'd listen to him – and they did.'

Bit by bit, we pieced together the story of Tierra del Fuego's gold. In 1885 – just a year before the first major strike in the Klondike – a young Romanian by the name of Julius Popper stepped off a packet steamer at Buenos Aires. He was a seasoned adventurer with an insatiable curiosity. While still a teenager he'd left home to study engineering in Paris, and subsequently found it impossible to settle in his home town of Bucharest, which seemed backward and dull. So he began to travel. At first he set his sights no further than Constantinople and Cairo; then, gaining confidence, made a voyage to the Far East. Finally, after a long vagabonding journey through the Caribbean and Brazil, he fetched up on the banks of the River Plate.

He found Buenos Aires bristling with rumour. A group of Patagonians had recently turned up in the capital carrying a tiny sack of gold, which they claimed to have sifted from beach deposits at Cape Virgins on the Magellan Strait. More was waiting, they promised, for anyone who cared to pick it up.

By a stroke of luck, Popper had some experience of mining, and a quick study of the Patagonians' story persuaded him that it wasn't a hoax. If there was gold on Cape Virgins, he told himself, there was every reason to suppose that it would be found under similar conditions further down the coast. A hunch led him to draw a circle round a small part of Tierra del Fuego.

Like others before him, Popper was also attracted by the legend of a lost Patagonian republic of untold riches – the 'City of the Caesars'. As recently as 1869 a small strike had been made on the banks of the Río de las Minas near Punta Arenas – the first in modern times. Two years later George Musters, reporting on his travels further north, rekindled the belief that an El Dorado might exist deep in the Andes opposite Chiloé. To anyone with a nose for geology or romance, it was obvious that Patagonia still harboured gold.

Popper at once approached the Argentine Government for prospecting rights on Tierra del Fuego. No one else had shown any interest in the island, so his request was granted. He found eighteen men willing to form an expedition, and to protect them from the Indians he asked permission to carry arms. This, too, was granted. Popper's next action – which he took without the precaution of asking permission – was to have eighteen army uniforms made up, in a pattern similar to those of his native Romania.

A ship took the party to Punta Arenas, where the men set up camp on the beach. Hearing of their arrival, the Governor went down to pay a courtesy call, and found to his surprise an armed sentry guarding each tent and a bugler standing by. Popper's men took their duties seriously, suspecting quite rightly that their master would have no compassion for laggards and traitors.

We've no record of how the Governor reacted to this violation of Chilean sovereignty, but I imagine he was somewhat relieved when, within a few days, the 'army' set sail for Tierra del Fuego. They quickly crossed the island to the place Popper had encircled on his crude map – a lonely promontory extending into the Atlantic, which the men dubbed El Páramo – 'The Wilderness'. For all his swank Popper must have been an astute geologist or else blessed with extraordinary luck, for more than half Tierra del Fuego's subsequent gold production has come from this spot. A combination of currents, it seems, had created a beach of gold-bearing sands which was replenished with every tide.

Popper spent seven years working the deposits. As more adventurers turned up to share his finds, he either had them summarily shot, or else press-ganged them into joining his ever-growing army which, after the purchase of a couple of luggers and a gunboat, had the support of a navy. At least twice he fought full-scale battles with prospectors from Punta Arenas. As time went by he came to consider the whole of Tierra del Fuego his domain, and seized every opportunity to quarrel with the Governor of Ushuaia. Fortunately in those days communications were so bad that for most of the time the Governor could ignore him.

In fact, output from the El Páramo workings wasn't all that great – a couple of pounds would be considered a good day's production. But in Buenos Aires the rumours became ever more exaggerated, and Popper and his men found themselves increasingly under armed attack. On one occasion the invaders actually succeeded in occupying his camp, and it was only by a surprise attack from the rear that he managed to drive them out. As his treatment of outsiders became more brutal, Patagonians began to call him the Dictator of Tierra del Fuego – amongst other unprintable names.

Not satisfied with an army and a navy, in 1889 Popper hit upon the idea of striking his own coins. Being of pure gold, they naturally proved popular with the farmers from whom the miners bought their meat. Cullen's receipt books for the period show sheep fetching six grams of gold, skins two grams. Naomi O'Byrne let me see a coin which she still kept polished in her kitchen. Against a background of pick and sledgehammer, it read 'TIERRA DEL FUEGO – POPPER – 1889'. Following the success of the coinage, Popper later started a postal service complete with stamps. Had he lived, one can only wonder what other governmental pretensions he would have aspired to. But a dictator's life is a hazardous one, and early one morning in 1893 they found his body slumped on a bed. The official verdict was a heart attack, but the men at El Páramo agreed that someone probably put arsenic in his bedtime nip.

After Popper's death, life at the camp disintegrated. Men used to taking orders found it impossible to maintain discipline without their leader. Jealousies erupted into fights, and newcomers were no longer kept at bay. Moreover, less and less gold was emerging from the washing-plants. Within a few years life on the peninsula – dismal at the best of times – became unbearable. By the turn of the century it had been abandoned to the seabirds once more.

On a day when an onshore north-easter made it almost impossible to stand up, Pat took me out to El Páramo in his old Ford. Black beach-sand had clogged the channels and the settling-lagoons, and without Pat's assurance I would never have believed this to be the place. The spit curved away to the south, a whaleback of shingle littered with the skeletons of skuas and fulmars, until it merged into the distant grey Atlantic.

'Look – over here!' shouted Pat above the gale.

I followed him to a spot where the ground had been ripped open, as if by an excavator. Some old bones lay rotting nearby.

'The cemetery!' he yelled. 'This was the miners' cemetery!'

For almost 100 years, Popper and a dozen of his men had lain undisturbed in this wretched place. Each grave, according to legend, contained a small cache of gold.

'The graves were still intact when I came here a month ago,' said Pat with a look of infinite sadness. 'Some son of a bitch has robbed them.'

King George Island

Before continuing north up the Atlantic coast, I wanted to make one more visit to Punta Arenas. 'I'll run you up to the border,' said Pat in a final display of Patagonian generosity. 'It's only 30 miles.'

The sun was already low over the Magellan Strait as I boarded the landing craft at the First Narrows. No more than a couple of miles separated the shores at this point, but as soon as it left the island slipway the vessel was hit broadside by a barrage of waves. Walls of black water rose on all sides, and an articulated container lorry rocked violently on its springs, threatening to crush the cars and pickups crammed between the bulkheads. Another truck, loaded with sheep, began to emit a foul stench as the animals vomited, first over each other and then over the vehicles alongside. Perhaps it was this smell which attracted four dolphins to swim round and round the boat, their black and white bodies knifing through the crashing waves and surfacing noisily to suck air from the troughs between them.

To the immense relief of the passengers – and most of all, I imagine, the sheep – the crossing was soon over. Within half an hour I was standing on the mainland, and late evening found me strolling once more down the brightly lit streets of Punta Arenas.

During my previous stay at this 'crossroads of Patagonia' I enjoyed the hospitality of a Canadian company called Adventure Network International. The name gave little clue to the firm's business. Founded in 1985 by a small band of adventurers, its aim was to bring together the expertise of climbers, bush pilots and tour operators with an interest in the polar regions. As well as running errands for a number of organizations operating in Antarctica, it had by 1990 achieved several Antarctic 'firsts', including a dogsled traverse of the continent and a commercial passenger flight to the South Pole. It had also ferried supplies for the Austrian explorer Reinhold Messner's Antarctic ski crossing aimed at promoting Antarctic conservation.

Canadians are second only to Patagonians when it comes to generosity, and one of my fellow visitors to Estancia Cristina, who happened to be a director of this company, had made an offer I couldn't refuse. 'We've got a smart office in Punta Arenas – there are even bedrooms attached. Give this note to Tony Piggot, the manager there, and ask him to put you in one of the rooms.'

For the brief southern summer, the office and its bedrooms had provided a base for the pilots of Twin Otter aircraft ferrying people and supplies to Antarctica. The company had won a contract with a Yukon-based firm which was building an airstrip for the British at Rothera Base on Adelaide Island. Its role in this operation was to provide an 'air bridge' for personnel and equipment between Rothera and the South American mainland. This involved a complicated juggling of planes, aviation fuel and people between Punta Arenas and the intermediate refuelling point on King George Island, 80 miles off the Antarctic Peninsula.

The office sat on the highest hilltop in Punta Arenas, its picture windows framing a gorgeous view of the Strait. On fine days the water stretched like brushed baize towards the Porvenir shore; and when wild weather approached from Dawson Island, which it did with almost clockwork regularity, the sheen would give way to rolling white horses and the toy ships would scurry inshore. On the finest days of all, I fancied I could make out the snowy outline of Tierra del Fuego's Darwin range, so distant and dim that I'm still not certain if it was real.

During my stays in this 'dream office' I became a part-time office boy, running errands and answering the phone calls which came in from all parts of the globe. The Twin Otter pilots, exhilarated and exhausted after their long and sometimes dangerous flights over the Drake Passage, had to be cosseted. Materials and fuel had to be hunted down, bargained for and taken to the airport. Visitors needed to be met, interpreting done. Daily radio exchanges with Rothera threw up some novel requests. One day I might be telephoning or faxing urgent personal messages to Canada; the next day I'd be buying contraceptives.

My stays were further enlivened by a constant stream of

visitors to the Adventure Network office. A *National Geographic* team was at work in the Antarctic, and occasionally its members passed through. They'd crowd into the hospitality room, quaffing the company's gin and luxuriating in the unaccustomed air of civilization. A cruise ship, fresh back from the Antarctic, produced a retired explorer who'd been acting as guest lecturer on the voyage. He burst in one day close to hysteria. 'If one more Wisconsin wrinkly asks me to explain about the ozone layer, I shall be hanged for murder!'

In between these duties as secretary, chauffeur, butler and nanny, I listened with growing curiosity to the stories of my new acquaintances. Antarctica, one of the last frontiers of exploration, was a continent to which I hadn't previously given much thought. It was a destination for others, outside my reach, like the moon. While this may have been the case ten years ago, I soon realized that changes had been taking place at the bottom of the world. The Rothera airstrip was one of several developments – scientific, political and commercial – which were bringing Antarctica closer to the mainstream of world affairs. Its pioneer days, ushered in at the beginning of the century by Amundsen and Scott and peaking with the heady discoveries of the 1950s, were now drawing inexorably to a close.

From my eyrie overlooking the Magellan Strait, I grew gradually more familiar with this new continent, and as I did so I was struck by a curious thought. The Antarctica of the 1990s recalled the Patagonia of the 1890s. As in those far-off Patagonian days, the period of initial exploration in Antarctica is now over. We have a clear notion of the continent's topography, and are learning quickly about its geology and mineral wealth. Communications are improving year by year, but – again as in old-time Patagonia – they still present a cost barrier sufficient to keep out all but a privileged few. Hence, like the Patagonia of the last century, Antarctica for most people today is more or less a blank on the map.

But what about settlement? With nearly 200 research bases, it could be said that Antarctica's settlement is well advanced. As in Patagonia, the impetus has been primarily an economic one, though diplomacy requires most countries to cloak their interests in scientific disguise. Hence individuals tend to be attached to specific projects and return home when their stint is done. But there do exist a few settlers of a more traditional kind; for just as the Chilean and Argentine politicians of the last century sought to beef up their Patagonian claims by encouraging settlement, so these and other nations are supporting civilian communities on the islands and mainland of Antarctica. Unlike their Patagonian forerunners, these late twentieth-century pioneers don't aspire to be self-sufficient. They are there at the behest of their governments; their presence has no practical purpose whatsoever. Faced with the hostile polar environment, they will always be dependent on supplies from outside. Another thing missing is the missionary movement – there being, of course, no indigenous population. But in most other respects, it seemed from my perspective in Punta Arenas that the ingredients of Patagonian and Antarctic settlement were largely the same.

Geologically, the Antarctic Peninsula – that rugged, snaking arm which reaches up from the heart of the continent towards the tip of South America – is a continuation of the Andes. Twisted by continental drift, its outline traces a great arc to the east of the Drake Passage, where the highest peaks break the surface in the icebound archipelagos we know as the South Orkney and South Sandwich Islands and South Georgia.

Perhaps it was this tenuous link that, one morning in the Adventure Network office, made me prick up my ears. An American voice was telephoning for Brydon Knibbs, a pilot who'd spent the summer on the King George Island–Rothera run. The voice introduced itself as belonging to Corporal Morey, pilot of an American Air Force transport plane which had just landed at Punta Arenas. The aircraft, one of the famous Hercules C-130s, was on its way to King George Island with supplies for the 40 American scientists who would be overwintering nearby. The corporal wanted to talk to Brydon about the state of the King George Island runway.

On Brydon's behalf, I arranged for the two to confer in the Los Navegantes Hotel that afternoon. A hunch made me ask if I could sit in on the meeting.

'King George is a dream,' Brydon assured the corporal. He was talking not about the island, but about the dirt landing strip which had been bulldozed out of the plateau near its western tip. 'It's a bit on the short side, but fairly flat, except for one great hump in the middle.' The co-pilot and flight engineer gathered round as he pointed out hazards and landmarks on their charts. After half an hour they were satisfied. Heart thumping, I broached the question that I'd come to ask: 'Would there be any chance of a lift to King George Island?'

Corporal Morey's reply wasn't what I expected. 'Sure,' he said immediately. 'If you can have your name put on the manifest, we'll take you with pleasure.'

Back at the office, the Adventure Network staff were sceptical. 'You'll never get on the manifest; the Yanks don't take aliens.' But the agent responsible for drawing up the manifest didn't see any objection. The plane had plenty of space, and would be coming back the same day. 'Why not?' he replied to my telephone call. 'I'll put you on the manifest right away.'

In a state of euphoria I packed my bag: just cameras, a tape recorder, a notebook and some extra clothes. Although the Hercules wouldn't be full, there was no point in burdening myself with more than the bare essentials. The forecast was for fair weather over the Drake Passage, deteriorating later around King George Island itself. After frowning over the matter for a few minutes, Corporal Morey decided that despite the uncertain conditions at our destination we would leave first thing in the morning.

Tossing excitedly in my bed, I reflected that Antarctica's links with Patagonia were not just geological ones. In 1940, the Chilean Government had issued a decree claiming a pie-shaped slice of the continent between longitudes 53° and 90° west, including the whole of the Antarctic Peninsula (known to the Chileans as Tierra de O'Higgins) and the South Shetland Islands. Citing, amongst other reasons, its geological and geographical links with the Chilean mainland, they announced that henceforth the area would be known as Chilean Antarctic Territory.

Their old adversary across the Andes was quick to respond. Since 1832 the Argentines had been arguing with Britain, not only over the Falklands, but also about a number of other South Atlantic islands which the British administered under the name Falkland Islands Dependencies. In 1942, using the principle of extrapolating lines of longitude from the extremities of its claimed territory, Argentina announced that it had annexed a slice of Antarctica between longitudes 25° and 74° west. A glance at an atlas will show that this extended over more than half the area already claimed by Chile, including the all-important Antarctic Peninsula which the Argentines knew as Tierra de San Martín. Like the Chilean claim, it extended right down to the South Pole. The new acquisition was to be called Argentine Antarctic Territory, and administered (notionally together with the Falklands and their dependencies) from Tierra del Fuego.

While the politicians in Santiago and Buenos Aires were busying themselves with these claims, the shadow of a third nation fell across the peninsula. Since 1908, when the Englishman Ernest Shackleton edged closer to the South Pole than anyone before him, Britain had asserted rights to a huge sector of Antarctica – a 60° slice between longitudes 20° and 80° west. Like the Chilean and Argentine claims, this included the peninsula, which the British called Graham Land after a one-time first lord of the Admiralty. For 35 years they'd maintained a low profile in the area, but despite Whitehall's preoccupations with Hitler the new annexations didn't go unnoticed. In 1943 a British warship anchored off Deception Island, a horseshoe-shaped volcano in the South Shetlands group. Landing from one of the ship's boats, its crew found to their surprise a sign pointing to a small brass cylinder, inside which was a copy, in Spanish and English, of the Argentine declaration of the previous year.

Frustratingly, history books don't record the more intimate details of what happened next. We know simply that the British obliterated the Argentine signs, hoisted the Union Jack, posted a declaration in the name of the King, and returned the cylinder to the Argentine Government. When, however, they visited the island again in 1944, they found their flag and declaration replaced by Argentine ones. I wonder if the crew appreciated the comedy of it all, as once more they removed the Argentine chattels and erected their own? The farce could have gone on for years, but with the ending of the war in Europe the Attlee Government decided to establish a permanent presence on Deception, which was later supplemented by bases on other islands and on the peninsula itself. The Chileans and Argentines did the same.

Despite the absurdity of the situation, and notwithstanding tensions between the three countries in other areas, the claims coexisted more or less peacefully for more than ten years. In 1952 an Argentine naval vessel fired over the heads of a British meteorological party which had landed on the peninsula, but later allowed them to carry on with their work. Then, in 1957, a moratorium was agreed on all political claims, both on the peninsula and throughout the continent, for eighteen months. By the end of this time the twelve nations involved had pledged in principle to shelve their claims for the next 30 years.

This unprecedented decision – embodied in the Antarctic Treaty and enacted in 1961 – was a diplomatic landmark with worldwide implications. For 30 years a whole continent was to become a military and economic no-go area, open to exploration by all nations but with an outright ban on weaponry, mining and drilling for oil. Scientific research would be encouraged if its intentions were peaceful and non-commercial; but international rivalries were to be set aside when a scientist – or, for that matter, anyone else – ventured beyond 60° south.

I knew that King George Island possessed the bases of no fewer than ten countries – namely Chile, Argentina, the Soviet Union, a still separate East Germany, China, Uruguay, Peru, Brazil, Poland and South Korea. The treaty was due to be reviewed the following year, and with controversies raging over a range of issues from pollution and tourism to fishing and, most of all, the future of the continent's minerals, the real interest of these far-flung nations was no secret. When the Prime Minister of Malaysia was asked what drove a country which consisted largely of tropical rain forest to carry out research on an icefield, he replied, 'I've heard the South Pole is made of gold, and I want my piece of it.'

My timing couldn't have been more perfect.

The crew of the Hercules, squeezed into the hotel's courtesy minibus, seemed quite unconcerned about having an alien with them. So did the officials at the grandly named Punta Arenas International Airport. As far as the Chileans were concerned the flight was an internal one, so there were no passport formalities. No one questioned why a foreign civilian should be following the flight crew through the deserted departure gate; nor was any interest shown in the manifest. My meagre luggage aroused as much curiosity as a shopping bag in a high street.

The plane's interior was a single cavernous space – dark, bulbous and dominated by aluminium ribs, sheathed cabling and stacked packing cases. It was like being in the gut of a whale. This was a cargo flight so there were no seats; the loadmaster simply pointed to some webbing bolted to the side of the fuselage, like a row of linked deckchairs, and told me to make myself as comfortable as I could. Then the engines were throttled up and all conversation became impossible.

The three-hour journey passed in a cacophony of ear-shattering noise. The Beagle Channel and Cape Horn passed unseen beneath the wings; and sooner than expected I felt the beginning of a buffeting descent through thick, snow-filled cloud. Conditions at King George Island were worse than expected, and with the cloudbase at only 200 feet Corporal Morey missed the runway on his first approach. We climbed steeply and turned, and I glimpsed an iceberg being lashed by massive waves. At the second attempt we succeeded in landing, though the plane hit the runway so hard that some smaller bits of cargo went skating down the fuselage.

The island's dirt airstrip was maintained and run by the Chileans, as part of their Teniente Marsh Base. The base commander stood beaming like a schoolboy at the bottom of the steps. Visitors were a rare and welcome distraction, and he promptly invited the Americans to join him for lunch.

'I'm sorry,' Corporal Morey told me. 'You're not included in the party. Meet us here this afternoon; we'll leave at 4.00 p.m.'

The weather was dank and overcast, but I was determined to do some exploring. At these latitudes April is a month of wildly fluctuating temperatures, and on this particular day it was a degree or two above zero. Banks of snow lay here and there, but on the windblown slopes and exposed flat ground I could see black volcanic soil flanked by rocks and tongues of scree. A track had been forged between the landing strip and a cluster of orange buildings grouped around a bay. I pulled up my hood and set off towards them.

This 60-by-20-mile island, pounded almost continually by the storms which sweep the Drake Passage, was one of the first Antarctic landfalls ever made. Though Captain Cook had reached the 71st Parallel during his daring voyage of 1772–5, he never sighted land, and it was left to nineteenth-century sealers and whalers to confirm that a continent did in fact exist. One of the first of these was Captain Clark of the British sealer *Lord Melville*, who in 1820 built a hut on the island's north shore at about latitude 62°. Eleven men subsequently spent the winter there; they named their desolate landfall after George III.

Hastening against a biting headwind, I pondered on the accomplishment of those eleven men. Poorly sheltered, ill-provisioned and with no idea what to expect, they committed themselves resolutely to the Antarctic winter. I wasn't sure that even with today's comforts I would willingly do the same.

Suddenly I saw a curious vehicle approaching up the track – the kind of beach buggy that marketing people call an 'all-terrain vehicle'. Driving it was someone I recognized. Bruce Palmer, a Californian sailmaker, had arrived in Punta Arenas a couple of months previously on board a two-masted ketch. He joined the Adventure Network staff and we quickly became friends; but then they sent him to Antarctica and I thought we'd seen the last of each other. Now here he was, sitting on a beach buggy and grinning at me from under a jaunty bobble hat.

Though our backgrounds were quite different, Bruce and I had found much in common. From his San Diego sail-loft he'd made several long voyages, mostly as crew on the same two-master which had just delivered him to Punta Arenas. The trips had taken him to more South Sea islands than I'd ever dreamed existed; but his most hair-raising adventure had been chasing the vessel down the South American coast, having been accidentally marooned and subsequently robbed in Costa Rica. All but destitute, he finally reached Peru, and made his way to Lima where he spent his last few cents on a bus to the port of Callao. The ketch was anchored in the bay. Being familiar with the crew's routine, he made a bee-line for the yacht club bar, where he found them draining their last round before sailing.

'What are *you* doing here?' Bruce and I hollered simultaneously.

Having already finished his work on the island, Bruce had asked the Chilean base commander to persuade the Americans to take him back to Punta Arenas. 'Your US passport should do the trick,' I assured him. 'They even took an alien like me.'

With three hours till the appointed take-off hour, he immediately offered to show me some of the island. In deference to its fragile ground cover we left the vehicle on the track, and set off through lichen-clogged mud. An hour's footslogging brought us to a headland – still unnamed to the best of my knowledge – where we came upon an extraordinary sight. The grey volcanic foreshore was littered with what appeared to be boulders – but boulders which, as you approached them, reared up and roared. They were elephant seals, monarchs of the seal family, the females wide-eyed, the males two tons of mottled, blubbering fury. Further along the beach, a group of young fur seals was playing and barking like mongrel puppies. An agile leopard seal rose on its flippers and looked on. And amongst them all, flapping like an agitated pensioner, waddled a two-foot Chin-strap penguin.

Seals are mammals, and come ashore to sleep. Not surprisingly they don't much appreciate being woken. Despite its ungainly bulk, a seal with a sore head can move fast and inflict a painful bite; so after tiptoeing amongst them for half an hour we left the colony in peace. By three o'clock we were heading reluctantly back to the airstrip, savouring our final hour in this compelling place.

Suddenly there came an unexpected sound. Growing louder every moment, it was unmistakably the roar of aircraft engines. Bruce and I looked at each other in surprise; as far as we knew, the only plane on the strip was the Hercules, not due to take off for another hour. Perhaps they were warming up the engines. But the sound quickly reached a crescendo, and it became clear that whatever was making it was not warming up but taking off. A moment later the Hercules appeared, already airborne and climbing. Before we could fully appreciate what this meant, the great plane lumbered over our heads, banked towards the north-west and was making off in the direction of Punta Arenas. Mutely, Bruce and I watched the steadily dwindling shape till it was no more than a speck in the afternoon sky.

We stared at each other, speechless as our predicament sank in. Finally Bruce broke the silence. 'I happen to know there won't be another flight for at least two weeks.'

I gazed wistfully north-westwards. 'And I didn't even bring my toothbrush.'

If you're going to be stranded in Antarctica, King George Island is a good place to choose. The bases of the various nationalities, manned by personnel who are often assigned for a year at a time, offer almost unlimited opportunities for a castaway to eat, drink, socialize and learn about Antarctic life. Bruce and I got a taste of this when we knocked on the door of the Chilean base commander who'd been entertaining the Americans to lunch. 'What happened?' we asked.

'Oh, they had a radio call from Punta Arenas. Bad weather approaching up the Drake Passage, so they got out while they could. It looks as if they forgot you.'

Commander Barrientos then introduced himself and offered us the freedom of the base. Luckily, Adventure Network had a small wooden hut nearby, and Bruce had already made himself comfortable there while doing his work. It was well stocked, so we could assure the commander that we wouldn't have to abuse his hospitality; we'd simply make use of the base's bathrooms. 'Oh,' I added as an afterthought. 'I don't suppose you've got a spare toothbrush?'

The hut occupied a magnificent position near the head of the bay. Though only half-finished it looked quite habitable. Glass windows had recently been put in, and inside were a couple of camp beds and a kerosene brazier. A cooking stove, the most recent acquisition, stood against a wall. 'All mod cons,' said Bruce, slipping naturally into the role of estate agent. 'Do you know, this is the only private house in the whole of Antarctica? Every plank and nail had to be flown in. It's worth millions.'

It's worth millions just for the view, I thought.

Being free of luggage, I soon settled in, and spent the rest of the afternoon exploring the bay. Stripped of its winter snow, King George Island couldn't by any stretch of the imagination be called attractive. Behind the black beach the ground supported a thin soil which, whenever the temperature rose above freezing, turned to dark treacly mud. On either side rose cliffs, in some places high and proud, in others denuded and shattered by repeated freezing and thawing. The higher forms of plant life – trees, shrubs, flowers and grass – were conspicuously absent from the scene, leaving the landscape bald and lunar. But on closer inspection the land was far from sterile. Lichens and mosses grew so abundantly that I crushed swathes of them wherever I walked.

That evening, we received an invitation to visit the two scientists who made up the total complement of the East German base across the bay. Though the Berlin Wall had been breached several months previously, a date had yet to be fixed for German reunification. Meanwhile, their building remained where it had always been, in the shadow of the huge Soviet Bellingshausen station. By the standards of our hut the accommodation was opulent beyond belief. As well as a small shared dining table and cooking stove, each had his own writing desk, together with shelves and a cupboard. Off the entrance hall was a washroom which doubled as a photographic darkroom. To complete the list of comforts, the pair had brought with them cushions, paintings and wall posters, and there was even a small tank of tropical fish: definitely the world's southernmost guppies.

Detlef Zippel and Joachim Ulbricht were cartoon-character scientists. Detlef was 35 years old, skinny and highly strung, with a shock of swept-back hair. Joachim was younger, stouter, bespectacled and completely bald. They'd been sent by the Communist authorities, in their turbulent final year of power, to study – of all things – birds. It had long been suspected that certain southern seabirds, such as the Giant Petrel, were particularly sensitive to human interference. With the help of previous records, the East Germans had shown that at one site the number of breeding pairs had halved in the five years since helicopters started flying overhead. They were now working to see if there was a direct connection. Waste and pollution were also growing issues: with each new scientific project came more people, more equipment and more rubbish. The Chileans on King George Island had already been observed dumping scrap metal in the bay; the Russians had littered the place with redundant tracked vehicles; and the Argentines had been responsible for Antarctica's first environmental disaster when their supply ship *Bahía Paraíso* hit rocks off Adelaide Island, spilling thousands of gallons of diesel fuel which fouled beaches and killed fish, birds and krill. Perhaps most deplorably of all, one or two of King George Island's glacial meltwater lakes, specifically earmarked for protection under the Antarctic Treaty because of their outstanding biological value, had been used as garbage dumps.

Over bierwurst and brandy Detlef and Joachim explained their own anxieties, as every day their shortwave radio brought fresh and cataclysmic news from home. What future would they face as scientists in a united Germany? After 45 years of impoverishment, how would East Germany's scientific institutions compete with those of the West? And what about their salaries? In East German marks these amounted to about 1,000 per month – insignificant compared with those of their Western counterparts. When prices rose following reunification, how would they live?

I asked about their families, and Detlef became morose. 'Joachim's lucky, he's not married. But I – well, I have a wife and child in Germany, yet for two years I'm supposed to live here on the other side of the world. I love my work, but you can imagine the difficulties for my family.'

Detlef had also been having some problems with his Soviet neighbours. 'This man, the – how do you call him? – quartermaster,' he hissed. 'He must be quite stupid. Twice we've asked him, politely and in Russian, not to put his timber and materials so close to our front door. Twice he's ignored us!'

In the Antarctic you can't afford to have enemies, and I wondered whether what was really irritating Detlef was his forced dependence on the Russians. Despite his and Joachim's efforts to disguise it, their building was unmistakably a Russian one. It had Russian fixtures, Russian furniture, and a field telephone link to the Soviet building 100 yards away. He stared miserably through the window across the darkened, icebound bay. 'I've done what I can, but these Russians simply don't understand,' he sighed. 'Every night I dream of Germany and home.'

Perhaps in that year of European turmoil some conflict was only to be expected between the East Germans, nervous of their future, and representatives of the nation which had been responsible for their ruin. The next afternoon I decided to judge the Russians for myself. None of the bases was corralled by walls or fences, so it was an easy matter to approach the cluster of steel structures which made up the Soviet one. I poked my head inside the largest building to find it heavy with the reek of Bulgarian tobacco and crammed from floor to ceiling with radio equipment. The grey cabinets studded with dials and switches gave the impression of a science-fiction spaceship – but one which had obviously met with some catastrophe, because there was nobody to be seen. After a good deal of calling I raised a young man who, using sign language and some words of German, explained that the staff were all in the sauna. Following his directions, I

142

ploughed through 50 yards of mud and entered a long, low building in which three generators were throbbing. Continuing across a catwalk and through damp communal washrooms, I finally came to a stifling dark-panelled antechamber. A man was towelling himself. 'Hello,' he said in English through the steam. 'You must be the visitor they just phoned me about. I'm Jury Gudoshnicov, station commander.'

The temperature in the anteroom was well over 80° Fahrenheit, and this seemed also to be the level in Jury Gudoshnicov's office, to which he later took me. 'We will drink vodka!' he proclaimed. The office was so thick with tobacco smoke that Jury could well have been generating it for the whole base. It was like walking into a bonfire. On the walls I could just make out heavy-framed portraits of Lenin and Gorbachev, carefully positioned for equal prominence, each staring sternly at the other.

Jury was in high spirits. His two-year posting was about to end, and a Soviet icebreaker would soon be arriving to take him home. He'd found Antarctic life professionally stimulating but, compared with his beloved Leningrad, rather philistine. He'd had enough. The base workforce was being expanded from 25 to 75, and he pointed through the window to the building being put up to accommodate the new arrivals. It was, like the others, squat and square – as characterless in its green-and-yellow livery as the Moscow tenements which had no doubt inspired it. The only difference, apart from size, was that to enable access through the winter snows this block stood on stilts.

After coffee, vodka and the inevitable Bulgarian cigarettes, Jury took me on a tour of the main building. The equipment I'd been admiring earlier – which turned out to be nothing more sinister than a shortwave receiver tuned to Radio Moscow – was only a small part of the extraordinary paraphernalia of this major Antarctic base. The electronics were all of an early vintage, generating a lot of noise and heat. 'Some of this stuff's primeval,' complained Jury. 'Look at this transmitter, for example – all valves and rheostats. It takes up far too much room and uses more electricity than we can really afford. Today's equivalents would sit on a desktop and probably run off an ordinary power point.' I passed from room to room, beset by images of the Cold War, until at last our more harmonious age seemed to reassert itself in the form of

143

a teleprinter side-by-side with a sewing machine. 'The chief engineer is a dab hand at embroidery,' said Jury.

Two hundred yards away, the Chileans had established their 'colony' of Villa Las Estrellas – the Village of the Stars. Slightly inebriated from Jury's vodka, I called on some of its 240 inhabitants. Unlike the Soviet Union, Chile has a territorial claim to King George Island, and the colony's real purpose was clear. Any pretence at research was limited to collecting weather data – the same data, as far as I could see, that the other bases were collecting. The important thing was that Chilean civilians should be seen to be living in Antarctica, so that when the treaty came up for review their sovereignty could be substantiated under international law. Villa Las Estrellas boasted everything from a post office and shop to a hotel, a tiny hospital and even a gymnasium. The 'colonists' worked as mechanics, radio operators, cooks, administrators, drivers, teachers or doctors. An important feature was that children should be born and brought up within the colony, and this had been arranged too. The primary school had eleven pupils and two teachers – the highest teacher/pupil ratio in Chile. Commander Barrientos' wife was said to be experimenting with hothouse vegetables in an attempt to make the base partly self-supporting; but apart from a few tomatoes and carrots she hadn't yet had much success.

The irony of the Chileans' costly and carefully thought-out effort was that less than 100 miles to the south, on the tip of the Antarctic Peninsula, the Argentines were doing exactly the same.

After a few days, life at the hut began to take on a pattern. There were jobs to be done, and to relieve our guilt about the provisions we were consuming Bruce and I threw ourselves into them with gusto. One morning we set out to shift fuel drums. Aviation fuel was the lynchpin of Adventure Network's operations, and while it was plentiful in Punta Arenas, the task of getting it to where it was needed was a constant headache. Each drum weighed a quarter of a ton. Fifty of them had been deposited on the beach by the Chilean supply ship *Piloto Pardo*, but the Twin Otter pilots would need them at the airstrip, a mile up the muddy track down which I'd walked on my first day. Bruce had noticed that the Chileans possessed a small lorry, one of the few ordinary vehicles on the island, and we asked Commander Barrientos if we could borrow it. 'On one condition,' he replied, pointing towards our hut. 'Before you leave this island, you must put a coat of paint on that disgusting shack.'

Unfortunately for us, the materials for carrying out the commander's instruction were in abundant supply. We did, however, have an excuse for not starting right away, for our work with the fuel drums was soon interrupted by one of the most violent blizzards I've ever encountered. The hut shook as if it were of cardboard. Venturing outside, I felt my face being strafed by horizontal streaks of rock-hard snow. After half a dozen sorties on various errands, I learned my lesson and the errands stayed undone. As night descended the storm continued to grow, and Bruce and I lay listening to it for several hours before falling into a fitful sleep. Occasionally the hut would lift slightly, and we would hold our breath for a moment until it settled back down. It wouldn't have surprised either of us if it had turned right over, bringing unthinkable quantities of timber, tools and groceries down upon our heads.

But morning brought blue skies, and the painting now proceeded at a brisk pace. Within a couple of days my time was my own once more. Behind the hut rose a steep headland, and a mile or so beyond it, the Great Wall Station of the People's Republic of China. It was too tempting to ignore.

The station chief, Zhang Jieyao, turned out to be a tight-lipped man who was obviously used to receiving visitors. He extended his hand without surprise or emotion, called for his interpreter, and ushered me into a reception room which looked more like a banqueting suite than part of an Antarctic research station. Woodcarvings and calligraphy adorned three of the teak-panelled walls, while the fourth was completely taken up with a tapestry of the station's namesake, the Great Wall of China.

Through the interpreter, Zhang informed me that eighteen Chinese scientists were carrying out research in nine different fields, from marine biology through glaciology to the effects on the human body of long periods in a polar climate. 'We're not duplicating other nations' work,' he emphasized. 'Unlike some, we have no territorial interests here. Our motivation is purely scientific.'

The station was like a fragment of China. In the communal areas, vacuum flasks of hot water offered continual refreshment, supplemented by packets of jasmine tea. The dining room contained a glass counter displaying tinned fruit and half a dozen bottles of Great Wall wine. I recalled the East Germans' bierwurst, the Russians' cigarettes and vodka. Like tortoises, King George Island's residents seemed to carry their homes with them.

I pressed Zhang on the changes in his country during the previous year, especially the events of Tiananmen Square. He dodged the question artfully. 'What changes do you mean?' he smiled. 'From what I hear, life at home continues smoothly.'

I raised the subject of Antarctic conservation. It was said that in constructing the base the Chinese had destroyed an important breeding ground for Weddell seals. Again Zhang sidestepped. 'I'm afraid I know nothing about this; it was well before my time.'

Eventually, defeated by his skill in avoiding controversy (an ability which may well have been written into his job description), I made my excuses and left. The Chinese station was certainly the cleanest of those I'd visited. The piles of scrap metal which marked the Soviet base, and the discarded fuel drums around the Chilean one, were nowhere to be seen. There was even an incinerator for combustible refuse, which helped to heat the buildings. But Zhang's claim not to be duplicating other countries' research was called into question by the meteorological instruments I passed as I left the base. Like all the others, the Chinese were monitoring the weather. Their records must have been almost identical to those of the Chileans, East Germans and Russians just a mile away, and not all that different from those being collected on the island's six other bases. It was a shame, I thought, that they couldn't cooperate on this simple subject.

The days passed quickly – some bright and clear, with the sun hanging low on the northern horizon; others dull and blustery, with heavy cloud pressing down and snow flurries coming in horizontally from a tumultuous sea. I explored whenever I could, wrapping myself in borrowed cold-weather gear and armed always with a weather forecast, updated hourly, from our Chilean neighbours. As I became more familiar with the terrain I ventured steadily further afield, until one day I established the limits of solo travel – at least in my ill-equipped state – when I came up against an icefield completely severing the island. But there was still plenty to see. Skuas and petrels circled continuously overhead, some approaching so close in their curiosity that

I grew used to ducking at the whoosh of their four-foot wings. Chinstrap penguins were in great abundance, scrambling up the rockier shores in preparation for their annual moult. With no natural enemies on land, they were quite fearless, and would waddle up to inspect human intruders, peering short-sightedly and flapping their stubby little flippers. Much of the island was blanketed in *Usnea antarctica*, a delicate pale green lichen which grows so slowly that in some places it only reaches maturity after 1,000 years. I dwelt guiltily on this statistic every time I stepped on it.

As I walked, I kept an eye open for fossils. Detlef and Joachim had already alerted me to the possibility of stumbling on these bizarre remnants of trees, shrubs and rodents made extinct by successive ice ages. On nearby Seymour Island biologists had unearthed a perfectly preserved fossil beech leaf, and the previous week Detlef himself had picked up part of a fossilized tree-trunk, its growth rings still visible after 40 million years. Ammonites, lobsters and sea urchins were among the sea creatures whose shapes had been preserved from those distant temperate days. Like the lichens, they were all too easy to destroy, and I was careful to leave my few discoveries as I found them.

It occurred to me, as I made these sallies across the island, that the human impact on Antarctica had only just begun. Stepping on lichens and fossils was one thing; building bases and airstrips entirely another. Already, the conservation campaigners Greenpeace had brought the world's attention to such atrocities as whaling and the destruction of penguin colonies – both supposedly justified in the name of research. Another concern was Antarctic tourism. Besides the relatively small-scale operations of Adventure Network, cruise ships were now bringing groups as large as 160 to the continent up to 20 times per year. Despite exhortations by on-board lecturers to take nothing away and leave nothing behind, these visitors were having an increasing impact around their landing places. With a surge of new interest expected in the 1990s, restrictions both on visitor numbers and on permitted landfalls would be the only way of protecting those parts of the continent which – unlike King George Island – remained unspoilt. Greenpeace and others had suggested that the best way to achieve lasting protection would be to declare

Antarctica and its islands a world park. The proposal had received widespread support. But while countries like Britain continued to build airstrips and gaze greedily at Antarctica's possible reserves of oil and gas, the prospects for such protection seemed slim.

As I took stock of what I'd seen and heard, I reminded myself that the Antarctic Treaty in its original form had just fourteen months to run. For those who cared about Antarctica, those months would be a time of agonizing debate. Several key governments – including the United States, Britain, West Germany and Japan – were openly nervous about locking up such fabulous wealth in the name of conservation.*

Bruce and I had been promised a flight back to Punta Arenas in a Hercules of the Chilean Air Force. On the eve of the appointed day there came a knock at the door of the hut. Outside, silhouetted against driving snow, Detlef stood clutching a bottle of brandy. 'There are some things I want to tell you before you go,' he said gravely. 'Let us drink!'

For two hours he entreated us to take ever larger tots of his lethal grog, and while a freshening blizzard rocked the hut our conversation ranged from acid rain through ozone issues to the question of dumping at sea. The drink strengthened both Detlef's accent and his powers of criticism, especially when it came to fellow scientists. 'So many people, all studying the same things!' he roared. 'I tell you, soon the ornithologists will be fighting each other to ring the birds!' He waved his arms, almost extinguishing our storm lantern. 'And the meteorologists! I don't know whether to laugh or cry about the meteorologists. They launch so many weather balloons, I'm surprised they haven't become entangled.'

Through an intoxicated haze I had a vision of Russian and Chinese balloons colliding in the upper atmosphere, ruining each other's statistics. But Detlef was in full torrent, and now he rounded on me. 'You, my friend, are a journalist. You have a special role to play. No one is reporting the truth about Antarctica: not the scientists, not the governments, and certainly not

* In the event, common sense prevailed, and just before the treaty ran out in 1991 they agreed to ban mining and drilling for a further 50 years.

the navies and air forces which man the bases and bring in the supplies. Each has a foot in the door and is determined to keep it there; so how can they possibly be objective? You must write in your book about these things. You must write about *all* these things. You must be passionate; you must tell the world!'

And on concluding this oration – the most impressive summary of Antarctica's predicament I'd heard since my arrival – Detlef threw back his head, drained the last of the brandy, bade us goodnight, unlatched the door, and staggered off into the blizzard.

I was now two weeks into a stay that had been intended to last four hours. Bruce had been on the island much longer. It was hardly surprising, therefore, that the next morning found us side by side at the airstrip a good hour before the Hercules was due to arrive. The control tower confirmed that it was on its way, and a snowplough had cleared the runway in readiness for its arrival; but while we waited the weather took a turn for the worse. First a cloudbank, then snow flurries, and finally a full-blown storm engulfed us. For nearly an hour we listened to the tantalizing drone of engines as the pilot circled, waiting for conditions to clear, but finally dwindling fuel reserves forced him to return to Punta Arenas.

It was now well into April; winter was virtually upon us, and for 36 hours Bruce and I faced the real possibility that the hut might be our home until the spring. The following day saw no improvement in the weather; but the day after that, to our delight and relief, we awoke to clear skies. The control tower called to say that the Hercules was once more on its way, and would attempt a landing shortly after midday. This time it was success-ful, and in the twilight of late afternoon we hurtled down the slush-covered runway, heading for home.

Five hours later I was strolling again through the streets of Punta Arenas. Sights and sensations flooded over me: the lights, the traffic, the well-dressed pedestrians, and most of all the seemingly subtropical warmth. In little more than a fortnight these things had become distant memories. I peeled off my layers of clothing and luxuriated in a bath. Someone brought me coffee, commenting that winter was on its way. I couldn't think what they were talking about.

Atlantic Coast

I'd come south down Patagonia's misty, forested western side; I wanted to return north up its arid eastern side. After his adventures on King George Island Bruce felt a need to return to more temperate latitudes, and soon I was on my own again, making my way up a winding gravel road towards the Argentine border. At a bleak border crossing high in the Sierra Dorotea I left Chile for the last time on a bus full of miners. The Río Turbio mine, though just inside Argentina, was staffed mainly by Chileans commuting from Puerto Natales. On the Chilean side the road climbed past cottages set in neat vegetable patches; but once in Argentina it descended into a valley whose soil seemed to consist entirely of slag. For half a century coal has been mined on the banks of the Río Turbio, and the locals joke that in all this time the operation has never made a profit. Perhaps this was why so little had been done to make the valley fit for its several thousand inhabitants, who lived in rabbit-hutch houses planted in rows like cabbages in the black desert.

A road and a goods railway run east from Río Turbio towards the Atlantic coast, and I set out to find them. Somewhere along the road was a farm called Morro Chico, and some friends in Punta Arenas had given me an introduction to its manager Victor Steel. At the railway depot, surrounded by hissing steam engines, a driver said yes, he knew the place. But amid profuse apologies he declined to take me on his footplate; so I filled my water bottle from a murky brook and plodded off down the road.

For two hours no vehicles passed. The mine receded and the soil returned from black to its natural beige. For the first few miles road and railway ran side by side; then the railway tracks swung behind a bluff and disappeared. Now not even a train would come by. My boots crunched on the gravel and I wiped my brow of sweat mixed with coal dust.

After a while a strange thing happened. I forgot about Morro Chico; forgot that I was listening vainly for the sound of an approaching vehicle; forgot that I was covered in coal dust; forgot even the unremitting, soul-destroying wind. I was in Patagonia, in the middle of nowhere, and it felt grand. I slackened my pace and looked around. Scrubby grassland grazed by grimy sheep rose towards nondescript boulder-strewn crags – an insipid scene by any standard, and it was too early in the day for lengthening shadows to work their magic. Yet walking down that gravel road, I wouldn't have swapped my surroundings for all the world's beauty spots combined, because the view was mine alone. For a few brief moments I had no origin, no destination, no future, no past; I would tread that road for ever.

It wasn't the first time on my travels that I'd experienced this unexpected joy. The feeling had arisen several times already in Patagonia, often without warning, welling up from deep inside when once in a while I managed to let go of plans and worries. Long uncomfortable journeys weren't essential to the process, but they helped greatly. So as I tramped eastwards I found myself in agreement with Julius Beerbohm, a young Englishman who in 1877 led his band of gauchos to a spot not far from where I was now:

I seemed to be leaving the old world I had hitherto known behind me, with its turmoils and cares and weary sameness, and to be riding merrily into some new sphere of free, fresh existence. I felt that without a pang I could break with old associations, renounce old ties, the pomps and the pleasures, the comforts, the bothers, the annoyances of civilization, and become as those with whom I was now travelling – beings with no thought for the morrow, and therefore no uneasiness for it either. . . .

Robert Louis Stevenson always said that he travelled not to go anywhere, but just to go. A more recent traveller, Philip Glazebrook, wrote that for him the thrill came from testing his self-reliance. John Steinbeck put it down to a more basic instinct, which he called 'the urge to be some place else'. I suppose many people seek adventure to escape from home, or to escape from themselves, or to prove themselves in some way, or to impress their friends with tales and slide-shows. Chris Bonington has pointed out that the spirit of adventure often springs from discontent: particularly for those in the developed world, a dissatisfaction with bland city life. He sees it as a modern phenomenon, quite distinct from the great explorations of centuries gone by. In those days explorers were strictly practical. Marco Polo went to do business with the Chinese; Christopher Columbus because his king sent him; Captain Cook, ostensibly at least, to make astronomical observations for the Royal Society.

My own travel inclinations come from a mixture of Glazebrook's self-testing and Bonington's discontent. As a boy I often used to browse through my school atlas and wonder what it would be like to pit my wits against the Andes, or the Hindu Kush, or that wonderful African range they called the Mountains of the Moon. But today I get more fulfilment from meeting people than from surmounting obstacles – and the more I meet, the more discoveries I make about myself. The stoic peasant, the arrogant city slicker, even the guidebook-toting tourist has his or her tale to tell. Travellers are often accused of being hopeless romantics, poking about under rainbows for the elusive pot of gold. I did my share of this, until one day I realized how much I was missing. What I'd been looking for was under my very nose!

Travellers are also thought of as a brave bunch; after all, don't we face impossible odds when we venture forth on foreign territory? Robbers, rapists and manic bus drivers must surely rub their hands with glee at the sight of our approach – and this is not to mention the perils of venomous snake-life and debilitating disease. But personally I think it takes more courage to stay at home – to face the daily challenges of work and family and the frustrations of a regular routine. In this sense, travelling for me is pure escapism. It's when I forget duties and deadlines and indulge in my life's true purpose, which (I realize on such occasions) is to perfect the art of drifting. So far, I've managed to pursue this indulgence without encountering too much mischief from saboteurs of either the human, the reptilian or the bacteriological kind. Of course this may have been just a run of luck; but it seems to me far riskier to spend one's life commuting on the M25.

At last a pickup sped past, and the driver must have noticed the self-satisfaction on my face, because after 100 yards it slewed to a halt and reversed to where I was still sauntering along. He was alone – a travelling salesman on his way to Río Gallegos. Would I like a lift? He seemed willing to take me wherever I wanted, but had no more idea than I did of the whereabouts of Morro Chico. After an hour we turned off the road and drove for miles down a rough track which he thought might lead us there. It didn't, but he drove cheerfully back without a hint of resentment. I was impressed.

Eventually we found the place – a scatter of red-roofed buildings on a featureless plain – and my benefactor dropped me off. 'We don't get many visitors here,' said a weatherbeaten Victor Steel. 'We're right at the end of the track.' And they were. The original approach from the Río Turbio road – itself carrying only a few dozen vehicles per day – had been abandoned since a bridge over the Gallegos River had been declared unsafe; to reach the farm we'd simply driven straight across the plain. The buildings lay up against the border fence with Chile, and when the wind wasn't screaming through the radio aerials I could make out the sound of lorries on the paved Chilean road from Puerto Natales. In one of those vehicles Punta Arenas, with all its bustle and hubbub, would be less than two hours away. But here across the fence in Argentina, Morro Chico was indeed isolated. To buy even a loaf of bread Victor and his wife Roberta had to walk or drive along seven miles of farm track, ford the river, then continue for another 25 miles on a road hardly wider than the track. After all this they could avail themselves of the half-dozen bars and shops of the hamlet of El Turbio. How frontiers distort our lives! Patagonians are naturally sociable people, and visit their neighbours often despite the distances involved. But Chilean and Argentine Patagonians move in quite different circles – like magnetic fields around opposite poles.

Roberta brought tea and fruitcake, and we settled in the parlour with the farm's owner, a Scot by the name of Andrew Gallie. Andrew and Victor were discussing the drought. Morro Chico had had no rain now for three years running; its lagoons had dried up, and the wind had redistributed the sandy lagoon-bed material over acres of surrounding land. Like Bedřich Magaš in Punta Arenas, many Argentines were putting the drought down to the collapse of the ozone layer, but Andrew wasn't so sure. 'We've had droughts before,' he pointed out. 'The difference with this one is the way it's affecting the farms. It's not the occasional drought that's killing Patagonia; it's deliberate and continual overgrazing. Year in, year out; the vegetation has no chance to recover, and the forage is getting frighteningly sparse.'

He'd already cut the Morro Chico flock from 25,000 to 17,000. 'I'm trying to think of the next century,' he said. 'Though from what they tell me, my neighbours are having difficulty thinking of next year.'

On an inlet of the Atlantic, 135 miles east of Morro Chico, stood the largest city in the far south. Founded in 1885, Río Gallegos was for many years no more than a tumbledown wool port – a collection of tin-roofed shacks set in streets so mean that A.F. Tschiffely, arriving in 1938, wrote disgustedly, 'They are merely strips of sand or dirt between straight rows of houses.' But for all its seediness, Río Gallegos in Tschiffely's day was a mecca for the surrounding farmers, who'd drive 100 miles or more for an evening at the Hotel Paris or the British Club. 'About a dozen of the buildings are well constructed,' he noted, 'and therefore greatly admired by the simple-minded inhabitants, in whose eyes Gallegos is the most important place in the world.'

A boost to the town came shortly after Tschiffely's visit, with the opening of the railway to Río Turbio. Though the line never carried more than a few passengers, its deepwater coal jetty became the focus of yet more ramshackle development, later to be supplemented by sturdier houses when the provincial government moved its headquarters from Santa Cruz. More recently, units of the Army and Air Force have made their homes there, boosting the population to more than 100,000. In 1982 its civilians may well have wondered if the latter move had been altogether a good thing, when they found themselves in the front line of the Falklands conflict. Río Gallegos spent two months under blackout orders. The airport, doubling as an air force base, was expected to be a prime target for British bombing raids, and as it was only five miles from the city centre the whole community felt at risk. One night a gas main exploded and a thousand people dived for shelter.

The early sheepfarmers were nearly all British: the children or grandchildren of Falkland kelpers. As the farms expanded, peons

154

were contracted – a few from Britain and Scandinavia but the majority from Chile – and a work system developed which can only be described as feudal. The labourers were housed in sheds, up to five in each thirteen-foot-square room, where they slept on rough cots draped with uncured sheepskins.

Peons weren't allowed to leave the farms without permission, and probably wouldn't have had the money to do so anyway, since their wages were next to nothing. At the end of the First World War a foreman could expect to earn just £14 per month. One Danish worker is said to have complained to his employer, 'Twenty years I've sweated on this farm, and what have I got to show for it?' And he held out his life savings of £40. But his boss was unsympathetic. 'You sup too much whisky, old man,' he replied. 'You waste money on clothes and travel. Why – I know for a fact you've been three times to Río Gallegos in those 20 years!'

Being scattered across Patagonia and held as virtual prisoners on their farms, the peons found it difficult to mount much opposition to their masters. The farmers themselves claimed they were being squeezed by big companies such as Swift International, which exported their meat and wool. But in 1920 a trade union called the Sociedad Obrera de Río Gallegos set the stage for a showdown with a thunderous declaration: 'Slavery, drudgery and servility imprisoned in irons, in dungeons or under the whip, vile plagues which have oppressed humanity through the centuries, and which today seem like figments of the imagination . . . are but a pale reflection of what has befallen the unhappy workers . . . in the territory of Santa Cruz.'

The man who wrote these words was Antonio Soto, a Spanish anarchist who, inspired by the Russian Revolution, had given up an acting career to stir up the workers of the world. Rather than face military service at home, he fled to Buenos Aires and took a job as a scene-shifter with a touring theatre company. A tour of the far south was arranged, and it couldn't have been timed more perfectly – Soto and Río Gallegos were ripe for each other. He quit his job, signed on as a docker and was quickly put in charge of the Sociedad Obrera, where his skill at oratory fed the flames of revolt. Bruce Chatwin, who studied the course of the next twelve months in detail, recalled: 'Attempts to silence him failed: nor could the jail hold him, for his faction was too strong. One night a knife flashed on an empty street, but the blade hit the watch in his waistcoat pocket and the hired killer fled.' Soto's escape seemed to confirm his sense of mission, for he immediately called a general strike, apparently not noticing that his support was beginning to fade. He joined forces with some Italian anarchists to form the so-called Red Council. 'With a band of 500 rough riders,' wrote Chatwin, 'the Red Council swooped on estancias; looted guns, food, horses and drink; freed the Chilotes from their inhibitions; left heaps of fire-twisted metal; and dissolved again on to the steppe. . . .

'Soto still believed the Government was neutral and ordered each commander to seize a stretch of territory, to raid and take hostages. Secretly he was dreaming of a revolution that would spread from Patagonia and engulf the country. He was not very bright.'

But of course the Government was far from neutral. In 1921 it sent a cavalry unit to pacify the territory, and after a winter of sporadic violence they confronted several hundred peons at La Anita (the farm which the Calafate travel agent had warned me was now a tourist attraction). The peons were no match for trained soldiers, and they knew it. Soto fled to Chile and the rest gave up without a fight. In return for unconditional surrender the commanding officer promised to spare their lives, but next morning, on the insistence of the farmers, he put 120 before a firing squad. It's said that each farmer had drawn up a death list, and personally watched it being carried out.

Little good emerged from Patagonia's revolution. After the first wave of strikes the farmers bought off the peons by doubling their wages, but on regaining the upper hand they halved them again. The executed peons were replaced by Chilotes, and this time the farmers made sure they employed only the most poorly educated ones. With no understanding of social issues – let alone trade unions – they could be relied on to work without complaint. Like the Russian Revolution which inspired it, the revolt was born out of the best humanitarian ideals, only to be sabotaged ultimately by extremists on both sides. But where the Soviet experiment would grow to influence the course of the twentieth century, Patagonia's worked itself out within fifteen months, leaving only resentment and spite. 'Bad business,' an Argentine

Scot summed it up to Chatwin. 'Bunch of Bolshie agitators came down and stirred up trouble.'

There can't be many schools in the world where a stranger can turn up unannounced late on a Friday afternoon, and with children streaming out for the weekend be given tea, cake, a key to the building, a mattress to sleep on, and an invitation to dinner with the headmistress. Admittedly, I had a slight advantage over the average stranger, for the school in question was the British College, where well-heeled Río Gallegans send their offspring to learn English. But my generous reception was to be repeated so many times in this drab town that I wondered if there was some connection between the extraordinary sense of compassion and the dreary surroundings.

The school was a rambling Edwardian bungalow, with a green pitched roof and cream-painted classrooms smelling of polish, chalkdust and juvenile sweat. On weekdays children pounded the corridors from dawn until well after dusk; but on Saturdays and Sundays the building was silent. The toilets were labelled not '*Caballeros*' and '*Damas*', nor even '*Niños*' and '*Niñas*', but 'Boys' and 'Girls'.

Saturday had been earmarked by the British Club for its Annual General Meeting. With no apparent trace of irony, my invitation asked me to be there at five o'clock, '*hora inglesa*'. Literally this meant 'English hour', but what it really signified was that I'd better not be late. Behind a mahogany bar, white-uniformed barmen were polishing glasses and serving malt whiskies to refresh the members after their journeys in from the farms. The men perched on barstools and called each other 'Archie old boy' and 'Oh come on now Henry'. Wives sat across the room in deep sofas under prints of dogs and sailing ships, their handbags on green baize tables by their sides.

Thirty of the club's 150 members had gathered for the AGM – a fair attendance, considering how far some of them must have come – and at the appointed hour they moved to a meeting room to face a committee of nine. The speeches, all in Spanish, were short and businesslike. Only when the chairman announced the next stage in the proceedings did the noise level begin to rise, for the next stage was the barbecue. Two whole sheep had been roasted, and we trooped into a back room to be greeted by a fog of charcoal smoke. Plates were hurriedly passed round, wine glasses filled, and within an hour the occasion was in full, deafening swing.

As the evening progressed, besuited and fur-coated figures streamed in from all points of the compass. I was introduced in turn to Naomi O'Byrne's brother Chris Kennard; to Jesse Aldridge who'd been British Vice-Consul in the old days; to crusty old Jim Halliday, grandson of the first kelper to come across from the Falklands; and to a score of Douglases, Camerons and Jamiesons whose faces were no more than blurs in the smoke.

I fell into conversation with a long-established farmer, and inevitably the subject turned to the drought. In a desperate attempt to conserve pasture he'd cut his flock by no less than 40 percent. 'I'm one of the lucky ones,' he laughed sourly. 'In this province, one farm in ten has already gone down.'

Despite his difficulties the farmer remained defiantly optimistic, and reckoned that the decline in Patagonia's grazing was coming to a halt. 'When I was young, I'd ride across the farm and the grass would come up to my stirrups,' he told me, indicating the level with an outstretched hand. 'Grass like that would soak up rain like a sponge. But nowadays, you know, it hardly grows above my ankles; so at least now the rain reaches the ground.'

'But how can you be sure things won't get worse?' I asked.

'Well,' he replied thoughtfully. 'Call me gullible if you like, but I'm working on the theory that when you've hit rock-bottom you can't sink lower.'

This farmer did have one thing to be thankful for. Since Perón's time the Government had been casting covetous eyes on the richer British-run establishments. His estate had been one of those singled out for expropriation. During the Falklands conflict his days as a farmer had seemed numbered, but after desperate lobbying Buenos Aires had agreed to put the matter on ice. He hardly dared believe his luck. In 1982 the farm would have provided a useful income for an ailing treasury; today, of course, it would be simply a liability. So for the time being he could rest assured, along with other farmers in the room, that the civil servants wouldn't come knocking at the door.

It was two in the morning when the last station wagon roared away into the night. A crew-cut teenager lounged outside an ice-cream parlour, watching the vehicle disappear down the empty street. Litter whirled in circles, and on a parched grass verge a row of saplings beat noisily against their slatted windbreaks. All were either dead or dying. To survive in Río Gallegos trees need more than windbreaks: they need the spunk of the Devil and the luck of the British.

May Day was a national holiday, but in the province of Santa Cruz the children holidayed all week because their teachers were on strike. The school year had already started late – in some schools a month late – because the provincial government couldn't meet the teachers' salary bill. When, in early April, some salaries had at last been paid for January and February, classes had struggled into action – only to be brought to an abrupt halt at the end of the month when the Governor announced that his administration was broke.

The situation, although grim, wasn't without international precedent. Five years previously the council of Liverpool, a city with five times the population of Santa Cruz, had become virtually bankrupt through its failure to set a rate. And a few months after the Santa Cruz affair the entire federal adminis-tration of the United States would come within a hair's breadth of insolvency. What made the Santa Cruz announcement unusual was that the year up to 30th April had seen Argentina's inflation rate spiral to no less than 16,900 percent. In such a situation salary-earners find it especially difficult to make ends meet, since their monthly pay rises, being awarded in arrears, never catch up with inflation. When, however, their employers begin defaulting not only on the rises but on the salaries themselves, the road to destitution is short and straight. For the teachers of Santa Cruz, bank loans were out of the question since the banks were short of liquidity themselves; and with teachers' salaries averaging only £75 per month, few had savings to fall back on. By the time of the announcement, some families were facing the very real prospect of hunger.

On 2nd May 500 angry teachers marched on the provincial offices in Río Gallegos. The police ringed the building shoulder to shoulder. After a good deal of barracking someone threw a brick. The police retaliated with tear gas and water cannon. There were injuries on both sides. Eventually the crowd dispersed, but the teachers' mood was ugly and Río Gallegos remained tense for the rest of the week. The Governor blamed the riot on the police; the police said the order to attack had come from the Governor. Both blamed the Buenos Aires government for failing to send money that had been promised months previously; but the Ministry of Education replied that, like the province, it was broke.

And so the accusations flew. Promises were made, broken, and made again. To curry favour with the Governor, the teachers agreed that the police had sparked off the violence, and at this the police themselves went on strike, pointing out that their salaries, too, were overdue. Finally both teachers and police joined forces in a call for the Governor's resignation. He stood firm.

I left Río Gallegos in an uneasy stalemate. As a simple observer I felt that the impasse might have been resolved by the dismissal, not of the Governor, but of some of the 1,000-odd political appointees in his inflated bureaucracy. Without the burden of these people on the payroll, he might have been able to spare a little more for the teachers; but I suppose some things are too much to ask for, however desperate you are.

A hundred and fifty miles from this confrontation, I found the old provincial capital, Port Santa Cruz, semi-comatose. A breeze rustled the few remaining leaves on the beech trees lining Avenida San Martín. The town's 3,000 inhabitants were nowhere to be seen.

When the *Beagle* landed here during her second voyage in 1834, Captain Fitzroy set out with a party of 24, including the young Charles Darwin, to explore the hinterland. For eighteen days they hauled their heavy whaleboats against the current of the Santa Cruz River, until 140 miles from the coast they rounded a bluff and saw, glistening on the western horizon, the Andes. What Darwin would have given to have climbed their foothills, observed their animals and examined their plants! But the party had already been for some days on half-rations, and their supplies were all but gone. That night he wrote in his journal, 'A light stomach and an easy digestion are good things to talk about, but very unpleasant in practice.' So they launched their boats into the stream, and so strong was the flow that within three days they found themselves back on the coast. Had they continued for just another 30 miles, they'd have been the first Europeans to set eyes on Lake Argentino.

I put my head inside a shop and asked for the house of Doña Eliza Lewis, the town's oldest resident. Born in Newfoundland in 1900, Eliza had come to Santa Cruz at the outbreak of the Great War. She married a Falklander, but he died in the 1920s and it was left to her – and later her sons – to run the family farm. In those days of horse transport communication was a real problem; neighbouring farmers would help out in an emergency, but longer trips, for example to visit the doctor, might take days or even weeks. Santa Cruz had only one motor vehicle – an Oldsmobile taxi – and even that had been shipped in by sea, there being no road from Buenos Aires until well into the 1930s.

After her marriage Eliza never left the province. 'When my husband died, people used to ask me, 'Why don't you go back to Newfoundland?' Well, maybe I could have paid a visit – but I'd always have returned to Patagonia. It's only natural, you know; it's my home.' Looked at objectively, her adopted country had deteriorated by almost any standard she cared to choose. The journalist Jimmy Burns commented in 1987 that it had few rivals as an example of collective social and political trauma. But Eliza had no complaints. 'I've got some land – sufficient to keep going, you know – and they can't take it away from me because the deeds were signed by Perón!'

At 90 years of age, she now lived in a prefabricated bungalow a few yards from the church. Her sons ran the farm and kept her larder filled. Stone deaf but still spry, she poured me cup after cup of strong milky tea. 'What a pity you didn't warn me you were coming,' she mused. 'I could have baked a cake.'

When evening came Eliza passed me on to Jack and Jean Halliday, a brother and sister only slightly less aged than herself, who ran a grocery business in a pink-painted shanty surrounded by waste ground. 'Seventy years old, this cottage is,' Jean told me in a sing-song Dumfriesshire accent. 'And when the wind blows from the west, I tell you it blows right through!'

The shop stayed open day and night. Customers arrived in a steady stream: old Adolfo Alvear for his special spiced sausage; Doña Julia for her daily bottle of Termidor wine; and the kids to buy sweets (or to steal them when Jean's back was turned).

Portraits of stern-looking parents hung high on the chipped blue walls, father John in his cravat and mother Catherine in crinoline and furs. 'We were a handsome family, don't you think?' laughed Jean, rocking gently in her chair as if such things weren't important any more. Jack nodded in agreement. His face still bore the strong jawline of the figures in the paintings, but his tattered clothes suggested that he, like his sister, had long since given up worrying about appearances. In his youth he'd been a maverick, well known for his horsemanship, business deals and accordion playing. But those days had passed, for as he gossiped with his customers I could hardly have imagined a more innocuous-looking man.

I slept in an alcove, and next day Jean took me to see Maurice Lewis (no relation, apparently, to Eliza) in his cottage by the sea. Shafts of sunlight fell on postcards of Moffat and the Tweedsmuir Hills. The house smelt of seaweed. Maurice stared out from his armchair across the estuary, rocking a little, his trim white beard nodding as he recalled 80 years of estancia life. For a second-generation Argentine he seemed almost too English to be true. A Beckenham and Windsor public schooling had endowed him with an old-fashioned southern counties accent, which he peppered unconsciously with Spanish words like 'bueno', 'claro' and 'tampoco'. I had the feeling that if I listened too long I'd forget which language was which.

After graduating from the Imperial Service College, he started his sheepfarming career in the unlikely setting of Bradford. The textile firm Dawson & Co. wanted a wool classer. What better way, his father argued, to learn about the wool trade? Maurice was appalled at the prospect; but he wasn't the rebellious sort, and by all accounts became a hardworking apprentice, spending much of the 1920s with Dawson's before returning to his father's Santa Cruz farm. After the damp, smog-choked Pennines, Patagonia must have seemed like paradise.

The Second World War came, and though now settled back in Argentina he followed the example of other young British expatriates and joined the Navy. His service took place mostly in the South Atlantic and Antarctica, and in 1945 he had the good luck to be demobilized in the Falklands, where he stayed for eight years before returning to the mainland and his father's farm.

'You should have seen the sheep drives in those days,' he told me. 'There were no lorries, so animals would be taken to the slaughterhouse on the hoof. Those coming from up in the Andes might take as long as two months, with half a dozen peons driving 1,000 sheep. Boy, could they raise some dust!'

Maurice's grandfather, a carpenter by the name of James Lewis, had left Bristol in 1869 to help Thomas Bridges in his evangelical work with the Fuegian Indians. His second son, Maurice's father, had been the subject of Tierra del Fuego's first-ever baptism, and in honour of this he bore the unfortunate name Frank Ooshooia. When the place of his baptism became more commonly known as Ushuaia, the boy sensibly followed suit. Frank Ushuaia Lewis rose to become mayor of Santa Cruz, and had a plaque erected and a street named after him. Maurice pointed these out to me from behind the wheel of his Ford Falcon, which he still drove, though both he and the car were quite unroadworthy.

'Have you met the Kemps yet?' he asked suddenly. 'Oh, you must meet the Kemps! Come on, I'll take you over.'

But Jean Halliday had been there before us: the Kemps were expecting me, and the table was set with a Scottish high tea. Mary and her 80-year-old mother Phillis lived together in a big Edwardian house, where Mary spent her days as a seamstress and her nights reading aloud from the Bible. Phillis, a cousin of the Hallidays, sat across the table in a rocking chair, making theological observations as her daughter sewed. 'Jesus will show you the way, my dear.' At each comment Mary would look up from her work and nod vigorously towards her mother's piercing china-blue eyes. 'Praise the Lord!' Both mother and daughter were evangelists – 'but not practising, you understand,' they told me firmly. 'Not like the Jehovah's Witnesses. Oh no, we'd never go from door to door.'

Although they lived in the middle of town, Mary and Phillis were so frugal and proud that during the bad winter of 1984 they'd nearly died of hypothermia rather than seek help. They believed the Gospel in its literal sense, and were now waiting for Armageddon as predicted in the Book of Revelation. 'The Son of Man will return, and the sinners of this shameful world will be cast to the Devil!' cried Phillis, her gaze directed pointedly at me. 'Glory be to God!'

Wandering the streets of Santa Cruz, I got the impression that it had always been a home to stubborn old ladies. On Avenida

Roca a statue of a stern-faced octogenarian, carrying what looked like a tablecloth, was dedicated 'TO DOÑA MARGARITA MANSILLA VDA. DE CLEMENTE, AND IN TRIBUTE TO ALL THE MOTHERS OF HER DAY'. These were no doubt the same energetic women who for 50 years had staffed the crumbling hospital on the seafront. Its roof bore a bold red cross, painted hurriedly in 1982 in the hope that it would somehow fend off British bombing raids which, in the event, never came.

Back at the grocery shop, Jean Halliday pressed a package into my hand. 'Some bread and cheese for the track,' she said. I was grateful for her thoughtfulness, because 100 miles of desert separated Santa Cruz from the nearest settlement in any direction. Continuing north, the next town up the coast was San Julián, Patagonia's most ancient port, where in 1520 Magellan had spotted the dancing Tehuelche giant and made his legendary declaration '*Ha, Patagón!*'

San Julián offers one of the few sheltered inlets on the whole Atlantic coast, and from Magellan's time onwards ships called in regularly for refitting or to shelter from storms. The South Atlantic tempests were legendary. For a whole month before taking refuge at San Julián, Magellan's fleet had battled against violent seas, making hardly any progress in their journey south. A ship's boat hit rocks, and one of the fleet nearly met the same fate itself. Eric Shipton, in *Tierra del Fuego: the Fatal Lodestone*, sums up for the twentieth-century reader what Magellan and his crew must have been feeling:

It is difficult nowadays even dimly to appreciate the courage demanded of these early explorers. The ever imminent destruction of their clumsy, fragile ships may perhaps be equated with that of the merchant convoys in the last war, the calculated risks with those of the astronauts; we may shudder at the months of exposure to cold and wet, or stand aghast at the hideous privation they had to endure; but, for the combination of all these factors, wrapped in the immensity, the terrifying immensity, of the unknown, for this we have no modern yardstick. Supposing it existed, this strait they sought; supposing against long odds they survived its passage; what terrors awaited them beyond? Pack-ice more dense than that of the Greenland coast? Storms more savage, doldrums more lifeless than any in the known world? What new land-mass might bar their way; why should they expect to be able to sail northward again to escape from this awful wilderness? Moreover, though the astronomers amongst them might have good reason to suppose that by sailing westward they would eventually return to the east, it had yet to be proved, and the large majority had to take this preposterous belief on trust.

Francis Drake, too, was dogged by gales when he reached the South Atlantic 58 years later, and like Magellan he spent the winter at San Julián. As we've seen, both Magellan and Drake executed crew members during their forced sojourns there: in Magellan's case to snuff out a pre-planned mutiny, in Drake's for the simple crime of wanting to go home.

Gibbet Point, where the executions took place, can be reached by rowing boat from the shingly seafront. And to be honest there isn't much else to do in San Julián, because in the best part of five centuries since Magellan dropped anchor there, nothing much seems to have happened. The main street – another San Martín – now has perhaps 20 blocks where until this century there were two; but walk 100 yards down any of the side-streets, and you'll find yourself in the desert once more.

It may have been for want of diversions that Donald Cameron, the 'Gringo Gaucho', fathered his seven children; for the family of this most famous of San Julián's citizens was a sizeable one, even by Patagonian standards. Born in 1877 near Inverness, he sailed while still a young boy to the Falklands, and at the age of fourteen continued by one of the new steamship services to Patagonia. There was plenty of work for a willing lad, and he soon found a job as a farmhand. But he didn't keep it long – there was too much of Patagonia to see – and it was only after marrying that he finally settled in San Julián. Donald Cameron was one of the few Britishers ever to 'go native' in Patagonia, and was never seen without his gaucho's outfit of accordion boots, *bombacha* trousers, baggy shirt, neckerchief and slouch hat. The townsfolk used to joke that he'd been born wearing them. But though his memories of Scotland grew dim with the years, he never quite forgot his roots, and from time to time could be found playing poker and reminiscing in the neatly whitewashed British Club overlooking the bay.

Cameron's story was related to me in a maisonette on the edge of San Julián by a son who was himself well into his seventies.

Like Santa Cruz the town seemed full of British pensioners. There was Lidia who devoted a whole day to driving me round and answering questions; Lionel who showed me the dried-up lake beds; Olive and Mary who fed me mountainous high teas; and Bessie and May, both well into their nineties, whose cottage had an outside lavatory, no running water, and a battle-scarred bust of Winston Churchill scowling from above the cast-iron stove. I could have spent weeks listening to stories from Model T days, but I still had a long way to go, and eventually bade farewell to the old-timers and set off north once more.

I was helped on my way by a couple in one of Argentina's ubiquitous Ford Falcons – a slightly more modern version of the Model T. José Antonio and Ethel had been visiting Punta Arenas on a buying spree. 'When we saw you, we thought you wouldn't want to squeeze in with all the boxes,' they told me. 'Then we saw your face; it was a picture of pleading.'

I settled down among the boxes and decided I must cultivate that look.

The lift was a long one, and while José Antonio drove, Ethel settled into conversation. A raw-boned sprig of a woman, she looked too young to have a nearly grown-up daughter as she claimed. But long hours spent teaching in a school for the disabled were beginning to haunt her eyes. In another 20 years, I thought, a matronly cynicism would overtake her. For the time being, however, she spent her spare moments strolling with José Antonio on the Atlantic beaches and across the pampa, picking up Tehuelche artefacts. I showed her some arrowheads I'd found, and she pointed immediately to a small one. 'This is real; do you see the marks where it's been worked?' She threw the rest aside. 'Those are just rubbish.'

The road carried us north, with not so much as a bend, for mile after mile across the flat plain. 'So what's an Englishman doing in Patagonia?' asked José Antonio.

I explained that I'd had a romantic vision of Patagonia, and had come to see if I was right.

'Of course you're right,' cried Ethel, thumping the dashboard. 'Patagonia's the most romantic place in the world!'

'Why's that?'

'Because of the people it's attracted over the years. Just look at us: runaways, dreamers – hopeless romantics, every one! Our immigrants left their homes and countries to throw their fate to the wind, and now their grandchildren are doing the same. If a Patagonian has a choice, you see, he'll always go for the unknown. He hates security, stability. He'll do everything he can to escape from it, to get out into the desert – even this useless desert of scrubby bushes and dried-up lake beds.' She thought for a moment. '*Especially* this useless desert.' She encompassed the horizon with a grand gesture. 'Some of our visitors complain that it's not just useless, but ugly too; but a Patagonian wouldn't worry about that. He accepts it for what it is – empty and barren – and you'll often find him living on some sheepfarm or cultivating his cabbages in the middle of nowhere. I grew up in the cordillera near Lake Viedma, so I'm a Patagonian, and I love Patagonia through and through. I dream that one day we'll claim our independence. Imagine – a Republic of Patagonia. Now wouldn't that be fine!'

Ethel and José Antonio insisted that I call in to meet their daughter, who'd prepared a special tea. She was seventeen, and wanted to be, of all things, an aeronautical engineer. Like many young Argentines she saw her future abroad, and was hoping to spend a year as an exchange student in Oklahoma – a state in which, I reflected, a Patagonian might feel quite at home.

I passed through Caleta Olivia, a seaside oil town whose approach was marked by rubbish piled alongside the road and the now familiar rotting plastic hanging from the bushes. A statue of an oilman towered over the central roundabout. There was something Soviet about the monument, and indeed about Caleta Olivia generally. The hulks of rotting concrete which passed for buildings, the open spaces which were yellow where they should have been green, and the sullen faces moving silently from block to block, conspired to make me feel small and sad. I walked north and tried to hitch a lift towards Comodoro Rivadavia, but the traffic sped past without so much as a wave. Darkness was falling, so after putting what I judged to be a safe distance between myself and the town I turned away from the road and pitched my tent in a hollow. It was like camping in a rubbish pit; and perhaps it was indeed a rubbish pit, for in the middle of the night a pack of scavenging dogs set up a vigil by my tentflaps and barked at me till dawn.

Comodoro Rivadavia, Patagonia's largest city, looked like a

bigger version of Caleta Olivia, and on first inspection seemed even more oppressive. Most of its 150,000 inhabitants lived in peeling tower blocks, some with belligerent names like 'Malvinas Argentinas', clinging to a crumbling bluff. But after an hour spent walking the steep streets I noticed a curious thing about the place: its inhabitants smiled. Maybe this was because at last, on my journey northwards, I was coming into a more gentle climate. The square even boasted a couple of palm trees – surely the most southerly in the world. Or perhaps the reason was that in all Patagonia this was the only town left whose people were still earning a decent wage. It was near Comodoro Rivadavia on 13th December 1907 that Patagonia's first oil was discovered; and the citizens are so thankful for that event that today, more than 80 years later, they still celebrate the anniversary with a public holiday.

I continued for 100 miles with Antolín, an unhappy man suffering from gripe. For the whole three-hour journey he wore an enormous pair of sun-goggles, with mirrored lenses bulging out of their frames. Trying to read his expression was impossible; it was like talking to a bluebottle. He left me in the middle of nowhere, but a travelling car mechanic called Vivian Jones took pity on me. Soon he was recounting lewd stories in Welsh as we bounced in his Citroën 2CV towards Trelew, and the valley which David Lloyd George called 'Little Wales across the Sea'.

Tea with the Welsh

The city of Trelew, christened 100 years ago after a Welshman by the name of Lewis Jones, has lost much of its Welsh charm over the years. In front of the old railway station – closed in 1961 – my eye was drawn to a granite obelisk standing incongruously by a palm tree. The inscription read 'CANMLWYDDIANT Y WLADFA GYMREIG YN PATAGONIA' – 'In memory of the arrival of the Welsh in Patagonia'. Today the monument is overshadowed by a much larger one to the soldiers who fell defending the Falklands in 1982.

Patagonia's Welsh colony served two purposes. For the Welsh,

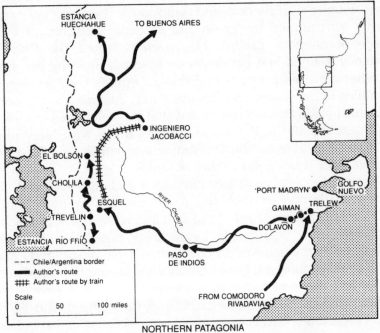

NORTHERN PATAGONIA

169

it was an opportunity to re-establish their religion, language and culture in a land not yet contaminated by the English. For the Argentines it was a means of confirming their sovereignty over a territory which, in the 1860s, was already in dispute with Chile. For some years the Argentine Government had been trying to attract what it called 'hardworking' immigrants from northern Europe. Large numbers had settled in and around Buenos Aires and the towns of the Pampas; but none had so far ventured south.

The idea of setting up a transatlantic Welsh colony, beyond the reach of their oppressive neighbours and landlords, was first put forward by Lewis Jones with the help of a Bala priest named Michael Jones. Initially they favoured the United States, but it soon became clear that a colony there would be surrounded by the hated English. At this point someone drew their attention to Captain Fitzroy's account of the voyage of the *Beagle*. Fitzroy had mentioned seeing driftwood and wild cattle in the lower Chubut Valley; this, they decided, could only mean trees and pasture.

The two Joneses lost no time in drumming up enthusiasm. A 'Colonizing Society' was set up, and its first act was to publish a handbook explaining in simple language what Patagonia had to offer. Fitzroy's driftwood and wild cattle became 'tall strong forests' surrounded by 'green and splendid pastures' in which 'herds of animals' grazed. His warning about the Chubut's tendency to flood was conveniently ignored. Splitting the difference between temperature and rainfall figures for Port Famine, 700 miles to the south, and Buenos Aires, 700 miles to the north, the handbook's authors concluded that the valley had one of the healthiest climates in the world. Temperatures were 'very pleasant and adaptable to the Welshman's constitution', they said. Rainfall, too, was similar to that of Wales.

The handbook was widely circulated and well received. The Society made contact with the Argentine Government, and in 1862 agreed that someone should go and have a look at the land they were intending to settle. Lewis Jones, together with another enthusiast by the name of Sir Love Jones-Parry, accordingly made a tour of inspection. Sir Love was shocked to find that the Chubut Valley had more in common with the Sahara than with Wales, and he advised the greatest caution in the venture. But by this time Lewis Jones had become quite obsessed. He embarked on a lecture tour, raising funds and rallying support. 'Wheat has been sown,' he announced emphatically to an audience in Aberystwyth, 'one crop yielding 45 times the amount sown.'

The lectures made a great impact on the increasingly dissatisfied Welsh. Those who didn't attend personally read the reports in the *Welsh Banner and Times*. Each settler, they learned, would be given 300 acres of lush pasture, together with five horses, ten cows, twenty sheep, some fruit trees, two or three pecks of wheat and a plough. Over the next couple of years interest continued to grow, and early in 1865 a small tea-clipper, the *Mimosa*, was chartered to take the first of the prospective colonists to their new homeland.

The Buenos Aires government was delighted that the Welsh had chosen Patagonia. Despite Chile's acceptance since 1856 of the principle that land east of the Andes could be regarded as Argentine, the legal basis of such sovereignty was shaky, to say the least. Government lawyers argued that recognizing the Welsh colony would put the claim on a sounder footing. Spurred on both by the Welsh and by his own superiors, Interior Minister William Rawson quickly pushed forward a plan to populate the region with 3,000 to 5,000 Welsh families within ten years. Each 200 families would be granted five leagues of land – about 50 square miles. Rates and taxes would be waived; and when the population reached 20,000 the area would be made a province. As an additional inducement the first group of settlers were to be presented with 3,000 sheep, 200 horses and 50 cattle, together with artillery to defend themselves against the Indians.

On 24th May 1865 the *Mimosa* left Liverpool with 163 men, women and children on board. They had names like Griffith Huws, Zecaria Jones and Thomas Davydd, and came from towns such as Bangor, Merthyr Tydfil and Mountain Ash. Most of them were poor folk – miners, craftsmen and farm labourers – and had sold everything to raise their passage. Some had already left their birthplaces in the hope of finding a better life; none had yet succeeded. Indeed, two of the *Mimosa's* passengers seem to have already tried their luck overseas, for the passenger list included a Mr Edwin C. Roberts from Wisconsin and a Mrs Rhys Williams from Brazil.

To understand what drove such people to leave their homes for an uncertain future on the other side of the world, it's important to appreciate what it was like to be Welsh in the 1860s. The Agricultural and Industrial Revolutions had, by and large, not done much for the ordinary Welsh. Thousands of families were at the mercy of English landlords, who by the simple threat of eviction could control their worshipping, their voting habits, even their language. The idea of a persecuted people seeking freedom in an unknown land already had a ring of familiarity across the water in Ireland. Over the next 80 years it would be heard throughout Europe, as the continent's disillusioned uprooted themselves to head west.

So what were they thinking, those 163, as the *Mimosa* cleared the Crosby Channel and headed out into the Irish Sea? A Bala man, Abraham Matthews, watched the Anglesey hills disappear over the horizon and fingered nervously at the ticket in his waistcoat pocket. I found the ticket, yellowing and creased, in the museum at Trelew:

CAMBRIAN EMIGRATION OFFICE, 41 UNION STREET, LIVERPOOL. PASSEN-GERS' CONTRACT TICKET. Ship: Mimosa, of 450 tons register, to take in Passengers at Liverpool for New Bay* on the fifteenth day of May 1865.

I engage that the Persons named in the margin hereof shall be provided with a Steerage Passage to, and shall be landed at the Port of New Bay in South America, in the ship Mimosa with not less than 10 cubic feet for luggage for each statute adult, and shall be victualled during the voyage and the time of detention at any place before its termination, according to the subjoined scale, for the sum of £48 including Government Dues before Embarkation, and Head Money, if any, at the Place of Landing, and every other charge, except freight for excess of luggage beyond the quantity above specified, and I hereby acknowledge to have received the sum of £48 in full payment.

The following quantities at least, of Water and Provisions (to be issued daily) will be supplied by the Master of the Ship as required by Law; viz. – to each Statute Adult, 3 quarts water daily, exclusive of what is necessary for cooking the articles required by the Passengers Act; to be issued in a cooked state, and a weekly allowance of provisions, according to the following scale; – 3½ lbs. Bread or Biscuit, not inferior in quality to Navy Biscuit, 11 lb. Wheaten Flour, 1½ lb. Rice, 1½ lb. Peas, 2 lbs. potatoes, 1¼ lb. Beef, 1 lb. Pork, 2 oz. Tea,

* Bahía Nueva, shown on modern maps as Golfo Nuevo.

1 lb. Sugar, ½ oz. Mustard, ¼ oz. black or white ground Pepper, 2 oz. Salt, 1 gill Vinegar.

    N.B. – Mess Utensils and Bedding to be provided by the Passengers.

Signed, James Lamb, On behalf of JAMES LAMB, of Liverpool.

                – LIVERPOOL, fifteenth day of May 1865.

The start was not auspicious. The *Mimosa* was smaller than the vessel originally promised, and some of the passengers had to be accommodated in makeshift shelters on deck. During a long delay in Liverpool, many of them had spent the last of their money, and had to sign IOUs for the balance of their £12 fares. As the days at sea became weeks, they warded off seasickness and boredom by singing John Wesley's sombre hymns to the swelling accompaniment of a harmonium.

When the *Mimosa* reached its destination on 28th July 1865, the colonists saw that Patagonia wasn't quite the green and pleasant land promised in the handbook. Its brown sandy loam supported plenty of thorn bushes, but of the promised trees and pastures there was no sign. Some of those on board must have been tempted to return with the *Mimosa* to Wales, but to their great credit none did, and the clipper sailed discreetly out of the bay, her decks and holds quite empty.

The first fortnight was a nightmare. Many of the settlers didn't even have tents, and to shelter from the winter gales they dug crude caves in the toscanite along the shore. Dafydd Williams of Aberystwyth lost his way whilst looking for water, and a search party came back empty-handed. His skeleton was found years later, not five miles away. A fifteen-month girl and an eighteen-month boy perished in their mothers' arms.

August came, and an expedition was raised to look for the Chubut River and the pebble spit which Lewis Jones had ear-marked for their permanent home. Without compasses or even the most basic direction-finding skills, they had the utmost difficulty finding the place. At one stage some of the party were feared lost, but they returned unharmed, thanks to a pool of muddy but drinkable water they'd stumbled on in a clay depression.

During that first winter of 1865 the colonists worked feverishly, and within two months they were able to inaugurate their first proper settlement, which they christened Rawson to acknowledge the Interior Minister's continuing efforts on their behalf. Later that year the Argentine Government pledged a monthly grant of £145 'until such time as the colony is self-supporting'. This was to prove vital, for the first five years were marked by a string of unmitigated disasters. The first wheat crop failed completely; the second produced enough to feed only six families. Drought alternated with flooding, and it was hard to say which was worse. In desperation, a farmer named Aaron Jenkins proposed a system of irrigation ditches which was ultimately to prove the colony's salvation; but it was to take years of backbreaking work before the benefits showed. Meanwhile in 1868 their supply ship, the *Denby*, sank with all hands while bringing emergency provisions from the north. The Government sent a replacement vessel, but on its maiden voyage this was irreparably damaged in a storm. In 1870 floods again wiped out the harvest, and a new hazard emerged in the form of the previously friendly Tehuelche Indians, who on one occasion stole 65 horses, leaving many of the settlers with no way to plough their fields.

But if the Welsh were short of almost everything else, they never lacked faith, and after seven years of setbacks their luck began to change. In 1873 they found themselves with a small surplus of wheat, which fetched a good price on the Buenos Aires market. The Government, ever mindful of Chilean pretensions, promised the colony yet more support, and in 1875 and 1876 it was swelled by a further 500 migrants from Wales and the United States. This boosted morale considerably, and after some discussion it was agreed that a party should be dispatched to the interior to prospect for a new settlement in the rainy foothills of the Andes.

If the initial voyage had been an act of bravery, this two-month venture was to be an epic. Led by Abraham Matthews' brother-in-law John Murray Thomas, a dozen hand-picked men set off for the cordillera on 21st July 1877. In the Trelew museum I rooted out Thomas's diary. The pencilled scrawl looked uncannily like my own, but his experiences could hardly have been more different:

Monday Aug. 6/77 – Got up before daylight, began our march about 8 am. Travelled until near sundown at a fair pace, made Some 18 miles towards a point SW by S.

Day began unfortunate. Severo lost his Boleadoras, lost nearly an hour looking for them, then the Carguero [saddle-pack] turned, another lost the pick, had to hunt for it and remake the pack. Kettle broken. Handle of pick lost. Pugh lost his handkerchief, piece of tent pole broken. Severo and myself caught an Ostrich 2 hares and a fox, came through a valley some 15 miles in extent. Very poor land, something like the hills near Chupat [Chubut], but more on a level with the river, since this morning the country seems to open, the hills seem to finish to a point, the land within a few squares to the river is very swampy and the whole place in rainy weather must be covered with water. Pugh grumbling because I went to hunt, answered I had Thomas Roberts to do my work, consequently I was at liberty to please myself.

Camped in a very poor place, damp and uncomfortable. Rather awkward without the kettle. . . .

Thomas and his companions returned to Trelew in September 1877, emaciated but alive, and after further expeditions and much hard bargaining the Welsh secured the right to settle on 50 leagues of the cordillera – about 500 square miles – which they affectionately christened Cwm Hyfryd or 'Pleasant Dale'.

Trelew today is an up-and-coming city, its tower blocks rivalling those of Comodoro Rivadavia. The Welsh have long been out-numbered by other nationalities; on the painted shop fascias round the square, Joneses and Thomases barely feature. One night I had supper with a 'Welsh' couple. 'William loves to talk about Wales,' his aunt had told me. But William and his wife spoke only Spanish, and our evening passed without a mention of Wales.

I'd heard that traditions were stronger in the countryside, so one Sunday morning I took a bus through the original 250-acre lots known as chacras. A veil of mist hung over the valley, wrapping itself around the poplars and coating their last remaining leaves with dew. On the back seat of the bus sprawled sleepy-eyed youngsters, their faces drawn and puffy from late-night partying in Trelew. At lonely junctions they got off one by one, dragging their feet past fields of withered sunflowers as they slunk home to face another week of hoeing, clearing ditches, tending beehives and feeding hens. Nothing else stirred; the chacras lay immobilized, waiting for the sun.

The bus dropped me at a crossroads, and I walked for half a

mile between hedges smelling of damp cowparsley. In a field behind some poplars I could make out the dim shape of my destination, St David's Chapel.

In 1878, as Gladstone was lampooning Disraeli at Westminster, a carpenter near Bangor fell from scaffolding and broke his hip. His name was Hugh Davies. To his dismay the wound failed to heal properly, and unable to continue with his carpentry he decided to take up the cloth. It happened that about this time the South American Missionary Society was approaching the peak of its endeavours. Hugh Davies was quickly signed up, and in 1883, at the age of 50, he sailed from Liverpool with his wife and four children. A surviving photograph shows a white-bearded giant of a man, with quiet, determined eyes. Initially his term was to have been five years, but the five became ten, then fifteen, and eventually he stayed in Patagonia for the remaining 26 years of his life.

The Davieses took a chacra in the heart of the valley, and Hugh set about building a modest chapel. The work couldn't have been easy; building materials were scarce, and though the walls could be made of adobe he needed corrugated iron for the roof. It wasn't until 1891 that the family finally stood back to admire the finished job: a shed-like building, quite plain, with six narrow windows and an eight-by-four porch to shelter worshippers from the perpetual wind.

For eighteen years the tiny congregation met every Sunday, until in 1909 a tornado ripped off the roof. Then, a few months later, Hugh died, and without anyone to repair it the chapel gradually fell to pieces. By 1914 it had become a liability, and under the direction of the church authorities a party with pickaxes demolished it in a single day.

A Welsh village without a chapel is like an animal without a heart, and it wasn't long before local farmers were raising money for a replacement. A bricklayer named Edward Lewis and a carpenter named William Williams were contracted to do the work. To symbolize the community's growing confidence the new structure was to be grander than the old, and when completed in 1917 it boasted a campanile with a bell shipped out from Llanllyfni near Caernarfon. After 300 years of ringing across Caernarfon Bay, it now began to peal across the Chubut Valley. The congregation was enthusiastic but still pitifully small; and when in 1947 the parson returned to Wales, no one could be found to replace him. The place sunk into dereliction. Only in 1989, after a long campaign by valley churchgoers, was it restored to use once more.

I arrived to find a small flock waiting by the church door. There was Hopkin Davies, great-grandson of Hugh, himself now over 80 and crippled by arthritis; Gerallt Williams, a quietly-spoken farmer from Bryn Crwn; Lottie and Sarah Williams ('no relation', they said); Eileen Insley from Trelew; and Isidora ApIwan, Hopkin's wife, with her sad watery eyes. As the sun broke through the clouds, the little group chatted softly in Welsh – not one of them under 50. Then Hopkin's daughter ushered us all inside, steering her father tenderly to his pew. 'He's completely blind, you know,' she whispered in my ear.

There was still no resident parson, so this morning the service was taken by one who'd come down from Bahía Blanca on the overnight bus. His name was Horacio García, and to the disappointment of the congregation he spoke no Welsh. Against a wall stood a harmonium, but no one was feeling well-practised so the hymns were sung unaccompanied. Gerallt led with his fine baritone voice, and the others followed where they could. The wind rattled the windows and howled round the campanile as the sun, having finally banished the morning mist, cast long yellow rays on William Williams' pitchpine woodwork.

Back in Trelew, on the last fine day of autumn, I called on one of the valley's more unusual couples. Nelia Humphreys, a generous, hardworking woman directly descended from one of the *Mimosa*'s passengers, was with her Algerian husband Aïssa Menina, locking up for the weekend at their bookshop on Calle Lewis Jones.

'Come out to our chacra,' she suggested. 'It's just the day for a barbecue.'

The place was on the banks of the Chubut, sheltered by golden poplars and an old cypress. A breeze swirled leaves in circles as the Chubut slid silently past. Nelia soon had mutton chops and black pudding grilling over a log fire, and as we sprawled in a circle waiting for them I asked Aïssa, a wiry 40-year-old, how an Algerian came to be living in Patagonia.

'Well, I only came here after trying everywhere else,' he

grinned, sipping maté from a gourd. 'I'd worked my way through Morocco, Europe, the Middle East – even India. I navvied on building sites from Switzerland to Iraq. Got kicked out of Libya; then landed in Rio and took a passage up the Amazon to Manaus. A man there offered me a lift to the Guianas, but his price was too high, so I came south. In all those countries I just worked to survive, but here in Argentina I found to my surprise that I could work and save. How? Because the Argentines hate work! They detest it; that's why the country's bankrupt. And that's why anyone who puts in any effort at all can make a killing.'

He turned the meat on the fire, refilled his maté gourd, and continued in a mixture of Spanish and his native French.

'Do you know that Argentina's one of the few countries in the world where you can arrive without a penny and in ten years be living like a prince? How? I'll tell you. First – inflation. This has been going on for as long as anyone can remember: 100 percent in a good year, 1,000 in a bad. To use inflation to your advantage you must invest your earnings in property. Land, buildings – anything that'll hold its value. This is precisely what Argentines don't do. Give them a million australes* and they'll spend a million and a half. Spend, spend, spend – it's the inflation mentality. They also spend, I'm afraid, because they're crazy about appearances; they can't resist a flashy car or a smart dress.

'Second, you've got to work. You don't have to kill yourself: just put in a decent day's grind. There are 97,000 acres in this valley – all irrigated – and do you know how many of them are properly farmed? Just half. The rest are more or less abandoned because their owners can't be bothered to till the fields. A few years back some Bolivians arrived and rented a few chacras, and what happened? They cleaned up! Potatoes, squashes and alfalfa began sprouting as if there were no tomorrow. And the fruit! You should have seen the fruit. Those peasants from goodness-knows-where on the altiplano sweated from dawn till dusk – but now for their pains they've got tractors, a smart house and a shiny new pickup. The Argentines hate them, of course; accuse them of all kinds of things. But those bumpkins saw an opening and grabbed it. I go past their place sometimes, and there are

* The currency at the time. When Aïssa was speaking, there were about 9,000 australes to the pound.

always one or two locals watching from the road, eyes popping out of their heads. Me, I keep my head down, but sometimes I have to laugh. These people here – what a bunch they are!'

We gnawed at the mutton chops, wiping greasy chins on our shirtsleeves and tossing the bones to an Alsatian dog. Mutton! After six months in Patagonia, how I hated it. Barbecued, it was almost impossible to digest, being burnt on the outside while still raw in the middle. I envied the constitutions of travellers like Tschiffely, who wrote:

Mutton . . . the only meat eaten throughout Patagonia . . . is of such excellent quality that I never tired of it; in fact, cooks often cut and prepared it in such a manner that I thought it was beef I was eating. Sheep are so abundant that ranchers do not care how much meat the men consume. In many cases it is amazing what *peones* can eat, and I could not help wondering where they put it all. For instance, on one ranch in Tierra del Fuego, I watched an Indian eat his breakfast. First of all he had a big bowl of coffee, next he tucked away a quantity of porridge which would have kept me going for three days, and then he was ready to start his meal in earnest. It consisted of a loaf of bread and seventeen mutton chops, all of which he put under his belt with the greatest of ease, washing the lot down with another bowl of coffee.

What I would have given for some *charquicán*, the delicately flavoured beef – sun-dried, roasted, ground to powder and mixed with ox-fat and chilli – which sustained San Martín's army in 1817 as it crossed the Andes to liberate Chile. Or the Christmas menu enjoyed by the gentlemen explorers of Hesketh Prichard's *Daily Express* expedition, during an age when sponsorship meant sponsorship:

LAGO BUENOS AIRES, 1900. CHRISTMAS DAY.

At 5 o'clock P.M.

NOTICE. – *Come early to get a good helping.*

MENU.

Common or Garden Duff à la Azulejo. Condiment au lait Suisse.

GRAND DUFF à la H. Jones avec muscatelles.

Bœuf.

Ostrich à la Patagonie.
(If you want it.)

Gigot de Guanaco.
(Order beforehand.)

Cocao au lait ⎱
Thé au lait   ⎰ Suisse.

Vieux Cognac avec vulcanite.

Plug Tobacco.

GOD SAVE THE QUEEN.

Suddenly Aïssa leaped up. 'And now I must work!' Minutes later he was out in the fields, clearing vegetation and turning the soil for all he was worth. This was certainly not just a man of words. In eight years, since arriving in Trelew with a dollar in his pocket, he'd got the chacra back on its feet and helped Nelia create a thriving bookshop. In 1984 he and Nelia were married. The locals' eyes must once again have been popping out of their heads.

Beneath the bulging panelled ceiling and slowly revolving fans of Trelew's Touring Club tearoom, I waited to keep an appointment with a Chubut woman who, for once, was neither English nor Welsh. After the service at St David's, Gerallt Williams had asked me to get in touch with his daughter-in-law, Irith Dorfman. 'You'll find her interesting,' he said.

On shelves behind the bar were ranged a hundred spirit bottles. Some clearly hadn't been opened in years. Their murky contents lurked poisonously behind mould-covered glass, waiting for the day when an innocent traveller might point across the bar and order a shot. Above this collection a clock counted the seconds with loud, measured ticks which echoed from wall to wall. Otherwise the tearoom was silent; the only other customers at this mid-morning hour were three old gauchos playing poker, and an anaemic-looking man seated at a corner table, dressed in a ragged suit and grumbling to himself as he read a week-old copy of *La Nación*.

Without warning Irith appeared by my side, a slight figure in dark glasses and mock fur coat.

180

'I'm here,' she said simply.

A stooping waiter in a frayed white jacket brought us coffee. For the first few minutes we talked about the Patagonians, about the people of Buenos Aires, and about how incomprehensible each finds the other. Then Irith suddenly threw me a glance. 'Do you believe in other civilizations?' she asked.

'Yes, of course.'

'No, I mean people not of this world. Beings who come perhaps from deep underground?'

I thought of Lucas Bridges' Ona Indians, and their belief that certain rocks and mountains harboured creatures of superhuman intellect and strength. 'Yes,' I said slowly. 'I do think there may be other intelligent beings besides human ones.'

Irith shot me another significant look. 'There certainly are. I know because I've met some of them. Actually I'm in touch with them quite often.'

I examined her face for a sign that she was joking, but found none.

'I meet them in my sleep,' she continued. 'Sometimes I have quite normal dreams – you know, the sort in which you go over what you've done today or what you'll do tomorrow. But many nights I dream that I'm flying, and on my flights I speak in strange languages with individuals who often don't have a physical presence at all. Sometimes they come from above, sometimes from below. They tell me the future.'

'Are they right?' I asked.

'Always.' She sipped her coffee, watching me intently. 'They've predicted many things in my life. I don't think they've ever been wrong.'

'What about more general things?' I asked. 'For instance, have they said anything about the future of Patagonia?'

'Ah, Patagonia!' she sighed. 'Yes, we do talk about Patagonia now and then. They think Patagonia has missed her chance. Her towns are spreading over the desert; factories are going up, producing things we don't need, put together by rookies from Mendoza or Tucumán. Meanwhile Patagonia's own people – the shepherds and cattlemen – are moving out because the farming corporations have ruined the land.' She examined her fingernails as if embarrassed. 'My friends tell me that Patagonia won't last. She has – how do you say? – had it.'

I thought again of the Ona Indians. Like Irith, they communicated with spirits and laid great store on what they were told. Lucas Bridges had dismissed their beliefs as superstitions, and it would have been easy to do the same with Irith's. But as she talked, I knew she wasn't pouring forth some kind of received dogma or holy grail; she was simply telling me her dreams. A cynic might have called them the product of an overactive imagination. But to Irith her excursions into the supernatural were real enough, and again I was reminded of the Ona and their legends.

If Irith's premonitions were correct, Patagonia in 100 years' time would be South America's Gobi Desert. She was by no means the first to predict this. More than ten years earlier, I'd read an article in the *Buenos Aires Herald* which concluded: 'Patagonia is dead, not dying. . . . Today we have a modern town with paved streets, mercury lights, speciality shops, *boîtes* and flood-lit plazas with expensive statues of our country's saviour. . . . Today we have 25 times as much government as we had 25 years ago, but everything else has dwindled to nothing, and Patagonia is dead.'

I'd met dozens of well-informed men and women who were predicting, if not Patagonia's actual demise, then an economic and physical decline unparalleled in her history. Economically she was far too dependent on meat and wool, and at the mercy of shifts in world markets. Physically her soil and vegetation simply weren't robust enough to withstand the vicissitudes of climate – a fatal weakness, brought dramatically into the open by the current drought.

From what I'd seen, I couldn't avoid the conclusion that Irith might well be right.

The Chubut Valley's commercial centre may be Trelew, but the nucleus of Welsh culture lies eleven miles upstream at the brick-built village of Gaiman. Here it is that the annual Eisteddfod is held, attracting Welsh singers and musicians from all over the world; and here, I'd been assured, I would find shelter and nourishment in teashops called Plas y Coed and Ti Gwyn. I arrived to find them both closed, but Euryn and Mair Owen called to me from their little pink-washed house overlooking the town. 'Come in, you poor boy, and have a cup of tea.'

The couple, who looked well into their eighties, ushered me into a small parlour where I sat on a sofa amid a scene straight from a Glamorgan miner's house. The room was crammed with dark-stained furniture of a bygone age. On the walls, ornamental plates sprouted like fungi; and a tiled mantelpiece carried snapshots of grandchildren propped up against postcards from Cardiff. In pride of place stood the harmonium, a beautiful model made in Boston, Massachusetts.

Euryn and Mair were a little hard of hearing, so our conversation took place at high volume. Like most of the valley's elders, they spoke Welsh with some Spanish but no English. Euryn's father had come out from Anglesey in 1880; Mair's people hailed from Capel Curig. She knew little of her ancestry, but pointed proudly to a photograph of Capel Curig in a Welsh Tourist Board guide which she kept by the radio. '*Es muy húmido,*' she told me. 'It's very wet.'

Neither Euryn nor Mair could play their harmonium, but Mair kept it well oiled and polished, and by way of compensation they took a walk every Sunday to the Old Bethel chapel across the river. 'We love the old hymns,' smiled Euryn indulgently. 'It's such a pity the youngsters don't learn them any more.'

I asked if either of them had been to Wales.

'Oh no, we could never have done that,' they replied in unison. 'Why, we wouldn't have known a soul!'

A few miles beyond Gaiman was Gerallt Williams' chacra. During our hymn-singing at St David's he'd invited me to pay a visit, and I wanted to take up his offer because this farm, Bod Iwan, was where Bruce Chatwin had spent Christmas 1974.

A Baptist missionary called Mair Davies drove me out from Gaiman. We pulled up in the yard and knocked on the door of the kitchen, where Gerallt was bottling jam. Like other Patagonians, Gerallt and his family had provided Chatwin with a rich source of inspiration for the characters who eventually found their way into *In Patagonia*. But whereas most of them kept their true names in the book, when it came to the Welsh it seems that Chatwin decided to play a few games. Sometimes he kept their forenames but changed the surname; once or twice he did the opposite; but mostly he altered both. Working out who was who provided me with several days' entertainment.

Bod Iwan had seen some changes since Chatwin's visit. Gerallt's mother Gwen Morgan, whom Chatwin called 'old Mrs Davies', had died in 1979, and in 1986 his wife Mariana Isabel had passed on too. On Mariana's death Gerallt and his brother Edmund had moved from the big family house to a mudbrick cottage which, though basic, was more manageable. Its bare floors and walls seemed to suit them. They went about their household chores slowly, deliberately, Gerallt humming hymns to himself and Edmund working silently, eyelids drooping heavily over his vacant brown eyes. Even at mealtimes they hardly seemed to speak, passing mutton and potatoes across the table with no more than a grunt here and a 'More?' there.

At first I thought Gerallt must be a very pious man. When I met him in the pews at St David's, he'd already been to one chapel service that day, and I was to find myself singing alongside him again the same evening at a place called Bethesda. But now, as he washed the dishes and lilted his way through Wesley's hymns, I realized that he really only attended for the singing. I warmed to him when he pointed to his forehead and confided, 'Last Sunday I was preached at up to here.'

Across the yard was the old house where Chatwin had stayed. It had been in the family since 1915, before either Gerallt or Edmund were born. When their mother died the brothers couldn't face sorting out her belongings, so they simply shut down the house as it stood.

Seeing my curiosity, Edmund found the key and prised open the front door. We stepped in amid a shower of dust. A Welsh dresser stood against a wall, its warped pine shelves lined with hymnbooks, and on a sideboard stood plates and cutlery ready to be laid out for tea. The fireplace was still piled with ashes, and in front of it hung a dishcloth, still drying after eleven years. A calendar, all in Welsh, was torn off at January 1976, three years before their mother's death. The grandfather clock had stopped at five past six.

I walked slowly round the chilly house, until my eye was caught by some ornaments on a mantelpiece. Propped against the chimney-breast were two silver trays, and in front of them stood a pair of pottery dogs flanked by jugs adorned with china roses. The sight triggered something in my memory. Later, back at the brothers' house, I delved into my rucksack and confirmed my suspicion; the arrangement had featured in a close-up photograph in Chatwin's book, and hadn't been touched or dusted since.

In the bedrooms more books lined the walls – all in Welsh, save for a singularly appropriate copy of *Great Expectations*. The iron bedsteads had been stripped of their sheets, but otherwise the ancestors in the wall portraits gazed down on a scene unchanged since their day. Above Gerallt's father's bed, a revolver hung from a nail. I didn't have the nerve to look if it was still loaded.

In a corner I found what had obviously once been the family's pride and joy – a Mason & Hamlin harmonium. A few pumps of the bellows produced a wheezy chord and a cloud of dust.

I asked Gerallt about the 1928 Dodge which had carried Chatwin and the family to the Christmas service at Bryn Crwn Chapel.

'Oh, that,' he sniffed. 'It got rather mangled in a crash on the road to Gaiman.' Then he paused, remembering. 'It's a shame – I miss that old wreck; but we still use our bullock-cart from time to time.'

Despite long hours put in by Gerallt and Edmund, it seemed to me that the farm was going gradually to rack and ruin. The brothers were no longer young. Edmund, now 55, was still a bachelor and unlikely to produce offspring to continue what his parents had begun. It was true that Gerallt had two grown-up sons, but neither was keen to take on such a run-down place. What would happen when they were gone? 'We try not to think about it,' said Gerallt.

After the Chubut Valley I was now keen to see the Welsh settlement at Cwm Hyfryd, 300 miles to the west, with its 'twin towns' of Trevelin and Esquel. Gerallt drove me to the main road; then a couple of peons let me ride on their tractor towards Dolavon, from where a farmer took me in his pickup to Paso de Indios, an adobe hamlet halfway to Esquel. The wind raised clouds of dust, blotting out the main street and bowling huge balls of dead thorn bush between the shacks. A crocodile of children filed out of the village school and were immediately lost from view. It was midday, and behind shuttered doors and windows the *campesinos* would be sitting down to mutton and

185

potatoes, to be followed by a lengthy siesta. Paso de Indios wouldn't be stirring again until four.

I settled by the roadside and read. Two hours passed; four hours; six hours. The sun cast long shadows, and still not a single vehicle passed through. I asked a couple of men about the likelihood of something going towards Esquel; but they pushed back their hats and scratched their old, bald heads. 'There might be something tomorrow, *señor* – or there again, there might not.'

I slept in the village graveyard, surrounded by tombs of cracked marble and protected from the wind by a low mud wall. One grave carried a photo of a moustachioed young man. In the lee of another lay a dead fox.

Next morning, billowing dust heralded the approach of a westbound lorry, and I was quickly ushered on top. Approaching Esquel after miles of monotonous desert, I found myself looking down on a toy town hidden deep in a green valley. Yellow and silver roofs pierced the canopy of cypresses, or stood framed by poplars in the last stages of shedding their leaves. To left and right, black mountainsides rose into even blacker stormclouds. Climbing down from the lorry, I felt the unfamiliar sensation of being rained on, so hurried to the house of Jack and Jean Halliday's niece Cristina. She'd promised a space for my sleeping bag among the discarded playthings of five children, two cats, and a husband who spent his spare moments turning out pine carvings. 'No, they're not for sale, just for fun,' he explained, leading the way through chippings and sawdust to a workshop which commanded one of the finest views in Esquel. 'I chip away and dream about how lucky I am.'

Like Trelew, Esquel has given up most of its Welshness, so my friends' eldest boy drove me in a wingless, bonnetless Citroën 2CV to the Trevelin road. Trevelin, 'the Place by the Mill', lay at the heart of the 50-league valley granted by the Government in 1888. In contrast to the lower Chubut, this was well-watered hill country – land which the Welsh could understand. Streams tumbled noisily from hillsides as green as the Berwyns or the Forest of Dovey. On the skyline, serrated crags recalled Glyder Fach; and the clouds in the sky were the scudding cumuli of Powys.

Although well east of the main cordillera, Cwm Hyfryd's

waters flow to the Pacific. With the Chilean frontier still, in 1888, very much undecided, the arrival of the Welsh didn't go unnoticed in Santiago. Had the Argentines the power to grant land rights in disputed territory? The matter cast a shadow over the growing community until 1902, when Sir Thomas Holdich's boundary commission turned up and invited the settlers to decide for themselves. The Chileans tried to lure them with land, but the prudent Welsh threw in their lot with their compatriots in the Chubut Valley. They would be Argentine.

In a spring-fed flour mill built of rose-red bricks, a woman named Alda Williams took me to a fourth-floor window and pointed to where a house stood alone on a bluff. 'If you want to learn more about this valley, take yourself off to that cottage. Pennant, they call it – "Head of the Brook". Its owner knows Cwm Hyfryd better than anyone else alive.'

The Welshman about whom she was talking was Freddie Green – cattle farmer, philosopher, writer and radio ham. I found him standing on his verandah, pink-faced beneath an unruly ginger moustache and what appeared to be permanently raised eyebrows. A paisley silk cravat was set off by a navy beret clamped firmly over a balding head. His neighbours called him the Red Fox, but in his dark glasses and sweeping cloak he seemed to me more like a figure dreamed up by Toulouse-Lautrec.

'Sent you from the mill, I dare say. That's right; they direct all the travellers to me. Sit down by the fire, say hello to Vera, and have a cup of tea.'

Vera nodded from the kitchen. Like Freddie, she looked in her sixties. Presently she brought tea and fruitcake, but returned to the kitchen, leaving Freddie to talk. If he received as many visitors as he suggested, she'd probably heard all his stories before.

Freddie's ancestors, though Welsh, had lived for many years in that most English of cities, Chester. At the age of thirteen his father Charlie had been sent to Patagonia to learn sheepfarming the hard way. 'It'll make a man of you,' said his parents. The year was 1889, and the colonists were only just beginning to turn the tables in their battle against the desert. At Port Madryn an old peon seated Charlie on his first horse and rode with him to

Rawson, where David Lloyd Jones, a friend of the family, gave him a job as a shepherd. Each Monday he would lead the animals out to graze; each Saturday he would return for clean clothes, fresh bread and Sunday chapel. His parents were right: the experience did make a man of him, and by the age of 21 he was master of 2,000 sheep.

Seeing that Charlie was capable of more than shepherding, Lloyd Jones generously presented him with half his flock, which Charlie exchanged for carts and wagons to launch a business with a partner named Myfyr Berry Rhys. They bought a plot at Los Altares on the road to Esquel, and built a general store. Trade must have been brisk, for within three years they'd sold the place and acquired a sheepfarm apiece – Berry Rhys away to the south, Charlie at Paso de Indios.

At about this time he met and married Gwen Berwyn, a Rawson girl, and in 1913 Freddie was born. His early life seems to have been rather perilous, for at the age of six months, while the family was moving house to Trevelin, Gwen had to throw him to safety from a runaway wagon. He survived this adventure unharmed, but tragedy confronted them again a few months later when Charlie died of typhoid.

'After that we always seemed to be moving,' recalled Freddie. 'My mother took me first to London, then to Wales, and finally to the Chubut Valley. She was a country lass – a "camp" woman through and through – and we stayed in the valley till the 1932 flood.'

After the war he married Vera from Trevelin, and set about building the house at Pennant. 'I've got 750 acres here, but really it's not a good place for sheep. Not like down in the Chubut. I lost so many to the pumas up here that in the end I swapped them all for beef cattle. Only 120, mind you – I try not to overgraze.'

He took me to a window and pointed. 'You see this valley? It used to be all forest. Now just look at those bare hills! My neighbours have burned down all their trees; they don't seem to realize how much damage a fire can do. I say, if you want to keep the land healthy, bring in the beavers!'

I was surprised at this suggestion, and mentioned the havoc I'd seen wrought by beavers in Tierra del Fuego.

'Stuff and nonsense! I've been to Tierra del Fuego and I know what beavers can do. They can be jolly useful if you keep them under control; and when they get too troublesome, you just cull a few. But beavers or no, we'll have to do something soon, or this valley will be a desert by the end of the century.'

Freddie kept in weekly contact with a radio ham in Cardiff, speaking in Welsh about their different worlds. 'He's a nice man, Geoff, but not too well up on Welsh affairs,' he complained affably. I guessed that Freddie would somehow keep well up on affairs both Welsh and Patagonian, and my hunch was confirmed when he showed me a book he'd written about the history of Patagonia. It was, of course, in Welsh.

He was a frank talker, fluent in Welsh, Spanish and English. For my sake he stuck mostly to the latter, with just a trace of his ancestral Clwyd, and when warming to a subject he became visibly excited. One such topic was the existence and location of heaven.

'Look here,' he exclaimed, leading me to a corner where a chart lay spread on a table. 'You see how big the universe is?'

The chart was an unusual one. It showed the known universe, which on closer inspection seemed to amount to 75 billion light years in every direction from earth. 'And that's only the bit we know about. Don't tell me there's no possibility of heaven somewhere in all that space!'

I had to agree that in a space of that magnitude, anything was possible. But my thoughts were on the chart. I'd never seen such a thing before. Did Freddie keep it spread out in this corner to help him with theological debate? Or was he in touch with radio hams even more distant than Cardiff?

I camped in a clump of pines behind the house, and in the morning Freddie drove me back to Trevelin. 'You mustn't leave without calling on Ralphie Hammond at Río Frío,' were his final words.

Estancia Río Frío, a showcase farm, lay in a broad valley near the Chilean border. Impeccably whitewashed buildings hid coyly behind belts of poplars, and the paths between them looked as if they were swept at least twice a day. Ralphie Hammond, a commanding figure in a wide-brimmed gaucho hat, was ear-tagging sheep in a corral. Six peons ushered the animals one by one into a pen, where a seventh caught each by the throat and held it deferentially while the master punched the hole.

'Good God,' he exclaimed when I introduced myself. 'The whole world has suddenly started writing books on Patagonia. Why, only the other day someone was sniffing round here taking photographs. What's got into you all?'

I was about to apologize for adding to his tally, when suddenly he relented. 'Look, I don't really know anything about local history; I'm just a sheepfarmer. But if you talk to my Uncle Frankie in Trevelin, he'll tell you all there is to tell.' He turned back towards the sheep. 'He's a nice old stick,' he added. 'You'll get on fine.'

A lorry was on its way back to Trevelin and the driver let me ride in his cab. Enrique Lukens was a small, wiry, talkative man, Chilean by birth but with a lifelong affinity for Argentina. He'd grown up in Trevelin, worked all his life for Argentines, married an Argentine, and was one of the few people I met in Argentina who had anything but contempt for the military governments of the past.

'Someone had to put things right after Perón,' he said. 'I'm not politically minded myself, but those Peronists kept the country in irons. If you wanted a job, you had to join the Party; it was as simple as that.

'Then came the backlash. Well, what else did they expect? The terrorists were as bad as the Peronists – just egomaniacs, really – only with them the arrangement was that you toed the line or they shot you.

'To get rid of them all, we needed a strong hand, and with the generals we got one. Yes, I know a lot of innocent people suffered; but no democratic government could have done what they did. The pussy-footers would have won the day.' And he made a cat-like gesture to emphasize the point.

'Mind you, I'm not against negotiating. Oh no! After we invaded the Falklands, when the British fleet was on its way, I – Enrique Lukens – said "Negotiate, negotiate!" If we'd negotiated and the British had still attacked the islands, then we might have had a bit more support from the United States. But oh no, we sang and danced in the streets, while the British professionals turned our poor conscripted *chicos* to mincemeat.' Enrique sighed and squinted sideways at me. 'Now, there was a strong hand for you! Your Iron Lady. How I'd love to have lived in Britain during those times.'

'Uncle Frankie' turned out to be the proprietor of the butcher's shop on Calle San Martín. He had a round red face which exactly matched the meat on his counter, and wore a big white smock smeared red. He listened to my questioning, then rocked back on his heels in merriment. 'You want to talk local history,' he chortled, 'and you haven't even asked about Butch Cassidy!'

Cops and Robbers

The photographs on the 'Wanted' poster dashed my illusions about the Wild Bunch. Paul Newman and Robert Redford were miscast. In real life, Butch Cassidy and the Sundance Kid bore more of a resemblance to Laurel and Hardy.

The poster lay hidden amongst other papers in the historical displays in Trevelin's old flour mill. Underneath the faded photos was a stern proclamation in Spanish:

> Argentine Republic, Federal Capital Police
> Buenos Aires, January 1906
> WANTED
> Jorge Parker, Harry Longabaugh, E.A. Place

> Warning – These persons, including the woman, are traders in arms and fire, and given their criminal records on the files of detective agencies and police, they should be approached with the utmost caution, because knowing the prices on their heads in the United States, it is certain that they will resist arrest.

The notice went on to list a string of bank robberies up and down the cordillera, from San Luis to Río Gallegos, which had shocked the locals and scandalized Argentina's law-abiding 'gringos' for more than a year. Exactly who staged the holdups, and what became of them, will probably never be known; but they bore the unmistakable hallmarks of one Robert Leroy Parker, alias George (Jorge) Parker, alias James Ryan, alias Butch Cassidy, and his long-serving partner Harry Longabaugh the Sundance Kid.

Wanted for a string of train and bank robberies in Utah, Nevada and Montana, and hounded by detectives from the

Pinkerton Agency, Cassidy made a rendezvous with Longabaugh and his girlfriend Etta Place in New York towards the
end of 1901. In the States they faced very long jail sentences or
even death, but in South America they could start a new life. It
wasn't a difficult choice. Signing their bills as James Ryan and
Mr and Mrs Harry A. Place, the trio spent a couple of weeks
living in style and eating in New York's best restaurants. The
two men lavished jewellery from Tiffany's on their apparently
rather stunning companion. Then, clutching leather suitcases
and hatboxes, they boarded the steamship *Soldier Prince* for
Buenos Aires.

Cassidy and the Kid left behind a five-year career, during
which their Train Robbers' Syndicate or 'Wild Bunch' came to be
the most feared band of outlaws in the West. For several months
Cassidy's name had headed Pinkerton's list of most wanted
criminals. The story goes that after they relieved the First
National Bank of Winnemucca, Nevada, of $30,000 in September
1900, the pursuit became so intense that South America seemed
their only option. Patagonia, they were told, was a land where
strangers could settle incognito. On arriving in Buenos Aires they
went straight to the government land office and laid down a cash
payment for the deeds to 25,000 acres of rough grazing in
Chubut. The place was up in the cordillera, 1,600 miles from the
capital, near a one-horse village called Cholila. There, they
reasoned, they'd be safe.

Early in 1902 the runaways reached Trelew, taking rooms at
the now-demolished El Globo hotel while they prepared for the
dusty journey to Cholila. As they rode into the mountains
they'd have felt increasingly at home, for Chubut is Wild West
country *par excellence*. Arriving at Cholila, they set up camp and
lost no time in starting work on a cabin and buying cattle and
sheep. Not surprisingly, this aroused much curiosity among
neighbouring ranchers, and during the first month they received
several visits from the authorities, including three from Milton
Roberts, the police commissioner at Esquel. But they diverted
him with talk of horsebreeding and he went away none the
wiser.

To judge from a letter home dated 10th August 1902, Cassidy
genuinely intended to go straight:

I suppose you have thought long before that I had forgotten you (or was dead) but my dear friend, I am still alive, and when I think of my old friends you are always the first to come to mind. It will probably surprise you to hear from me away down in this country but U.S. was too small for me the last two years I was there. I was restless. I wanted to see more of the world. I had seen all of the U.S. that I thought was good. And . . . another of my Uncles died and left $30,000 to our little family of 3 so I took my $10,000 and started to see a little more of the world. I visited the best cities and best parts of South A. till I got here. And this part of the country looked so good that I located, and I think for good, for I like the place better every day.

For three years Cassidy's famous *ménage à trois* farmed peacefully at Cholila. Their neighbours found them congenial. When the Governor of Chubut visited, the Sundance Kid played his guitar and Cassidy danced with the daughter of a local dignitary. No one thought they might be outlaws on the run. Pinkerton's wrote to the Argentine police, warning that it was only a matter of time before they fell back into their old habits, but the police chief in Buenos Aires took one look at the map of Patagonia and put the letter in his pending tray.

In 1903, the stage became set for the reconstitution of the Wild Bunch when one of their old partners broke out of a Tennessee jail. When there was killing to be done, Harvey Logan had always responded to Cassidy's call. Before long he turned up in Cholila. In 1905, urged on by Logan and with their funds now running low, the gang burst out of hiding to stage the most daring bank robbery Argentina had ever seen. Eyewitnesses in Río Gallegos said they swaggered into the Banco de Londres y Tarapacá, pulled guns on the assistant manager and a cashier, and lifted 20,000 Argentine pesos and a cashbox full of pounds sterling. A patent medicine salesman remembered having given them directions as they rode into town; and another man later claimed they'd told him they were going to camp at Lake Argentino before riding on north.

But the Wild Bunch were nothing if not professional, and they still hadn't been traced when, two years later, they staged a second daring raid in the central Argentine province of San Luis. This time things didn't go so well. Etta Place, though dressed as a man, was recognized from posters circulated after the Río

Gallegos raid. The bank manager resisted, prompting Harvey Logan to shoot him in the head. And as the robbers left town at full gallop, the Kid was hit by a bullet and only just managed to stay on his horse.

Now the heat was on. Pinkerton detectives arrived in Buenos Aires and began sniffing round Chubut. Then Etta (so it's said) became pregnant in an affair with an English neighbour by the name of John Gardner. In December 1907 the gang sold the estate and scattered into the cordillera – the Kid and Etta heading north, Cassidy and Logan south. Their neighbours never saw them again.

What happened next is pure conjecture. Of the nine separate versions of their death, the shoot-out at San Vicente, Bolivia, portrayed in the Twentieth Century-Fox film is the least likely. Cassidy, eager to be thought of as dead, may even have started the rumour himself. He almost certainly returned to Utah in 1908, possibly to live under yet another false name, but more probably just to visit his family before heading back to South America. Pinkerton's closed their files on the Wild Bunch after the Uruguayan police recovered three gringos' bodies from a shoot-out in 1911. If, as another report goes, Cassidy and the Kid were by that time working at the Concordia tin mine in Bolivia, they must have danced a jig when they heard the news.

For my money, none of these stories is true. There's an uncanny similarity – too close for coincidence – between the Wild Bunch raids and three others which took place in Patagonia after they supposedly fled. The first was in January 1908, when two gringos using the names Bob Evans and Willie Wilson robbed the Casa Lahusen general store in Comodoro Rivadavia. An eyewitness account said they were accompanied by a woman dressed as a man.

The second followed in December 1909, when the same two men held up the Chubut Mercantile Company's trading post at Arroyo Pescado near Esquel. The manager (a son, as it happened, of Michael Jones, the Bala priest who helped sell Patagonia to the Welsh) had been expecting a delivery of gold sovereigns to pay for the wool clip. But the robbers struck too soon, and all they found in the safe were a few pesos belonging to local Indians. Backing out of the store, the man who called himself Wilson tripped and fell, and the manager seized his chance. He went for

Wilson's gun – but Wilson was too quick for him, and shot him through the heart.

The third and final story began in March 1911, when two men calling themselves Wilson and Evans robbed a sheepfarm in Tiro Canyon south of Trevelin. A month later the same farm lost some cattle. For the police this was the last straw. A manhunt was ordered, and in June the gangsters escaped by only minutes when they were flushed out near the Chilean border. For six more months they continued to evade the law, but in December 1911 a patrol finally tracked them down near Río Pico and surrounded their camp. According to one of the constables, interviewed 60 years later, what happened next was pure Hollywood. The sergeant shouted 'Hands up!', but Evans responded with a volley of bullets which killed one officer and wounded another. The police returned fire and Evans fell. Wilson leaped from his tent to make a break for it, but the police let off another fusillade and he, too, hit the ground. Later, while searching the bodies, they found two gold watches from Tiffany's, and a photograph which the constable described as being 'of a very beautiful woman indeed'.

The sergeant was convinced he had the bodies of the 'Banda Yanqui', for which Pinkerton's was still offering $5,000 per head. Anxious not to let the reward slip through his fingers, he cut off their heads and asked a local farmer for some preserving alcohol. The farmer sent him packing, and told his peons to dig two shallow graves overlooking the cordillera, marked by a rough wooden cross which can still be seen. If the corpses really were those of Butch Cassidy and his partner, it's just the sort of place they'd have wanted to be.

The road to Cholila led through an upland valley of lakes and forests. I made my way slowly, accepting lifts when they were offered, but mostly walking, because this was a magic region, only lightly touched by human hands. The natural features had retained their marvellous-sounding Mapuche names, like Futa-laufquen, 'the Great Lake'. The wayside cafés and guesthouses also had Indian names – such as Pucón-Pai ('Door to the Sky') or Quimé-Quipán ('Welcome And Go Safely On Your Way') – but these were fakes, strictly for tourists, like the Welsh teashops owned by Italians. How capricious is the conqueror, that he can despise and exterminate a people and then attach their words to his developments!

I felt an irresistible urge to get closer to the Mapuche. I walked deep into their forests, on tracks almost obliterated by the fallen trunks of redwood and southern beech. Now, at the very end of the Patagonian autumn, the ground was spongy with their leaf-mould and the fallen trunks alive with fungi of every conceivable shape and colour. I sniffed the air and thought of damp cellars stacked with rotting cider apples. At this season, few woodland creatures were about; those not migrating would have settled down to hibernate, so the forests were still and silent save for the dripping of rain, relentless and hypnotic, from the canopy high above.

Did the Mapuche, pushing through this same dank under-storey in their guanaco skins less than 200 years ago, have a premonition of their impending demise? Did a youngster ever stop on his path, look up at the moss-encrusted boughs, and wonder what future lay beyond his lifetime? Did it occur to a hunter on the upper slopes that his language, developed over so many centuries, would be reduced to a few names swinging from chintzy motorists' drive-ins? Probably not, for the Mapuche were above all a practical race; tomorrow's cooking-pot would almost certainly have been the main thing on their minds.

On the second day, the rain turned to a wet snow, and I thought again of the Mapuche in their meagre animal skins. I tried to imagine what it would be like to trudge through the same deepening puddles of freezing mud in rough-sewn moccasins instead of my insulated, watertight boots. And winter here hadn't even begun! The more I considered it, the more respect I felt for those who'd extracted from such scanty resources the means to survive. Accomplishments aren't the prerogative of the mighty. At the time of their decimation, Patagonia's native races were scorned by the civilized world; but times change, and now we – the civilized ones – look back on our conquests with shame. When I thought of some of today's 'accomplishments', I had absolutely no doubt that one day they'd be equally reviled.

'So you want to see the cabin of the *bandidos*?' said the woman in Cholila. 'Yes, I can tell you where it is. Follow the Epuyén road for five miles and you'll see it over by the river, 100 yards to your left.'

Her directions led me through pine trees, not to a cabin but to a stone house advertising Welsh teas. Confused, I knocked on the door, and was ushered into a kitchen by an elderly grey-suited man. 'Oh yes, I know the place of the *Yanquis*. I'll show you in a moment. But first, sit down and have some tea.'

Miguel Calderón was only a quarter Welsh, and his wife Victorina could trace no Welsh blood at all, but this hadn't inhibited them from building up a thriving business in the name of the principality. Miguel showed me the tearoom, pretty and fussy, with a chiming wall clock and a pair of pottery clogs. 'The customers love Victorina's cooking,' he told me proudly. 'Her speciality's something called . . .' – but he'd forgotten the name.

'Welsh rarebit?' I suggested.

'That's it!'

Apparently no one had ever broached the question of Victorina's credentials.

At the cabin of the *Yanquis*, Aladín Sepúlveda was sipping his first maté of the day when I knocked on his rough plank door. The hut was surrounded by the fallen leaves of autumn, and as he ushered me in I saw that some had found their way through the glassless panes of what had once been a window.

The old man hitched up his sheepskin *bombachas*, pushed back his gaucho beret and looked me over silently. He seemed ancient, but having overcome his initial reserve he insisted, somewhat testily, that he was no more than 60. Born in the cabin, he'd shared his childhood there with brothers, sisters and various cousins; at one time, he grumbled, fifteen people had been living in its four small rooms. His father had acquired it from a cattle cooperative, which in turn had bought it from Butch Cassidy in 1907. He knew it had been built by 'the *bandido*'; but was dismissive of its construction, pointing out the gaps between the old logs, which had been steadily widening over the years.

When Bruce Chatwin turned up here in 1975, Sepúlveda's wife was still with him. Chatwin wrote: 'She was short and stout and had a bad time with her husband and the rotten cabin. Señor Sepúlveda was grogged out of his mind, half-sitting, half-lying by the kitchen stove.'

By 1990 the woman had left him, his children had moved

away, and the old man was living out his days alone. He was sober when I called, but had clearly lost whatever zest for life he may once have had. The place was a mess. Cardboard had been stuffed into the holes in the walls and windows, and also formed a makeshift tablecloth which bore a pile of filthy, mouldering dishes. Against one wall a stove was roaring nicely, but in front of it several days' worth of ashes spilled out over the rotting floorboards. The room smelt of mutton fat.

'No – I don't remember the Englishman,' he told me firmly. 'But I know what he wrote. Look, I've got it here.' And he showed me some photocopied pages from *In Patagonia*, both English and Spanish editions, which had been sent from the States with the relevant bits ringed in red. Despite his claim, he clearly hadn't understood either version, and in view of Chatwin's remarks it was possibly just as well.

'Do you get many visitors?' I asked. 'Other foreigners, perhaps?'

'No,' he replied. 'No one ever comes here.'

Forty miles north of Cholila I found the scene of a more recent drama. The valley known as El Bolsón ('The Sink') saw its first scattered homesteads in the 1880s, but only after 1930 did there emerge any real centre of population. Although mostly Chileans, the early settlers quickly began to look to Buenos Aires for their supplies, and the potential for travelling merchants came to the attention of some new arrivals from the Middle East. Soon several of these so-called *mercachifles* were trading in the valley. Though usually referred to as 'Lebanese', some came from Syria, and an early police muster-roll even included a Bedouin Arab.

For 30 years El Bolsón discreetly stagnated. Its residents, being neither particularly rich nor particularly poor, attracted little attention from the outside world. The occasional adventurer or bandit would pause in his journey, replenish his provisions at the general store, and pass on without a second thought.

But in the mid-1960s this tranquillity was brought to an end by the arrival of a wave of youngsters on the run from Buenos Aires. No one knows what triggered the influx. The valley's mild, wet climate, its fertile soils, and above all its complete isolation had already attracted one or two beatnik couples. But suddenly young people were coming in numbers, disillusioned with the heady life of the capital, and eager to experiment. After Perón's death in 1974, the wave became a flood as the famous and well-to-do found themselves being ruthlessly blackmailed by hired kidnappers and assassins. Parents packed off their teenage children like wartime refugees. Communes appeared in and around the little town, their membership quickly swelling, and a hippie fragrance drifted over the valley.

Some of the newcomers, inspired by their Californian counterparts, made a genuine effort to farm the land and achieve a measure of self-sufficiency, or at least enjoy home-grown produce. Others simply relied on their parents' monthly cheques to keep them in food, alcohol and dope. The already established settlers were, by and large, well disposed towards the youngsters, but sometimes tempers flared, and the resulting incidents found their way into the Buenos Aires newspapers. As the years went by, El Bolsón acquired the reputation of a Kathmandu laced heavily with Soho.

The woman I met in La Bolsonesa general store wasn't one of the 'poor rich kids'. Growing up in a working-class Buenos Aires suburb, Teresa had been drawn south by a genuine interest in 'green' issues. She'd come to the valley in 1976 with a man called Julio, and for seven years they scraped a paltry but happy existence, cultivating their plot and doing odd jobs to keep them in basic provisions.

But in 1983 two things happened: Teresa had a baby boy, and Julio walked out. She was thrown off the plot, and to make ends meet took on more and more jobs – making, mending, carrying, selling, and turning the soil for her neighbours. Luckily El Bolsón is gentle with people down on their luck, and she made friends in every corner of the valley. Later, the boy Daniel lent a hand. Mother and son drifted from home to home, sometimes squatting, sometimes house-sitting, and despite the upheavals Daniel grew into a strong and likeable boy. In lieu of proper schooling, Teresa kindled his curiosity about forest mushrooms and berries, taught him woodworking, and showed him how to play the flute.

I spent an evening with them both, huddled round a stove in an old log house. As the wind whistled through cracks in the walls, Teresa took her guitar and experimented with a song she was composing:

Cops and Robbers

Sunlight has more beauty when it's softened by a cloud;
My love for you will grow after we've weathered a few storms;
For now that I am older, I find dull the midday glare;
Oh take my hand and let me feel the tempest. . . .

Hours later, she was still plucking tentatively at the strings when I stepped out into the blustery night. I walked slowly across the valley to where I'd pitched my tent in the forest. My mind was filled with her music, and as I settled into my sleeping bag I realized why it had moved me so. Teresa's was the voice of Patagonia.

Back in Esquel, exhausted by days of bouncing in old lorries, I made my way to the terminus of one of Patagonia's few surviving railways. The engine was wheezing in a siding, spewing sparks and steam in the pre-dawn darkness like a dragon with bronchitis. Its four wooden carriages sat on the narrow-gauge rails at various angles to the vertical, like toys discarded by some giant child. A couple of dozen passengers, mostly Mapuche Indians, dozed in the dimly lit second-class carriages or mooched around the platform kicking old beer bottles. The first class was conspicuously empty.

I bought my ticket – a small wedge of thick card like train tickets ought to be – and proffered it to a uniformed official who seemed to be the guard. To my disbelief, he touched his peaked cap before ushering me aboard. Then, blowing his whistle and holding aloft a rusty lantern, he stood back as the train began to move. This, I thought, is how to run a railway.

With anguished puffing and a showy spin of wheels, the improbable affair began to gather speed. The last carriage cleared the platform and the guard leaped onto the running board. My fantasy was complete. As morning sunlight touched the snows of the Andes, the Old Patagonian Express heaved its way out of Esquel, its destination Ingeniero Jacobacci and the main line.

Of course, the people who run and use this weekly train don't call it the Old Patagonian Express; that was a name dreamed up in 1979 by the writer Paul Theroux. Old it may be; express it certainly isn't. Although scheduled to do the 250-mile run to Ingeniero Jacobacci in 13½ hours, it often takes 16 or more. Recently one train took 24. But the name is a good one, because the train is so small that even at 20 miles per hour, belching smoke and shooing sheep and ostriches from the track with deranged whistle bursts, it has all the high-speed drama of an InterCity 125. The locals call it *La Trochita* – 'Little Track'. But for its occasional English-speaking passengers, the Old Patagonian Express it will always be.

The line has never paid its way. It took 20 years to build – the company kept running out of cash – and in 1945 when they laid the final section using secondhand rails, the cynics dubbed it *La Trocha Económica*. Of the 38 original locomotives, less than a dozen were still working; a maintenance team kept them patched together by creatively recycling bits from a nearby scrapyard. But with the Argentine railway system losing £300 million per year the Government was poised to axe the line, so new parts were out of the question.

My second-class carriage was painted a sickly pea-green. Slatted bench seats warned of discomforts to come. Halfway down one side, a woodburning stove fought a losing battle with blasts of icy air which shrieked through the carriage sides. The stove was fed with beech logs, and my fellow-passengers devoted a great deal of time to keeping it alight, because apart from warming the carriage it provided hot water for the all-important maté. As the little carriage swayed across the desert, cans of water bobbed and hissed on the hob, enveloping those nearest in a cocoon of clammy steam.

The Indians watched as if hypnotized, speaking little. As the miles slipped by, they reached forward from time to time to refill their maté gourds, but it was impossible to tell what they were thinking, if indeed they were thinking at all. Impassive Mapuche faces stared at the stove, or at the ceiling, or at their feet. Thorn bushes and grazing guanaco slid unnoticed past the windows. Time seemed to stand still.

Suddenly the spell was broken. The train lurched round a bend, a door swung open, a cloud of steam rose hissing from the stove, and the window next to me banged down in its runner, nearly chopping off my fingers. I looked round anxiously at this log cabin on wheels. It seemed to be held together mainly by its panelling, and from time to time the ceiling took a different course from the rest of it, weaving along in sympathy but slightly out of time. The walls kept tenuous contact with the floor. I

202

glanced at the doorframe leading to the first-class carriage and saw it squeeze and release its door, which squealed like a pig in pain. It was a wonder the windows didn't drop out, and perhaps indeed some had, for several of the panes were cracked. In the first class they'd been replaced with fresh ones, and I glimpsed seats upholstered in rich Córdoba leather, but the carriage itself looked just as jerry-built as my own. When viewed from the running board, the whole train seemed to be oozing along quite independently of the rails.

At an oasis called Fitalancao – four cottages and a school – the inevitable happened. The train gasped to a halt, and after consulting gravely with the driver the guard announced a delay. A brake had been overheating and was in danger of setting us on fire. I looked towards the now red-hot stove – a fire hazard if ever I saw one – and decided that the problem must indeed be serious. 'Don't worry,' said the guard. 'Argentine Railways have a plan for every contingency. A *mecánico* has left the depot and he'll be here within the hour.'

Two hours later the mechanic arrived in a pickup, having driven 60 miles across the pampa. After some strenuous work with a jack and crowbar he stood back and signalled to the driver, and the train steamed cautiously into the gathering dusk.

A full moon rose, and we pulled up at a wayside halt which seemed quite devoid of habitation. Here, inexplicably, most of the Indians left the train. Grumbling loudly, they hauled sacks and packing cases off into the desert night. Perhaps they'd decided it would be faster on foot, and perhaps they were right, for an hour later we stopped again, this time truly in the middle of nowhere, and the guard informed us that we'd run out of steam. The remaining passengers accepted this without murmur or expression, and passed the next hour staring silently across the plain.

At last the driver raised sufficient steam for us to creep forward to the village of Ojos de Agua, where a crowd of city lads boarded. Despite their long wait they were in bumptious mood, and provided a colourful contrast to our earlier Indian companions by singing and laughing until two in the morning, when the train finally slunk into its destination, exactly four hours late.

Ingeniero Jacobacci exists for the railway. What the Great Western did for Swindon, so Argentine Railways did (and still do, just) for Ingeniero Jacobacci. Founded in 1916 when the broad-gauge tracks arrived from the Atlantic coast, the town looks to the trains for its employment, its supplies and its few visitors. Clearly the latter don't often arrive on the Old Patagonian Express, for the Grand Hotel – a mean-looking place near the station – was locked and dark. My fellow-passengers melted into the empty streets. There were no trees to sleep under, no hedges to offer shelter from the wind. Even the cypresses in the square were stunted like Japanese bonsais.

I thought of pitching my tent on a vacant plot, but a frenzied barking quickly changed my mind. This was Patagonia at its cruellest. I shouldered my rucksack and tramped off miserably to camp in the moonlit desert.

Patagonia in midwinter is utterly forbidding. At 9.00 a.m. the sky remains pitch dark, and when the sun does eventually present itself it reveals a land seemingly without life; for Patagonians, whether of the human or the animal kind, don't go out in winter unless they absolutely have to.

Striking camp in a grey dawn, I bent into the wind and walked slowly towards the west. I'd been wondering why there were so few vehicles in Ingeniero Jacobacci. Now I understood. Tracks radiated in all directions, but to reach anywhere of significance you'd have to spend several hours bouncing through potholes, circumnavigating bluffs and inhaling the fine ochre powder of the desert.

A storm burst upon me, the rain tearing horizontally through the thorn bushes. It stung my face and made runnels down my neck; then, as quickly as it had arrived, gave way to clear skies. The air grew cold, and I began to feel ice crystals in my breath. Suddenly I realized how late it was. I'd been walking since dawn – no great feat in the short days of midwinter – and had yet to see a vehicle. The sun cast long tangerine shadows down the road, turning its surface lunar. Ahead, a break of slope looked as if it might offer some shelter, but on crawling up to it I found the wind fiercer than ever. Cursing, I threw up my tent by the roadside, struggling in vain to find purchase for the tentpegs in the sandy soil, and slowly prepared myself for a long cold night.

I've often wondered what makes me choose such uncomfortable ways of getting from A to B. Some people travel like this to break free from a cosseted home life; others to meet people in new circumstances or see places from a different perspective; yet others, I suppose, to explore something within themselves. I think I'm driven by a bit of all three. But there are times on every journey when I can find no meaning whatsoever in the rain, wind, cold, loneliness and fear that envelop me alone in a small tent. What on earth, I ask myself, drives me time and again to leave the cocoon of home, family and friends? The reason (as I realize soon afterwards) is that these times of difficulty are an essential part of every journey – a yardstick by which to compare the less demanding moments, and without which such moments would be meaningless. This night was to be one such benchmark, and if the thought had crossed my mind it might have given me some solace. But it didn't. I lay miserably in my sleeping bag, dreaming only of home, a shower, a pizza, a friend and a bottle of wine; and soothed by these fantasies I shivered myself to sleep.

When I reach this depth of despair, forces are often already at work to save the situation. Next morning, even before the sun had made its belated appearance, I'd been woken and served coffee from a thermos flask, and within 20 minutes was being sped on my way. My unexpected deliverance was due to the keen eyesight of an Italian-Argentine clothes salesman doing his rounds of the southern provinces. On spotting my tent he'd skidded to a halt, and quickly helped me dismantle it before setting off again at high speed towards the Limay River and the province of Neuquén. He was eager to talk, and after such generosity I was quite content to provide an attentive ear.

The subject of our rather one-sided conversation was Argentina's economic woes, which my rescuer blamed squarely on the Indians. 'Those farmers down south had the right idea,' he thundered. 'Off with their heads!' Given that the Indians in question were now down to a few hundred half-castes, he seemed to be crediting them with extraordinary powers. The car boasted a huge dent in its side – a result no doubt of his tendency to let it drift off the road, which he did several times during our journey, while backing up his tireless arguments with great sweeps of the hand.

Neuquén, the northernmost of Argentina's Patagonian provinces, spills down from the 12,400-foot cone of the volcano Lanín, extending in sinuous forested ridges towards the plains of Zapala. The forests are a tangle of southern beech, bamboo, and – in a few unbelievable square miles – monkey-puzzle trees. In the glacier-gouged troughs which separate them lie cobalt lakes with Mapuche names like Currhué and Hui-Hui. Some people have questioned whether this fantasy-land, now being discovered by European and North American holidaymakers, should really be considered part of Patagonia. On the whole I think it shouldn't. But in Neuquén's eastern plains you can find quintessential Patagonia, for here the familiar scrub-covered slopes are topped by flat *mesas*: breezy plateaux stalked by foxes and scanned by circling condors. These tablelands end in basalt cliffs, whose caves and crevices contain Mapuche burial tombs with rubric messages in amber and russet. Clambering out of one such cave, I found myself on an airy ridge with not a trace of our own civilization in sight.

Some friends had invited me to stay at a farm in the heart of the *mesa* country. Huechahue came into British ownership in the 1930s, when George Wood, the son of a Berkshire sheepfarmer, bought deeds to a couple of valleys west of the Aluminé River. Years spent working for his father in southern Patagonia had given him an eye for what the land – and the market – could bear. Today his descendants had to be even more alert to the changing scene. To free the farm from the millstone of plummeting wool prices, they'd recently sold off its sheep, given the land over to Hereford beef-cattle and launched a programme of estancia-style riding holidays.

I arrived to find George's granddaughter-in-law Jane Williams running the farm. Experience told her exactly what I needed. Within an hour of showing up I'd been showered, talcumed, watered, fed, and laid out on a deep-cushioned sofa to the strains of Debussy. In a stupor of luxury I reached out to a coffee table and picked up an English-language copy of *Cosmopolitan*. Inside, an article considered the merits of locking up all men under 35. After the insights of my journey through Peru, Chile and Argentina I couldn't help being attracted by the idea; but it crossed my mind that they wouldn't have dared print such a piece in the Latin American edition – it would have sparked a riot.

That afternoon, across the world in Italy, the first games were being played in the World Football Cup. Argentina had been drawn against Cameroon. President Menem had set aside matters of state and flown to watch the match, and there was some discussion as to whether the day should be declared a national holiday. In the event it was agreed that it shouldn't, but most offices and shops pulled down their shutters anyway. From the Chaco to Tierra del Fuego, enthusiasts gathered in darkened rooms and watched in horror as Argentina lost the match. The nation was paralysed by grief.

For me, the magazine and the football match were reminders that after almost eight months in Patagonia I was on the verge of returning to the outside world. In Europe the period had been an eventful one. The Berlin Wall had been breached, prompting the populace of half a dozen countries to break the shackles of 40 years of subjugation. And in Britain a groundswell of opinion was gathering momentum against the woman who, in different ways, had redirected both British and Argentine history.

In Patagonia, by contrast, the same eight months had seen few meaningful changes. A meteorologist would have described the region as fractionally drier; an economist as slightly poorer, especially on the Argentine side. With drought and financial troubles looming, its immediate prospects weren't rosy. But when I turned to the more distant future, I found myself haunted by the words of the Trelew spiritualist Irith Dorfman. Had she been right to give Patagonia no place at all in tomorrow's world?

In the Argentine capital, 700 miles to the north-east, I hoped to find some clues.

The sun was shining on the small town of Ezeiza, 25 miles from Buenos Aires, as a lorry-trailer combination dropped me at the railway station. It was the Day of the Flag, a public holiday, and families were strolling together down the high street and in the park, enjoying the warm breezes of a perfect winter's day.

'You can get a train from here,' said the driver. 'They run every half-hour.'

I bought a ticket to Constitución, the terminus serving the south. The train was a broad-gauge electric one, and after the Old Patagonian Express it seemed both huge and ridiculously fast. I found a quiet carriage and settled down to enjoy the last few miles of my journey to the capital.

At the next station a man sat down opposite. He was young, handsome and leather-jacketed, and he was panting.

'Nearly missed it,' he grinned amicably. 'Where've you come from?'

'The south – Patagonia, actually.'

'You're joking! Most folk use this train just to go to work.'

He seemed relaxed and had an honest smile. My curiosity got the better of my reserve. 'Is that where you're going?' I asked.

'Mmm.'

'What do you do?'

He grimaced. 'I'm a sort of policeman. Plain-clothes – "SIDE".'

The *Servicio de Inteligencia del Estado* is Argentina's equivalent of MI5. I smiled to myself at the thought of meeting a spy-catcher – or possibly somebody pretending to be one – and prepared myself for a grilling. To my surprise it didn't come. Instead the young man recounted, factually and without apology, the headaches of his job; and told me how much he'd enjoyed the single perk of his career so far, a month-long training course in the United States. Then he enquired gently about my own trip, my impressions and my plans. By the time the train drew into the terminus I not only believed his story; I even rather liked the man.

'Lots of foreigners come to Argentina expecting to see tanks and shooting,' he continued as we crossed the station concourse. 'I try to convince them that we've moved on from those times. But the images persist, no?'

'Yes, they do,' I said. 'And it's really not fair, because I haven't seen a tank since leaving Europe.'

'Then tell your readers, tell them! Tell them the gangster days are over. Let them come and see for themselves.' He gave me a sharp look as we shook hands outside his office. 'They'd be amazed,' he concluded.

I had to admit that they would.

They say the typical Argentine is an Italian who speaks Spanish, thinks he's French, but would really like to be English. Nowhere does the national schizophrenia show itself more clearly than in Buenos Aires. Bruce Chatwin uncovered a fair slice of the city's history simply by leafing through its telephone directory. Radziwil, Romanov, Rommel, de Rose and de Rothschild – five names taken at random from amongst the 'R's – suggested to him stories of exile, disillusionment and anxiety behind lace curtains. For Chatwin the city also brought reminders of Russia – 'the cars of the secret police bristling with aerials; the women with splayed haunches licking ice-cream in dusty parks; the same bullying statues, the pie-crust architecture, the same avenues that were not quite straight, giving the illusion of endless space and leading out into nowhere.'

But both Russia and Argentina have moved on since Chatwin's day; and in Buenos Aires the bullying now comes not so much from statues as from a citizenry with an irrepressible sense of its own importance. Porteños (as Buenos Aires folk are known) make up fully one-third of Argentina's population. The city is ten times the size of its nearest Argentine rival, and vies with São Paulo for the distinction of being the most populous in all South America. Polluted and decaying, its infrastructure falling apart, its economy spiralling dizzily out of control, it gazes upon its own progressive collapse with a cocksure indifference.

I was still in touch with a couple of Porteño friends from a previous visit. They'd generously offered me the run of their flat, on the eighth floor of one of the many tall blocks overlooking the River Plate. In view of what later happened, I'll call them Antonio and Estela, though these aren't their names. Antonio was an architect and interior designer, Estela a radio and television announcer. Like all Porteños they lived life vigorously, often eating and drinking late into the night, yet still somehow managing to present themselves wide awake for work next morning without the help of matchsticks.

Midwinter's day came and went, and I thought how my friends down south would welcome the slowly lengthening days. In Buenos Aires I was now closer to the equator than I would have been anywhere in Europe, so the solstice held less significance. Some days I could even go out without a coat.

On 23rd June Estela drew my attention to a newspaper item. 'At 11.00 a.m. tomorrow, President Carlos Menem will arrive in San Martín Square to inaugurate a memorial to the 650 combatants who died in the South Atlantic War of 1982.'

'I think you ought to include that in your recordings for the BBC,' she suggested. 'With my contacts, I'm sure I could get you in.'

It was an opportunity I couldn't miss. I'd already recorded the views of many ordinary Argentines on the conflict and its aftermath, and hoped to include them in a radio programme on my return to Britain. The inauguration would be a chance to put their opinions in context and perhaps find out the latest government viewpoint.

After the announcement, it emerged that 24th June was a day when Argentina would be playing a vital game in their World Cup bid. The opponents would be their traditional rivals, Brazil. Well before noon, the nation would be gathering in front of its television sets once more. The ceremony was hurriedly brought forward by an hour, with the result that Estela, I, and scores of others turned up just as it was finishing.

But in one way our timing was perfect. As President Menem swept off in a limousine, the crowd began to disperse and the security cordon was relaxed. Recognizing two prominent politicians, Estela quickly buttonholed them and asked if they would speak to the BBC. To our surprise they agreed. Antonio Salonia, Minister of Education and Justice, and Néstor Perl, Governor of the front-line province of Chubut, both talked willingly of the importance of forgetting the past and renewing broken ties. Whilst emphasizing their conviction that the Falklands were legally Argentine, they thought the time had come for a dialogue which, in time, might lead towards a negotiated solution. I hadn't expected to hear such conciliatory words.

After these interviews, three women came up to me. Each had lost a son in the conflict. I switched on the tape recorder and they made an impassioned plea for an end to armed conflict, not just between Britain and Argentina but throughout the world. Fighting back tears, they put forward points that any mother would understand, whatever her feelings about the merits of the dispute. 'War doesn't solve anything,' they concluded. 'Ever.'

By this time I was close to tears myself, and made a move to break out from the ring of 30 or 40 passers-by who'd gathered round to listen. A young man tapped me on the shoulder. 'I'm an *ex-combatiente* – a war veteran,' he explained. 'I'd like to say something too.'

There was a touch of rancour in his voice, but I failed to pick it up. 'Of course,' I said, and switched on the tape.

At first his tone was reasonable; then, without warning, it

became hostile. 'Of course, you British are all Nazis really. You're killers; assassins. You're all the same, you know.'

I could scarcely believe my ears. The fellow was obviously hoping for a reaction, but when I failed to give one – more out of surprise than anything else – his manner became more threatening. 'Nazi. Fascist! You're just like the rest of them. We're going to get our islands back, whatever your friends in London think. And now we're going to show you what we think of assassins.'

Events then moved quickly. Those nearest in the crowd took up the chant. 'Nazis! Killers! We're going to get you.' I saw Estela running for help. I remember, for some reason, switching off the tape. Then a young woman's hand reached forward and grasped the microphone. Another snatched the tape recorder itself, wrenching it away with such force that the shoulder strap snapped and flew up in my face. From behind I felt a soft blow to the head, and someone started kicking me.

In the few seconds that the incident took, I remember thinking simply 'Oh my God' – then the police arrived. 'War veterans, let's go!' shouted the woman who had my microphone, and my assailants dissolved quietly into the crowd.

The four officers who finally elbowed their way up to me listened sympathetically but seemed powerless to help. 'They stole your tape recorder?' asked the sergeant. 'Then you must come to the *comisaría*, the police station, and make a statement!'

'But look!' shouted Estela. 'There's the woman with the microphone. Over there!'

It was true. Fifty yards away, she was standing with a group of young men. Estela almost dragged the policemen over to her, but of course the microphone had gone. 'What microphone?' the woman asked the sergeant. 'I don't know what you're talking about.'

The crowd had followed us and swelled. Everyone craned their necks to get a better view of the Englishman and his Argentine companion. A voice in my ear whispered 'Bastard!' and I turned to see a skinhead glowering at me. 'A skinhead in Argentina?' I thought. 'I must be dreaming.' Then the microphone-woman turned to the sergeant and said, 'This Englishman isn't from the BBC at all. I happen to know he's an American spy.'

Now I knew I was dreaming. Estela and I waited, stunned, while the police discussed what to do with us. The throng around us continued to grow. Fifty? Eighty? More seemed to be arriving by the second.

Finally they decided. 'Accusers and accused – you must all come to the *comisaría*,' announced the sergeant. 'A patrol car will be here in a moment.'

As we waited by the roadside, our tormentors grew steadily more frenzied. Cameras clicked, feet kicked, and a boy began to pull Estela's hair. 'Nazis, Fascists, assassins!' he yelled. The police nervously consulted their watches, waiting for their car.

A thought occurred to me: 'What if one of these lunatics has a gun?' In desperation I tapped the sergeant on the arm. 'Look, the Sheraton Hotel's just across the road. If your car's really on its way, why can't we tell them to meet us there?'

'Quiet, sonny,' came the reply.

After ten minutes the mob was frantic. 'Bastards! Bastards!' they yelled. At last the sergeant seemed to accept that the patrol car was not going to turn up. He instructed one of his colleagues to stop the eight lanes of traffic on Calle San Martín, and with that accomplished Estela and I were frogmarched to a taxi rank. We tumbled into the first cab and quickly locked the doors as the mob surrounded us. The sergeant climbed in beside the driver. '*Comisaría 15*,' he told him curtly; and to a thunderous hammering on the roof we sped away. My last memory is of a young face at the rear window, contorted with rage, brandishing a blue and white Argentine flag.

We reached the police station and the taxi was dismissed. The police offered no payment, and the driver knew better than to ask. As Estela and I stepped into the station, we joked that we'd never before been so pleased to see the inside of such a place.

But our troubles weren't over yet. Through the walls of an interview room we could hear the microphone-woman complaining loudly. 'The Englishman isn't a reporter. He works for the CIA! He was asking about the Mothers of the Disappeared. He's a subversive; a spy; an enemy of the *patria*. You must arrest him!'

Listening at the door, the sergeant looked heavenwards and told me, 'Don't worry – if she presses any charges against you, we'll nobble her for robbery with violence.'

But a few minutes later it was Estela who was being accused of violence. 'That *puta*, that whore – she broke my rosary necklace!' we heard through the wall. 'Look!'

We could hear her rattling her smashed rosary at the interviewing officer. Both Estela and I had noticed it round her neck – a symbol quite out of place, we thought, on this wantonly aggressive individual – but neither of us had touched it. She must have broken it herself.

The officer tried to calm her down. 'So the Englishman is a spy, is he? Well, we'll check him out with "SIDE".' He came out of the room looking weary. 'The kid's just overexcited. I'll give her half an hour, then send her packing.' He sighed. 'That's democracy for you. We never had to put up with this sort of thing when the military was in power.' Then he turned to me and added in a more sinister tone, 'You know, you shouldn't go around asking about the Disappeared. That's a closed issue. The mothers claim that 30,000 were tortured and murdered, but that's ridiculous; half of them didn't disappear at all. If you want my opinion, their mothers are wailing because they ran away from home.'

Back at Antonio and Estela's flat, we pieced together what had happened. It seemed likely that the attack had been planned from the moment we arrived. Since the Falklands conflict, some war veterans had joined an extremist group called the 2nd April Movement, whose aims were to sabotage negotiations with the British, bring down the current Argentine regime and retake the islands by force. Members of this group had come to the ceremony looking for trouble. During the President's speech they'd been urging the crowd to join them in chants of 'We will return, we will return,' followed by 'Those who don't jump are English'. So when a real Englishman arrived, he must have seemed heaven-sent.

Argentine public opinion is almost totally against retaking the Falklands, but the war veterans are a special case. In 1982 most were youngsters of seventeen or eighteen, doing their compulsory national service. With hardly any training, and ill-supplied with clothing and provisions, they found themselves being pitched into open battle. Some were injured, others so traumatized that they couldn't subsequently lead normal lives; but until 1990 successive governments had failed to help them in any way. Their resentment and bitterness were intense, and the 2nd April Movement was the perfect outlet.

Ironically, Menem used the occasion of the inauguration to announce that veterans not covered by private health schemes would in future receive free state medical treatment. 'We will rescue the neglected and forgotten youths who were once summoned by the fatherland, and on whom other ungrateful people later turned their backs,' he gushed. The Movement replied that it was all part of a plot to restore his flagging image.

Although Patagonia seemed worlds away from such rhetoric, I could see that its isolation was already something of an illusion. Patagonian issues are increasingly taxing the minds of politicians in both Buenos Aires and Santiago. The Beagle Channel islands will still be available to any future Argentine president wanting to pick a quarrel with Chile. Sensitivities about offshore mineral rights – more immediate with the prospect of discoveries of oil and gas – can be relied on to add to the tension. And until a genuine and lasting settlement of the Falklands question is reached, the bristling British defences there will continue to taunt the more bellicose of Argentina's generals.

Wider international issues are closing in on Patagonia too. Chile and Argentina are now front-line protagonists in the debate over Antarctica, with whose future Patagonia is becoming increasingly linked. Will Antarctica's overlapping territorial claims be revived, drawing Chile, Argentina and Britain into yet another diplomatic wrangle? Amongst other pressing matters, the southern hemisphere's ozone layer is in poor shape; and Patagonia's grasslands, already drought-stricken and chronically overgrazed, will be badly hit by any further climatic change. Finally, as other nations' wool and meat compete ever more effectively in a stagnant world market, Patagonian farms may face decline for the simple reason that they'll find it so much more difficult to sell their produce.

Yet incredibly the legend persists. Some years ago, Argentina's distinguished writer Jorge Luis Borges spoke, I suspect, for a multitude when he gave his opinion that 'you will find nothing in Patagonia. There is nothing there.' Today, despite all the changes and publicity, people still tell me that they think of Patagonia as a terrestrial black hole – a cross between the Sahara and Siberia. The idea of actually going there seems as far-fetched as flying to the moon.

For some, of course, this has always been its great attraction. In 1845 Darwin noted that 'in calling up images of the past, I find that the plains of Patagonia frequently cross before my eyes; yet these plains are pronounced by all wretched and useless. They can be described only by negative characters; without habitations, without water, without trees, without mountains, they support only a few dwarf plants. Why, then . . . have these arid wastes taken so firm a hold on my memory?'

Darwin himself thought the answer might lie in the free scope which Patagonia gave to the imagination. W.H. Hudson, another nineteenth-century naturalist, agreed. 'The old charm still exists in all its freshness; and after all the discomforts and sufferings endured in a desert cursed with eternal barrenness, the returned traveller finds in after years that it still keeps its hold on him, that it shines brighter in memory, and is dearer to him than any other region he may have visited.'

For Hudson, Patagonia came to be a vital refuge from an increasingly depressing world. Safe from the unutterable ills of Europe, he found himself gaining a new self-awareness:

During those solitary days it was a rare thing for any thought to cross my mind. . . . Elsewhere I had always been able to think most freely on horseback. . . . This was doubtless habit; but now, with a horse under me, I had become incapable of reflection. . . . To think was like setting in motion a noisy engine in my brain; and there was something there which bade me be still, and I was forced to obey. My state was one of *suspense* and *watchfulness*: yet I had no expectation of meeting with an adventure, and felt as free from apprehension as I feel now when sitting in a room in London. The change in me was just as great and wonderful as if I had changed my identity for that of another man or animal; but at the time I was powerless to wonder at or speculate about it; the state seemed familiar rather than strange, and although accompanied by a strong feeling of elation, I did not know it . . . until I lost it and returned to my former self – to thinking, and the old insipid existence.

It's this appeal as a refuge, I think, that has drawn many of Patagonia's settlers over the last hundred years. For the Joneses and Davieses escaping from the English; for Butch Cassidy and his partners on the run from Pinkerton's; and for more recent arrivals such as the Hopperdietzels from the Sudetenland or the

Mattars from Lebanon, its deserts and forests have offered a haven – a tough one, granted, but one which no one could take away. If you worked hard and stayed on the right side of the law, Patagonia would look after you. The process by which these pioneers selected themselves – the fact that they not only dreamed of a new life, but took steps to bring it about – guaranteed that they'd be a resourceful and dogged bunch. Their children, grandchildren and great-grandchildren, to judge by those I met, come largely from the same mould.

Patagonia has also had a fatal attraction for oddballs. The crazed characters of Orllie Antoine the King of Araucania, Julius Popper the gold miner, and Antonio Soto the anarchist, were only the most conspicuous of many. There was George Greenwood, a hermit of the 1870s who lived for years on a diet of guanaco and ostrich meat near Paso del Roble. And Jim Daniel, who arrived about the same time from North America (he never said exactly where) and used to sell guanaco carcasses to passing ships. Or Ascencio Brunel, 'the Wild Man of Santa Cruz', who was said to have become deranged after a broken romance, and roamed the plains in puma skins, rustling horses. Then there was 'Mister Jack' Harris, an Irishwoman who lived alone towards the end of the last century on a farmstead near Lake Argentino. She appeared from time to time in Río Gallegos, dressed as a man, with a revolver at her hip and a large briar pipe between her teeth. An American who worked for her refused to believe she was a woman.

Did these characters come to Patagonia because they were odd, or was it Patagonia that made them odd? Its remoteness has certainly attracted a number of desperadoes and misfits; but this doesn't explain why so many perfectly sane new arrivals subsequently became unhinged. Bruce Chatwin wrote movingly of Patagonia's *tristesse* – of 'white faces behind dusty windows' – and it certainly still has its fair share of abandoned souls. But so, it must be remembered, has Britain. The difference in Patagonia is that people pass by too rarely to turn the other cheek.

By far the majority of the Patagonians I met struck me as having adjusted perfectly to their inclement home. When not discussing the drought or the economy, they seemed to have a natural peace of mind which has been lost in more congested parts of the world. Anyone who has reached this page of the book will know that my most stirring memories of Patagonia are of its people. Above all, I noticed that they took an immense pleasure in helping strangers. 'Travelling ought,' said Darwin, 'to teach . . . distrust; but at the same time [the traveller] will discover how many truly kind-hearted people there are, with whom he never before had, or ever again will have, any further communication, who yet are ready to offer him the most disinterested assistance.'

The motto of Billy Two Rivers, a Canadian Mohawk chief, sums up for me the Patagonian's attitude to life. 'Love many; trust few – and always paddle your own canoe.'

Further Reading

(Original editions are quoted first, followed by British and/or paperback editions where different)

Exploration, adventure and other travellers' accounts

Andrews, Kenneth R., *Drake's Voyages* (Weidenfeld & Nicolson, 1967)

Beerbohm, Julius, *Wanderings in Patagonia: or Life among the Ostrich-Hunters* (Chatto & Windus, 1879)

Chatwin, Bruce, *In Patagonia* (Jonathan Cape, 1977; Picador, 1979)

—— and Paul Theroux, *Patagonia Revisited* (Michael Russell, 1985)

Coan, Titus, *Adventures in Patagonia: A Missionary's Exploring Trip* (Dodd Mead & Co., 1880)

Darwin, Charles, *Voyage of the Beagle* (Henry Colburn, 1839; Penguin, 1989)

Dixie, Lady Florence, *Across Patagonia* (Bentley & Son, 1880)

Hudson, W.H., *Idle Days in Patagonia* (Chapman & Hall, 1893; Dent, 1984)

—— *Far Away and Long Ago* (Dent, 1918; Century, 1985)

Mason, Michael H., *Where Tempests Blow* (Hodder & Stoughton, 1933)

Musters, George Chaworth, *At Home with the Patagonians* (John Murray, 1871)

Pigafetta, Antonio (trans. and ed. R.A. Skelton) *Magellan's Voyage: A Narrative Account of the First Navigation* (Yale University Press, 1969; Folio Society, 1975)

Prichard, H. Hesketh, *Through the Heart of Patagonia* (Heinemann, 1902)

Shipton, Eric, *Land of Tempest* (Hodder & Stoughton, 1963; republished in *The Six Mountain-Travel Books*, Diadem, 1985)

Swale, Rosie, *Back to Cape Horn* (Collins, 1986; Fontana, 1988)

Theroux, Paul, *The Old Patagonian Express* (Hamish Hamilton, 1979; Penguin, 1980)

Tilman, H.W., *Mischief in Patagonia* (Cambridge University Press, 1957; Grafton, 1988; republished in *The Eight Sailing/Mountain-Exploration Books*, Diadem, 1987)

Tschiffely, A.F., *This Way Southward* (Heinemann, 1940)

History and politics

Allende, Isabel (trans. Magda Bogin), *The House of the Spirits* (Jonathan Cape, 1985; Black Swan, 1986)

Bridges, E. Lucas, *Uttermost Part of the Earth* (Hodder & Stoughton, 1948; Century, 1987)

Burns, Jimmy, *The Land that Lost its Heroes* (Bloomsbury, 1987)

—— *Beyond the Silver River* (Bloomsbury, 1989)

Graham-Yooll, Andrew, *The Forgotten Colony* (Hutchinson, 1981)

—— *A State of Fear: Memories of Argentina's Nightmare* (Eland/Hippocrene, 1986)

Shipton, Eric, *Tierra del Fuego: the Fatal Lodestone* (Charles Knight, 1973)

Timerman, Jacobo (trans. Robert Cox), *Chile: Death in the South* (Knopf, 1987; Picador, 1987)

Williams, Glyn, *The Desert and the Dream: A Study of Welsh Colonization in Chubut, 1865–1915* (University of Wales Press, 1975)

Natural history and other background

Adams, Richard (ed.) *Antarctica: Voices from the Silent Continent* (Hodder & Stoughton, 1990)

Andrews, Michael, *The Flight of the Condor* (Collins/BBC, 1982)

Betenson, Lula Parker, *Butch Cassidy, My Brother* (Brigham Young University Press, 1975; Penguin, 1976)

Doyle, Sir Arthur Conan, *The Lost World* (Hodder & Stoughton, 1912; Macdonald Purnell, 1989)

Fogg, G.E., and David Smith, *The Explorations of Antarctica* (Cassell, 1990)

Goodall, Rae Natalie Prosser, *Tierra del Fuego* (bilingual) (Ediciones Shanamaüm, 1978 – available in Buenos Aires and on the island)

Jones, Tom P., *Patagonian Panorama* (Outspoken Press, 1961)

Llewellyn, Richard, *Up, Into the Singing Mountain* (Michael Joseph, 1963; New English Library, 1976)

Mainwaring, Michael, *From the Falklands to Patagonia: The Story of a Pioneer Family* (Allison & Busby, 1983)

Moorehead, Alan, *Darwin and the Beagle* (Hamish Hamilton, 1969)

Ralling, Christopher (ed.) *The Voyage of Charles Darwin* (BBC, 1978)

Guidebooks

Ball, Deirdre (ed.), *Argentina* ('Insight Guides' series, Apa Publications/Harrap, 1988)

Box, Ben (ed.), *South American Handbook* (Trade & Travel Publications, updated annually)

Hargreaves, Clare (ed.), *Backpacking in Chile and Argentina* (Bradt Publications/Hunter Publishing, 1991)

Samagalski, Alan, *Argentina: A Travel Survival Kit* (Lonely Planet, 1989)

—— *Chile and Easter Island: A Travel Survival Kit* (Lonely Planet, 1990)

Index

221

Index